Life and Death on Little Ross

The Story of an Island, a Lighthouse, and its Keepers

by
David R. Col...

Whittles Publishing

Published by
Whittles Publishing,
Dunbeath,
Caithness, KW6 6EG,
Scotland, UK
www.whittlespublishing.com

ISBN: 978-184995-359-7

Also by the author:

Kirkcudbright, an Alphabetical Guide to its History, (2003), ISBN 09533907-6-4

Kirkcudbright Shipping 1300–2005, (2007), ISBN 978-0-9551638-5-2

Kirkcudbright Sailing Club, the Early Years, 1956–1974, (2007),

Kirkcudbright's Prince of Denmark and her voyages in the South Seas, (2013),
ISBN 978-184995-088-6

This book is dedicated to my granddaughter,
Ailsa Alexander Collin

Printed by Melita Press, Malta

CONTENTS

Acknowledgements

In carrying out the necessary research to enable me to write this book, I have had great help from a variety of institutions and individuals in Scotland, England, the Isle of Man, New Zealand, Japan, and the United States of America.

The staff of the Stewartry Museum, Kirkcudbright – curator Anne Ramsbottom, retired curator Dr. David Devereux, museum assistants Denise Briggs, Vivien Dania, and volunteer helper Professor Donald Cowell – all responded positively and promptly to my many enquiries. Donald Cowell's painstaking work in cataloguing letters concerning Little Ross lighthouse was invaluable and led to new light being shed on the relationships between various members of the Stevenson family. Property manager Sheila Faichney and library assistant Sarah L. Jackson of Broughton House, Kirkcudbright, went to exceptional lengths to track down a particularly elusive photograph, and Ian Riches and Marcin Klimek of the National Trust for Scotland facilitated the granting of permission for its use.

In Fraserburgh, Liz Louis of the Museum of Scottish Lighthouses gave considerable assistance and encouragement. Throughout my lengthy research process, Lorna Hunter of the Northern Lighthouse Board (NLB) was always helpful, diligent, and encouraging. Graeme Macdonald and Barri Millar of the NLB also devoted much more time than I had hoped to finding photographs and details of works carried out at Little Ross during the processes of automation and conversion to solar power. Sarah Dutch of the Royal Commission on the Ancient and Historical Monuments of Scotland helped me to locate an obscure reference to Little Ross lighthouse in one of Thomas Stevenson's notebooks, and Dave Shawyer of BT Archives supplied information regarding the telegraph line to Little Ross. Mr. D. A. (Ali) Morrison of Conon Valley Builders in Dingwall gave a fascinating first-hand account of his firm's involvement in the lighthouse's conversion to solar power, and used his wide experience of lighthouse work to give authoritative answers to my many questions. David Hawker, Chris Miles, and Dr. Dylan de Silva of Scottish Natural Heritage helped greatly in tracking down an elusive archived report regarding the island's biodiversity, prepared by David Hawker in 1989.

One of my greatest challenges was finding information about the lighthouse keepers and their wives and families, in order to illustrate the nature, not only of their careers, but also of their domestic and leisure activities at Little Ross. Catherine Mackie Quirk in the Isle of Man and Ian Begg in Edinburgh generously made available the diary and family photographs of assistant keeper George Mackie, together with additional information about his father-in-law, principal keeper William Begg. George Mackie's diary is an extremely rare and delightful expression of the thoughts of a lighthouse keeper and a heart-rending account of his troubled early life. Details of the astonishing career of assistant keeper Joseph Dick were provided by Hiroshi Nakata in Japan, Professor Neil McKelvie in the USA, Roger Cliffe and Angela Davis in England, and by John Dick, the late Alison Kay, Keith Smith, Jan Smith and Ashlay Smith in Scotland. Richard Brunton gave some useful information about his distinguished forebear, also named Richard Brunton. Family details and insight to the character of assistant keeper Peter M. Gow came from his daughter Nancy Muirhead in Kirkcudbright, and information about the family and background of principal keeper Charles J. McNish was provided by John McNish. Jean and John Johnston in New Zealand helped me to find out more about their unfortunate ancestor, assistant keeper Robert Watson. The last principal keeper at Little Ross was John Thomson, and a unique account of his life and times there was provided by his nephew, the late James D. Thomson. Thomson family photographs were located and kindly made available by Harald Thomson, John Thomson's great-nephew.

Information about the enterprising builder Robert Hume came from Dr. David Steel and the late Antony Curtis Wolffe MBE in Gatehouse of Fleet, and from Robert Hume's descendent Susan Beale. Details about the Finlay family and agriculture at Little Ross came from Tony Finlay at Ross Bay and from James Finlay at Rainton Farm. My local knowledge of Kirkcudbright in general and Little Ross in particular was supplemented by input from David M. Hawker, Sir David Hope-Dunbar Bart., the late John King MBE, the late Ian McNeillie, Norman Parker, Daniel Shackleton, and Captain W. D. Shepherd.

I was delighted to have the opportunity to talk to and receive great assistance from former assistant keeper Charles J. F. Gifford, now living in Shetland. I have also had lengthy correspondences from and several telephone conversations with former assistant keeper Ian Summers and his wife Isabel, now living in Perthshire. The anecdotes they were all able to provide about the happy times they spent at Little Ross will, I hope, add greatly to the authenticity and interest of my account of the island's story.

I am greatly indebted to Dr. and Mrs. S. Roger Wild, and to Douglas Molyneux. They have given me much appreciated hospitality at Little Ross Island and in Edinburgh, and have done everything in their power to answer my endless questions. Perhaps every bit as importantly, their enthusiasm for all matters related to their beloved home on Little Ross Island encouraged me to persist when new sources of information and answers to outstanding questions were becoming harder and harder to find.

Whittles Publishing have skilfully converted my draft text and random illustrations into a finished production without fuss. It has been a great pleasure to work with them again, and to have the benefit of their encouragement and guidance. I am extremely grateful to Dr Keith Whittles and his team for their friendly and professional help.

Lastly, I must thank my wife Janette for, among many other things, saying, 'you had better hurry up and tell this story, because if you don't do it soon, someone else will beat you to it!'

Preface

Small islands have a special fascination for many people – the lesser the landmass, the greater their ability to relate to it. Many of us perhaps yearn to live somewhere so small and so clearly defined that we can know and understand every part. A deep-rooted fear of oppressors and predators may have influenced our thinking, as the defensive advantages of living on land surrounded by water are obvious. Unfortunately, most tiny islands lack the necessities to sustain life, such as sufficient quantities of fresh water, arable land, and grazing for sheep, goats, or cattle. Many islands are also by their very nature difficult and occasionally dangerous places to gain access to or leave from, particularly during winter. Despite the difficulties described, for centuries, several islands and islets off the west coasts of Scotland and Ireland have become homes to a mysterious range of hermits, recluses, and holy men, who have managed to survive, for a time at least, in conditions of the utmost deprivation.

Until the middle of the 20th century, it was possible for rather more practical people to realise the dream of living on such an island by seeking employment as a lighthouse keeper. Scottish lighthouses, and those on the Isle of Man, were built, owned, and managed by the Edinburgh based Northern Lighthouse Board, known from 1798 until 1835 as the Commissioners for Northern Lights. The original name continues to appear on the brass plate at the door of their head office in Edinburgh and is still widely used. Being a lighthouse keeper was a respected occupation, and service with the Lighthouse Board provided a career which many generations and branches of the same families were often proud to follow.

I was born on St Mary's Isle, Kirkcudbright, and although it is a peninsula rather than an island, it protrudes into Kirkcudbright Bay, and its long finger points southwards to the tiny island of Little Ross at the mouth of the bay, between Torrs Point and Meikle Ross. The island seems to guard and protect the bay; its lee provides an anchorage for visiting ships either to find temporary shelter or to await suitable tidal conditions to proceed up the River Dee to the safe but tidal harbour of Kirkcudbright. Throughout my childhood, the island and its lighthouse were the focus of the views from all the inlets, beaches, woods, and hills which were my territory. To my friends and me it was an inaccessible place of mystery and allure.

My home is now a little cottage on the shore at the Sandside, situated at the head of an arm of the River Dee's estuary, known as Manxman's Lake. It lies to the east of St Mary's Isle and is only a few hundred yards away from where I was born. When I open the curtains each morning, the first thing I see is the island of Little Ross, and when I close them each evening, the last thing I see is a friendly and reassuring flash every five seconds from Little Ross lighthouse. The lighthouse has been in almost continuous operation since 1 January 1843, and its dedicated and diligent keepers have served mariners and the community in general in accordance with the traditions and high standards established by the Commissioners for Northern Lights. The beam of light that the lighthouse emits is paradoxically now much weaker than it was when the lighthouse first went into service. Oil lamps, lenses, and mirrors, combined with ingenuity and great skill, generated a light that was visible for far greater distances than is now considered necessary. That fact, combined with the expense of providing the constant attention and maintenance necessitated by Victorian engineering, has led to the use of an automated solar-powered light, which though weaker, is more efficient.

As a child in the early 1950s, I occasionally spent weekends with a school friend in the mansion house of Balmae, one of the closest mainland residential properties to Little Ross. I vividly remember the excitement and romance of the lighthouse's beam raking across the bedroom wall every five seconds. Sadly, the mansion house of Balmae has since been demolished, leaving no trace of its existence.

There has only been one occasion when the light at Little Ross has been extinguished. I was at the lighthouse on that day, the 18 August 1960, and therefore have first-hand knowledge of the violent and tragic happenings that brought about the end of a previously unbroken record of 118 years of devoted service by 26 principal keepers, 35 assistant keepers, their families, and an unknown number of occasional and relief keepers. In this book, I attempt to tell the story of the island and of the men, women, and children who lived there. To almost all of them, it was a beautiful, peaceful, and much loved home. Wherever possible, direct quotations from people who had first-hand experience of either life on the island or incidents that took place in the vicinity have been used, without any attempt to alter the original spelling or grammar. The words of these people, and those of many other contemporary writers, paint a vivid picture of a vanished lifestyle which, although occasionally blighted by sadness and misfortune, was largely happy, purposeful, and rewarding.

CHAPTER 1

Little Ross Island

The south coast of Scotland stretches from the Mull of Galloway in the west to the head of the Solway Firth in the east. The mouth of the northern side of the Solway Firth is at Abbey Head, a few miles to the east of Kirkcudbright, and all shores to the west are exposed to the open waters of the Irish Sea. The coastline is indented deeply by Luce Bay, Wigtown Bay, and to a lesser extent by Auchencairn Bay and the estuaries of the rivers Cree, Fleet, Dee, Urr, and Nith. It is generally a very attractive and unspoiled coast, with no large towns and no heavy industries to pollute its rivers and beaches. Near to the village of Dundrennan however, 4,700 acres of former agricultural land have been used as a military testing area since 1942. The 'range', as it is generally known, is now more properly referred to as Kirkcudbright Training Area, and includes an area of sea 15 miles by 19 miles, into which projectiles are sometimes fired. There are currently considerable local concerns about future pollution occurring from the firing of shells containing depleted uranium. The range safety launch *Gallovidian III* is usually anchored off Little Ross Island when firing is in progress, and its skipper, Gary McKie, has the lonely task of standing by in almost any weather to forewarn the skippers of passing vessels of any activities which may affect them.

The mainland landscape consists largely of rolling agricultural land fringed with cliffs and a rocky shore. In the more protected areas within the main estuaries are several attractive sandy beaches, and due to the extreme tidal ranges that prevail, large expanses of sand and mud are exposed at low tide. The Borgue coast, which includes Little Ross Island, is a site of special scientific interest, but no records are published of any specific features of the island. A short distance inland, hills such as Screel, Bengairn, and Criffel provide relief from the pastoral landscape, and distant views of the Galloway hills add grandeur. There are a few islands close to the Scottish coast, but none close to the coast of north west England. The Isle of Man lies 23 miles south of Little Ross Island, basking in its unusual status as a self-governing British Crown Dependency which is not part of the United Kingdom.

The main islands off the Scottish south coast are the Isles of Fleet at the mouth of the estuary of the River Fleet, consisting of Ardwall Island, Barlocco Island, and Murray's Isles; Little Ross Island at the mouth of the estuary of the River Dee; Hestan Island at the mouth of the River Urr, and Rough Island in the estuary of the Urr. The Scares Rocks are prominent at the mouth of Luce Bay but consist only of bare rocks with little or no traces of vegetation, and are visited only by seabirds, seals, and the occasional intrepid ornithologist.

Little Ross, Hestan, Ardwall, and the larger of the two Murray's Isles have all been inhabited at some time in their histories. Hestan, like Little Ross, now has an automatic lighthouse, but it was formerly taken care of by attendant boatmen rather than full-time keepers, the attendants living for a time in a cottage which was originally built to accommodate copper miners. The cottage still exists and is now used as a holiday home. There is also some evidence at Hestan of the island's occupation in mediaeval times. Ardwall and Hestan are both known to have been used by persons involved in the smuggling trade, and in the case of Ardwall, this activity centred on a cottage on the island, which is now used as a holiday home. Ardwall was also the site of a mediaeval chapel, hall house, and burial ground. The ruins of a small stone cottage still stand on the larger of the two Murray's Isles. It was probably used as a seasonal bothy for fishermen in Fleet Bay.

Of the islands mentioned, only Little Ross and the Murray's Isles are true islands wholly surrounded by water at all times, albeit fairly shallow. The other islands, and a few smaller ones, are relatively accessible to walkers at low tide, though local knowledge and great care is advisable in the interests of safety. Little Ross, Hestan, and the Murray's Isles all provide useful anchorages for small vessels of limited draft, but only the anchorage at Little Ross enables vessels of moderate size to lie in safety in all but the most extreme weather conditions.

Little Ross Island sits at the mouth of the River Dee, in Kirkcudbright Bay, a quarter of a nautical mile from the headland at its west side. The island measures approximately 550 yards along its north-east/south-west axis, and 220 yards along its north-west/south-east axis. The bay, which is one and a half nautical miles wide at its mouth and has an average width on one nautical mile, runs northwards from its mouth for approximately four and a half nautical miles. St Mary's Isle protrudes southwards down the middle of the bay for one nautical mile and ends with the tiny island of Inch at its southern tip. The River Dee flows southwards down the west side of the bay, but cuts sharply to the southeast, passes the southerly tip of the Inch at St Mary's Isle Point, then continues until it is close to the eastern shore of the bay where the RNLI Station now stands. At that point it again turns sharply southwards and merges with the waters of the Irish Sea. The shores of the bay are wooded and the western side is particularly attractive and unspoiled, most of its shore being accessed only by a footpath. At the southern end of the west shore, Ross Bay opens out to the west. Ross Bay is shallow, but enables small vessels to dry out comfortably at low water on soft mud and in good shelter from northerly and southerly winds. Ross Bay is however partially exposed to westerly winds due to the low-lying nature of the land to its west; it is completely open to the east. Opposite the point of St Mary's Isle lies Dhoon Bay, a pleasant sandy beach accessible by road from Kirkcudbright. Above Dhoon Bay, the road turns inland towards the village of Borgue, five miles from Kirkcudbright.

The old harbour at Kirkcudbright, circa 1900

The southern end of the eastern shore of Kirkcudbright Bay is rocky, with high cliffs and several sea caves adding to its appeal. North of the lifeboat station however, the ground falls away to a belt of agricultural land and a public road that leads eventually to more woodland and the town of Kirkcudbright. The harbour of Kirkcudbright is in the heart of the town, on the south bank of the river. The harbour quay dries out at low tide but is still heavily used by fishing vessels of up to 100 ft. in length, and occasional coasters of up to 248 ft. in length. A small marina only a short distance downstream enables pleasure craft and smaller fishing vessels to lie afloat at all stages of the tide:

> Wee Ross - One of the best known islands belonging Galloway; it stands at the mouth of the Dee, and is about two miles in circumference; the Isle of *Heston,* [sic] in the *Bay of Balcarry,* [sic] is about the same size, and swarms with rabbits; there are none of these animals on the *Wee Ross,* but there are plenty of rats, which burrow amongst the rocks, and live on *partons, pirr-eggs,*

3

etc; it is called the *Wee Ross,* because the bold headland, termed the *Big Ross,* is right beside it, and forms, from its height, a famous landmark for sailors; between the two lands is a rock, termed *Janet Richardson.* This was a poor woman who belonged to *Clauchendolly,* and who went on to the rock at ebb-tide to gather a *powkfu' o' mussles;* while so employed the sea flowed round the rock, unobserved by her, at length noticing it — she '*kilted up her coats, aboon the na'el,*' as the saying is, plunged in, but the *buldering* waters of the sound hurried her off her *feckless shanks,* but she having a *farkage o' claise* about her, they keeped her *aboon broe,* until she was driven ashore on the *Milton Lands* [sic]; from such circumstances is the rock named, and that name will likely remain as long as if it had been given by Cook or Parry.

Beside this isle is a tolerable place for ships to anchor in, when they come from off the sea, at a wrong time of the tide, and must wait for *water* flowing of depth, to swim them up the river. However, if the storm be a hurricane, the shelter is not so great, and it requires a ship with the best holding tackle to ride secure.

The Scottish Gallovidian Encyclopedia by John Mactaggart, (1824).

In comparison with many of the magnificent islands off Scotland's west and north Coasts, Little Ross Island might reasonably be described as unremarkable. It has not been an inspiration for famous authors, poets, or composers, and it does not seem to have been the subject of either traditional music or folklore. There is a relatively modern Scottish Country Dance entitled 'Little Ross Light', but how it came to be thus named is unknown. Little Ross Island has certainly featured in the work of many of the distinguished artists that have either been resident in, or visited, Kirkcudbright since the mid-19th century, but has mainly been in the background rather than forming the main subject of their drawings and paintings. Like many other places where there are Stevenson designed lighthouses, its dramatic setting and lonely splendour may have provided inspiration for Robert Louis Stevenson's books. Perhaps Thomas Stevenson told his son stories of his long period of hard and lonely work there, while deprived of many of the comforts of city life. But Kirkcudbright's mariners have always regarded 'The Ross' with great affection, and at least one of them named his vessel after his 'home' island.

The 100 ton schooner *Little Ross* was commissioned by Captain Andrew Morrison of Kirkcudbright and was built by McPherson and Sons at their Friarton yard in Perth, from where she was launched in February 1870. She was subsequently based at Liverpool, but few details of her history are known. In November 1879, one of her crew, Murdoch Maddison, was charged with smuggling three pounds of tobacco from Amsterdam and fined one pound, twelve shillings, and sixpence. Two years later, on 10 February 1881, *Little Ross* was driven onto rocks at Blackhills, near the 'Bullers o' Buchan' in Aberdeenshire, and dashed to pieces. Her master and three crewmen, all from Skye, were drowned and only one man survived, having been rescued by three men on shore who each received a silver medal for 'Sea Gallantry', in recognition of their bravery.

The summit of the island, on which a lighthouse now stands, is 123 ft. above sea level, yet even that modest height provides an excellent vantage point from which to enjoy a panoramic view of the surrounding sea and nearby land. To the north are the relatively sheltered waters of Kirkcudbright Bay, to the northwest the cliffs and rocky shore of the parish of Borgue, and to the northeast, the cliffs, heughs, and rocky shores of the parishes of Dundrennan and Auchencairn. Further to the east, the seascape is dominated by a wind farm at Robin Rigg in the Solway Firth, but to the southeast, the view of the hills of the English Lake District remains almost unspoiled. The Isle of Man can be clearly seen to the south, southwest; in good weather in the hours of darkness, distant flashes from the lighthouses at the Point of Ayre and Maughold Head are often visible. In common with many other islands close to the mainland, Little Ross seems to enjoy a little less rain and a little more sunshine than the neighbouring mainland. In the absence of resident lighthouse keepers, there may no longer be statistics to prove this, but it is common to find that Little Ross is bathed in sunshine while a mass of low cloud hangs over the mainland, bounded by the edge of the coast. In 1906, dramatic proof of the anomalous weather at Little Ross was provided when 28 inches of rainfall were recorded at Little Ross at the southern extremity of the Stewartry of Kirkcudbright, compared with 60.2 inches at Glenlee in the north.

The shores of the island are generally rocky, and although there are only fairly modest cliffs, the rocks are sufficiently steep and jagged to make it advisable for vessels to keep well clear, particularly from the southern tip of the island. In stormy weather, and particularly when the wind is from the south east through south to the south west, seas break heavily on the island, throwing salt spray high over the rocks. Apart from stony beaches at the north–eastern and north–western tips of the island, there are no natural safe places on which to land.

Malcolm McL. Harper provided an interesting paragraph or two about Little Ross Island in his book *Rambles in Galloway,* published in 1896:

> From this point [Mutehill] is obtained a beautiful glimpse of the estuary of the river, apparently landlocked by the Little Ross Island, which lies off the great "Ross," signifying a promontory running into the sea. A narrow passage of 480 yards separates the Ross Isle, which is nearly a quarter of a mile in greatest length from the mainland. The island is somewhat oval in form, and a mysterious cavern or underground chamber in it is worthy of mention.

Rambles in Galloway by Malcolm McL. Harper, (1896).

The 'mysterious cavern' referred to in the above extract cannot now be located with certainty, but a rocky fissure on the east side of the island, the roof of which has now collapsed, is probably that described by Malcolm Harper. To find it, one must follow the line of the north wall of the garden adjacent to the forge and adjoined buildings in an easterly direction towards the sea. This leads to a deep, open-topped, and rather dangerous fissure where the grassy heughs give way to rocks. The fissure extends all the way from there to the sea and part of it is still roofed by both natural and loose rock. It is presumed that in 1896, the open-topped section was still wholly or partly bridged over. At that time it would therefore have been a well-concealed cave of some depth, which may have been relatively dry at its upper end.

Detailed geological information is rarely available about small, insignificant, and rarely visited islands, but Little Ross was the subject of the following paper, presented to the Wernerian Natural History Society on 8 April 1843 by Thomas Stevenson. Thomas was the youngest son of Robert, the founder of the Stevenson dynasty of engineers. Thomas's report on the island's geology uses clear, non-technical language to explain his subject in a manner that is stylistically as acceptable today as it was when written 172 years ago. Perhaps it is not surprising that his son, Robert Louis Stevenson, became one of Scotland's most famous writers:

> Remarks on the Geology of the Island of Little Ross, Kirkcudbrightshire. By Thomas Stevenson, Esq., Civil Engineer.
>
> Having been for some time resident on the island of Little Ross, whilst superintending the erection of a sea-light and other works on that coast, I had an opportunity of examining the geology of the island; and as my observations have led to results which, to myself at least, were unexpected, I have ventured to draw up a short account of them.
>
> Little Ross is situated at the mouth of Kirkcudbright Bay, and is about 1500 feet long by 800 feet broad. Its distance from the nearest point of the mainland is not more than 340 yards; and although there is a depth of about 20 feet at high water, there is nevertheless a narrow ridge by which, in many low spring tides, it is possible for foot passengers to cross over, not, however, dryshod.
>
> The district in which this island is situated has been generally supposed to exemplify the Cambrian group of the Transitional class; and accordingly the Little Ross Island, at first sight, presents the usual appearances of the greywacke of that geological epoch. It exhibits also a singular scene of disruption, torsion, and upheaving of the strata, which attain a height of 100 feet above the level of the sea. At the north-west extremity, or that most sheltered from the sea, there is a beach called the White Bay, [now known generally as the White Beach] consisting of shingle; while at all other points the rocks expose surfaces varying from low angles up to the perpendicular. There is but a thin covering of sod over the surface, below which may be found angular fragments of the mouldering rock, embedded in loam or earth resulting therefrom; and lying on this are erratic boulders of granite, compact felspar and porphyry, as well as a few water-worn pebbles of greywhacke.
>
> The rocks themselves consist of beds of greywhacke, alternating with conformable greywhacke slates, or, as they are there termed, *Slate-band*. The greywhacke beds vary in fineness, from the coarsest conglomerate or breccia, up to a nearly homogenous blue and sometimes greyish rock. And first, I may notice the composition of the conglomerates, which consist of water-worn boulders of greywhacke, embedded in a softish matrix of the same rock, or at least in an argillaceous rock of very similar description. This may

perhaps favour the conclusion that these deposits belong to the more recent of the transition class. With regard to the breccia, it is proper to state that it should more strictly be termed a *breccia-conglomerate,* as it consists of embedded fragments, partly angular, partly rounded. These conglomerates are often permeated by veins of yellowish, and sometimes red carbonate of lime, tinged probably by manganese.

Next in fineness comes a very coarse greywhacke, consisting of small pebbles of quartz, fragments of jasper, Lydian stone, pieces of clay-slate, etc. This rock is pervaded with dries, which separate it into triangular prisms. The other greywhackes have all a rhomboidal fracture (of from 70 to 80 degrees obliquity), and are of various degrees of fineness, and invariably shew specks of mica. They are all more or less cut up by dries or cutters, and are also pervaded in every direction by what appear to have been cracks or splits, which are occupied by carbonate of lime tinted red. These cracks, some of which intersect each other, give the rock, when cut for building purposes, a beautiful variegated or veined appearance. Besides these, there are brittle shales, which the action of the weather has in many places reduced to a mass of disconnected prismoidal fragments, that moulder away into a ferruginous earth. The regular beds of greywhacke are of two kinds — the one blue, the other whitish, and liable to weather red, so as to resemble, externally, beds of red sandstone. These two kinds seem to alternate with *slate-band* possessing corresponding characteristics. The blue alternates with dark-blue slates, having glossy sides, and of a fine and sometimes silky texture; while the whiter variety alternates with greyish-white slates, which weather still whiter.

Several of the slates have the peculiarity of unconformable cleavage-planes. The angles which the planes of cleavage make with the line of stratification, are generally about 30 degrees.

In some of the rocks above described, I have found embedded small pieces of *anthracite.* Quartz-veins do not occur, but carbonate of lime is very common; and sulphate of barites is not unfrequent. In one or two instances, I have found in crevices, small quantities of *bitumen* or *mineral pitch,* galena, and in one instance, steatite, which shall be afterwards described. In some parts also there are traces of copper-ore.

These constitute all the stratified rocks which this small island affords. Of trap rocks, we have several varieties. At the beach called White Bay, and at the top of the island, there are dykes of reddish coloured greenstone, in some places passing into a granite rock; while, at others, they resemble a compact felspar rock. Besides the greenstones, I have seen two dykes of compact felspar base, with here and there crystals of hornblende or augite interspersed. In a small felspathic dyke, on the south side of the island, there are brilliant specks of iron-pyrites.

In contact with these igneus intruders, the strata have undergone the usual changes. The greywhacke has become crystalline, so as to resemble greenstone, and the slates have become, in some cases, a sort of Lydian stone. In others, they are converted into flinty slates, of a yellow or creamy colour, and in both the edges of fragments are translucent, and the fissile property is destroyed. Near the trap-dykes the *altered rocks,* in some instances, contain specks of iron-pyrites.

Such then are the rocks of which the island is composed; and the characteristics which render them interesting, are the following:

On the eastern side, close to the sea, at a place where stones were quarried for the lighthouse works, there is a range of rocks tilted up at a high angle, and of which the quarrying operations have afforded a section. Among these is a bed, the upper side of which appears to have been exposed to diluvial action at some time posterior to its consolidation, as the surface is uneven and rounded. Conformable with this, and superior to it, is a series of very thin (1/16 inch) layers of slate-band. These layers of slate have obviously been deposited after the lower bed has been wasted, as they not only rest conformably with it, but have followed all the salient and re-entrant angles which its water-worn surface presents. This renders it probable that some considerable period had elapsed between the deposit of this member of the series and the incumbent shales.

In the finer sorts of greywhacke, I found very good specimens of the *graptolite* or *sea-pen*. The offshoots or feet are visible on one side only, so as to give the fossil very much the appearance of a saw. I have also found one specimen of the double graptolite, such as was observed in Norway by Dr. Beck of Copenhagen.

On the western side of the island I found a quantity of steatite investing the irregular masses of the whiter sort of greywhacke; nor does it traverse the rock as a vein, but seems confined to one spot. Some parts of it are translucent, of a greyish-yellow colour, with a shining oily lustre, and streaked appearance externally; while other parts are of a very dark green, or blackish colour, and massive.

In the coarser greywhacke, formerly described as a closely aggregated rock, containing a variety of fragments and pebbles, my friend Mr. J. T. Syme, civil-engineer, who spent some time with me on the island, found part of a shell; and I have since then procured many specimens that appear to be of different species; but I have found only one entire *shell,* which was unfortunately lost soon after I had got it. So far as I could judge from the imperfect examination that I had the opportunity of making, it appeared to belong to the genus *Terebratula.*

In the same sort of rock, which is certainly the last, both from its structure and the coarseness of its texture, that anyone would think of examining for organic remains, I have observed small circles of carbonate of lime, having a black spot in the centre, with apparent radiation, which on the whole closely resemble fragments of the stalks of Encrinites. But as I have seldom met with this appearance, I am not prepared to state that *Encrinites* are to be included in the list of the organic remains of the island. It is important to remark that the rock where these occur bears no mark of having been stratified, having no cleavage plane, and being every where pervaded by dries, which separate the mass into triangular prisms, and in some cases into other symmetrical solids. The occurrence, however, of organic exuviae alone, independent of the rounded pebbles which it contains, are, of course, absolutely conclusive as to its being of mechanical origin.

Mr. E. G. Fleming of Kirkcudbright shewed me a fossil which he had found several years ago in the solid greywhacke rock, at a point on the mainland nearly opposite to Little Ross Island. This fossil I found to be an *Orthoceratite*; and another specimen has since been found in the same spot, which confirms its identity.

There remains one point of interest to be mentioned, and that is the occurrence of an *elevated sea-beach*. As formerly noticed, there is but one beach on the island, at a place called the White Bay. It consists of oval-shaped shingle, of a size which, in Lancashire, would be called *single stanner*, and it is principally composed of greywhacke, with here and there travelled boulders of porphyry, of various colours. This shingle has assembled itself into two little bays, with a connecting spit between, the top of which is covered with lichen, and it is composed of the same sort of shingle as the beach below, but is considerably above the range of the highest tides. At the top of this spit the grass line occurs, and to appearance the beach here seems to end, but in reality the boulders are found in a decomposing state, and bedded in the loam resulting from that decomposition, for at least 20 feet above the present highest tide-mark. The grassy part has also the same slope and contour as the uncovered part of the beach. In cutting through this bed for a road, I found, at a depth of 4½ ft below the surface, *cockle, periwinkle,* and other shells, which still inhabit the neighbouring shores.

Here, then, is a beach whose level and appearance prove the gradual elevation of the island. Unlike many other similar relics of the sea that are found without anything intermediate to substantiate the connection, this beach presents a uniform continuation of the existing shore to the height of 20ft above the range of the highest tides, and thus would seem to provide strong presumptive evidence, that the land at this place does, or at least did, *gradually* emerge from the ocean, the general shape and contour of the present bays being easily recognisable on the grass-grown land.

I am sensible that the foregoing observations are in some respects but very imperfect, yet I feel justified in giving this sketch, as the facts which happened to come under my notice seem to favour the conclusion that the Silurian system, as characterised by Mr. Murchison in his work on the Silurian system, exists in Scotland.

Records of the Wernerian Natural History Society, two volumes of minute books (Jan 1808–Apr 1858) Edinburgh University Library GB 237 Coll-206 loc. Dc.2.55-56. Image from the Biodiversity Heritage Library. Digitised by Edinburgh University Library. www.biodiversitylibrary.org

Thomas Stevenson mentions that some of the stone used in the construction of the lighthouse station was quarried on the east side of the island, and signs can still be seen of that activity. Kirkcudbright expanded rapidly in the early to late 19th century, and most of the buildings of that period feature either random or coursed whinstone walls with dressed sandstone lintels, window margins, and quoins. Examples include the Sheriff Court House and Jail, the Parish Church, and both the original and the replacement Town Halls. Some of the whinstone is generally believed to have come from Little Ross Island, the Isles of Fleet, and various other places along the Borgue coast, brought to the intended building sites by small wherries based at Kirkcudbright.

The only building that is known to have existed on the island prior to the construction of the lighthouse station was situated northeast of the present beacon tower, at the head of a deep and narrow gully running down to the rocky shore. The building appears on early 19th century maps as a ruin, and no references have been found regarding its former use. Its purpose would seem to have been residential rather than as an observation post, since it is sited in perhaps the most protected location on the island, sheltered from the prevailing wind by the rocky hillock on which the beacon tower is built, but without the commanding view available from higher on the island. The rocky shore adjacent to it would not have been an ideal place to either keep or launch a boat, so a fisherman's bothy or store does not seem a particularly plausible explanation for its existence. It may simply have been a shelter for anyone stranded on the island, or for anyone tending crops or livestock there. Only a few fragments of collapsed stonework now remain, much overgrown by nettles. The possibility that it might have been the recluse of a hermit, or even a monk is intriguing and merits some archaeological investigation. The presence of early Christian settlements on Ardwall Island and at the Isle of Whithorn, each of which is within ten miles from Little Ross, might be significant.

One of the caves situated close to the east side of the mouth of Kirkcudbright Bay, now known as Torrs Cave, has been excavated and shows evidence of nine layers of human habitation having taken place between the Iron Age and medieval times. A similar cave on the mainland three miles to the west of Little Ross, now known as the Bone Cave of Borness, has also been excavated and has yielded large quantities of finds indicating human habitation dating from the first and second centuries AD. The archaeologist Frederick R. Coles recorded cup and ring markings on rocks at Little Ross Island in 1895, but subsequent searches for them in 1911 and 1965 failed to identify any such markings. Rather oddly, the original observation by F. R. Coles was noted as being on rocks that were below the high water mark. There is a current feeling among experts that natural markings may have been mistaken for those made by men or women. Frederick R. Coles was however an experienced observer of such symbols, having lectured and written widely on the subject. Perhaps he was wrong, but it is also possible that later quarrying of stone removed or obliterated what he saw in 1895.

Little Ross Island would have offered substantial security to people in lawless times, with the opportunity to observe, from the summit of the island, the approach of anyone who posed a potential threat from any direction and to prepare accordingly. Unusually for such a small island, it also offered some arable land and a fresh water supply in the form of one or two small springs. Fishing from the rocky shores would have been relatively easy and large quantities of mussels, limpets, and crustaceans were available from around the nearby rocks. There was nowhere on the island that offered a convenient harbour for small boats, but the stony beaches at the north and north-western extremities of the island would have made carrying small dugout canoes or similar craft to safety and concealment relatively easy.

There is as yet no firm archaeological evidence of any other early human habitation on the island apart from the buildings already described. There are some signs of rig and furrow cultivation, but no indication of the period from which they date. At the time of writing, traces of a possible circular building site with a raised rim at its edge which incorporates some stonework have been noted, and a theory that this may be evidence of a Bronze Age round house has yet to be investigated.

Members of the Finlay family were tenants of Ross Farm, at the head of Ross Bay on the mainland, from the 1840s until 1971, and became owners of it in 1971. The tenancy of Ross Farm included grazing rights on Little Ross Island, but when the farm was sold, the grazing rights reverted to St Mary's Isle Estate. James Finlay recollects that his grandfather kept six to ten black Galloway cattle on the island, leading them back and forwards to the mainland as necessary during extremely low spring tides. The grass on Little Ross however did not agree with the cattle's digestive systems, causing them to become constipated, so their diet had to be supplemented with linseed oil cake. Later, up to 30 black-faced lambs, known as hoggs, used to be taken across to the island for the summer months to fatten them up. The grass on the island at that time was fresh and sweet, as the large population of rabbits kept it close-cropped through the winter months, promoting strong new growth in the spring. The lambs were dipped before being taken to the island, and the chemicals used at that time were so strong that they kept the lambs free of 'fly strike' all summer without them requiring any attention.

James Finlay and his sister helped their father on one occasion to lead the lambs back to the mainland, following the same route used by his grandfather at low tide. But the tide ran more swiftly than they had anticipated, causing them to lose control of the lambs, which then began to panic and to swim in circles as their coats became heavier and heavier. Although the Finlays all came ashore safely, the lambs were swept away and drowned. James referred rather ruefully to the fact that many people dined on roast lamb in the following few days. After that incident, lambs were only taken to the island by small boat, with their feet tied together. Black-faced sheep and lambs are known to be good jumpers, and are therefore difficult to keep securely in fields unless fences are particularly high, or dykes are appropriate and in good condition. The island therefore seemed to offer a conveniently safe home for them. It transpired though that the lambs that lived on Little Ross became so skilled at climbing over the island's rocks that they developed even greater acrobatic abilities than their mainland-based relatives, and were very difficult to contain on their eventual return to conventional fields. The brand of sheep dip that enabled the lambs to be free of 'fly strike' was eventually banned because of adverse effects on the environment, and no lambs were kept on the island after the late 1960s.

James Finlay describes an occasion on which he and his brother Brian spent a long day on Little Ross, shearing lambs and tending generally to their needs. When the time came for them to stop for a much needed lunch break, Brian, who was according to his brother a 'fussy eater', was irritated to find that his sandwiches contained cheese, and stuffed them down a rabbit hole in disgust (this is rather surprising, as the dairy at Ross Farm produced the best cheese I have ever tasted!). By late afternoon James was hungry, but Brian was ravenous. Brian's hunger eventually drove him back to the site of their picnic lunch, where he succeeded in identifying the correct rabbit hole then recovered and ate his previously spurned sandwiches.

It is James and Richard Finlay's impression that when the lighthouse station was built, it would have been practical for the keepers to keep a cow or two on the island to produce their own milk, butter, and cheese, and that pigs might have been fed on domestic waste and whey. James also believes it to be likely that a pony or two could have been kept on the island to haul carts carrying stores and provisions from the landing places to the island's various buildings.

The low profile of most of the lighthouse keepers and their families and the absence of any known human occupants prior to 1841 has made Little Ross, for most of its known history, an unofficial sanctuary for wildlife. After automation of the lighthouse in 1960, the island was completely uninhabited for 27 years, and during that time the gardens diligently cultivated by the lighthouse keepers became overgrown, as did a small putting green and many of the island's paths. The winches and timber mooring posts at landing places rusted and rotted, and the island became a lonely place, abandoned by humans but home to great numbers of other species.

Deer often swim across the sound to Little Ross, and groups of up to six have been seen on the island. There is very little natural vegetation to provide cover for them, but they are adept at hiding behind rocks and ensuring that they are on the opposite side of the island from any intruders. To come upon one at sea is quite disconcerting; when they are swimming, their heads and necks are well clear of the water's surface and they bear a close resemblance to images purporting to be that of the Loch Ness Monster. This is particularly evident when the sea is very calm, and a 'V' shaped wake spreads from the swimmer's neck.

Keepers tried hard to control the rabbits by shooting, which also provided a valuable source of fresh and nutritious meat with which to supplement their rations. Myxomatosis was introduced to the island at some point after 1960 and effectively wiped out the entire rabbit population for a time. Sadly, there is evidence that attempts to gas the rabbits were also made, and may have resulted in the unintentional eradication of some nesting puffins. Nowadays, in the absence of the keepers' fresh vegetables, rabbits do not seem to be quite so tempted to set up home at Little Ross, although they initially prospered in their absence. Contrary to the situation reported by Mactaggart in his *Scottish Gallovidian Encyclopedia* of 1824, rats do not seem to be a problem today. However, mice, shrews, and voles are flourishing, and their burrowing has made much of the ground tussocky and difficult to walk on safely. The island's owls seem to greatly appreciate their presence.

Richard Finlay recalls that when the lighthouse keepers were in residence, their domestic waste was dumped on the shore at the south-east side of the island, where it attracted a lot of rats. Those rats also reduced the bird population by eating their eggs. In the late 1970s, mink became common on the island and these ferocious predators soon wiped out both the rats and the few rabbits which had survived the introduction of myxomatosis. Mink were also seen to occasionally attack and kill gulls and to pull their bodies into abandoned rabbit holes. A research project based on the island's population of mink was undertaken by two students from the University of Durham in about 1990. A male and a female mink were tagged with radio transmitters and their movements were followed. Mink had disappeared from the island by the 1990s, after presumably disposing of virtually all the rats and rabbits. A lone dead fox was found on the island by attendant boatman/keeper George Davidson during the years he visited the island after the automation of the lighthouse.

The island's bird life splits into two categories: the birds that breed there, and those that can be observed from the island. Detailed records of sightings in each category were made by several keepers and are quoted in chapters 9 and 10. The records show a great variety of species, including some of considerable rarity. A report, 'The Breeding Birds of the Solway Islands', listed the following breeding pairs of birds as being observed on Little Ross Island in 2005: cormorants, oystercatchers, ringed plovers, common gulls, lesser black-backed gulls, herring gulls, greater black-backed gulls, skylarks, rock pipits, wrens, carrion crows, and linnets, but some of the birds listed, such as cormorants and crows, probably nested on the nearby mainland cliffs. There are no present day records specific to Little Ross and no-one today has as much opportunity to make such observations as was enjoyed by the lighthouse keepers, so it is difficult to make an accurate comparison of the situation then and now. One fears that it would be difficult to record such a variety of sightings today as was recorded by the keepers anyway. Some fairly rare species not recorded by the keepers, such as spoonbills and ospreys, have nevertheless been seen in Kirkcudbright Bay, not far from the island, and other common species such as herons are plentiful all around the shores of the bay. Gannets are also now frequently to be seen fishing close to the island and within the bay.

Fishermen from Kirkcudbright have worked in the vicinity of Little Ross Island for centuries, setting creels in which to catch crabs and lobsters, but they have also line-fished and trawled for many different species of fish. The late John King MBE, Kirkcudbright's best-known commercial fisherman, spoke of catching mackerel, whiting, cod, plaice, spotted dogfish, spur dogfish, tope, coal fish, pollock, john dory, blochans, conger eels, dabs, lemon sole, skate, lobsters, and crabs in the area surrounding Little Ross.

Creatures such as seals, otters, porpoises, and bottle-nosed dolphins are often seen around Little Ross, the latter sometimes in considerable numbers. In the early 1970s, while sailing very close to the east quay at Little Ross in a 22 ft. sailing boat, I passed within six feet of a basking shark which was as large as my boat. The experience was a little unsettling, as the shark appeared to move closer to me to satisfy its own curiosity. When alongside, it even rolled on to its side, enabling its eye to look directly up at me. On 9 August 2003, a leather-backed turtle is recorded as having been seen by Karen Upton, 28 metres off Little Ross Island, alive and swimming eastwards, and her sighting was confirmed by other similar reports. A few years later, the body of an orca was found on the rocks close to Torrs Point, and on 3 August 2011, I and two Kirkcudbright fishermen working in the area saw a fin whale, approximately 40 ft. in length, swimming close to the island. I had just passed through the Little Ross Sound heading southwards, and was travelling west, close inshore, when an unusual sound attracted my attention and I saw the whale spouting while passing between me and the shore, moving eastwards.

A detailed examination of marine life occurring between the high and low water marks was made a few years ago, concentrating on two separate locations on the shores of Little Ross Island. The report is of a rather specialised and technical nature, and has therefore not been included here, but an extensive list of the findings made can be found in *Species point records from 2000 Reach, Little Ross Island (Kirkcudbright bay) littoral survey,* published by Joint Nature Conservation Committee (JNCC) (custodian).

As mentioned by Thomas Stevenson, the island is rocky, with only a thin covering of soil, although its grassy cover is green in all but the hottest and driest spells of weather. Plant species that thrive on the island are limited generally to those capable of tolerating high winds bearing considerable quantities of salt, and there are few trees or shrubs which have chosen to grow there. A few apple trees survive close to the garden walls from early plantings by the lighthouse keepers, and they still bear fruit, despite being small and stunted. Occasional clumps of small conifers were planted after the lighthouse cottages came into private hands and can still be seen struggling to survive. Site monitoring of the island's plant life was carried out in 1989 by David Hawker, and was part of the research necessary as a prelude to the setting up of the Borgue coast SSSI (Site of Special Scientific Interest). His report, made for the Nature Conservancy Council (now Scottish Natural Heritage), which includes some references to bird and animal life, is included in Appendix V.

It is not easy for members of the general public to gain access to Little Ross Island, and this has helped to maintain it as a rarely disturbed place, where only the owners of either working boats or pleasure craft can come ashore to stretch their legs, or to have a picnic with their families. Neither the island's owners nor the Northern Lighthouse Board have ever taken any steps to restrict access, and the military activities referred to earlier have not affected passage to or from the island. On occasions, private charter services can be arranged to gain access to the island in suitable conditions of weather and tide. Enquiries regarding this matter are best made initially to the harbourmaster at Kirkcudbright.

CHAPTER 2

Captain Skelly's Beacons

Prior to 1820, it would have been very difficult for the master of any visiting vessel approaching the Port of Kirkcudbright to identify the entrance to the channel of the River Dee at its junction with the Irish Sea, close to the mouth of Kirkcudbright Bay. Few navigational aids existed, and although a pilot with local knowledge would have been able to assist, the only means of establishing communication with potential pilots would have involved a considerable lapse of time, during which weather, daylight, and tidal conditions may well have become less favourable. Many masters in such circumstances were forced to make decisions that would ultimately lead to considerable loss of life and property, as a consequence of the grounding of ships, damage to vessels and, in the worst cases, shipwrecks.

The channel was sporadically marked upstream from its mouth by timber 'perches' – tall wooden posts inserted in pits dug at low tide on the muddy sides of the channel, with traditional top marks of bunches of withies above high tide level, indicating whether they were port or starboard hand markers. For port hand markers, the bunches of withies had the fine ends of their twigs pointing upwards and for starboard hand markers, they pointed downwards. Such perches however were vulnerable to damage by high winds and heavy seas and required constant maintenance and frequent replacement. It was not practical for them to be placed close to the mouth of the channel because of the severity of conditions there during adverse weather.

Clearly, what was needed was a simple system of highly visible leading marks, which a ship's master could align to guide him directly on to the most advantageous course by which to enter or leave the navigable channel. Such marks are common in many ports throughout the world, and usually involve a prominent feature such as a church steeple close to the sea front brought into line with a cairn or tower on high ground inland of the port. Kirkcudbright Bay has few obvious sites for such marks on the mainland, but has in Little Ross Island an ideal location, which has the advantage of proximity to the hazard concerned and the resulting enhanced visibility.

Local mariner, ship owner, and ship builder Captain James Skelly campaigned for years to raise public awareness of the need for beacons to mark the entrance to the channel of the River Dee and to raise the necessary funding by public subscription. His efforts were eventually successful, and this already well-respected and popular Kirkcudbright man became something of a local hero. Part of his life story is told, along with the story of the beacons, in the following extract from a tribute to him, published by his nephew John C. Mackenzie on 30 November 1880:

> Tribute to the memory of Mr. James Skelly, Ship-carpenter, Master Mariner, etc.
>
> On the *Wee Ross* stand two *land-marks,* erected by the wisdom of *Skipper Skelly;* they point out to sailors the *land's lead* and the *Dee's Channel.* I must not pass over this worthy *Skipper Skelly,* slightly; his honest and feeling mind has been exerted in behalf of the sailors, a class of men, perhaps, as much respected as any on earth, and apparently for good cause. Whatever the skipper sees he can do for them, that he doth, even to hurting himself; his daring mind is *backed* out by that of every wise man's, and all his plans have originality and good in them; well may I term him the Gallovidian marine engineer for the same reason that I term *Gladstone* (an ingenious millwright in Castle Douglas. One of his daughters became the wife of Ivie Mackie, esq., of Auchencairn) that of the land. After his *land-marks* were built, a curious *poet* fancied he addressed them thus:

> Some time ago when I was wont to cross
> The Solway Firth, and trade in coal and lime,
> Often I found myself at no small loss,
> To know the Dee in many a stormy time-
> Deep rolling river always grand, sublime-
> From others stagnant full of sludge and dross,
> Which vomit round it in the sea their slime;
> Twas then methought that from these jumbling gross,
> Skelly should mark it yet upon the Little Ross

> So I with you, ye brothers square and high
> Have had my wish, I glory in your birth,
> Stand unscar'd beneath the sulky sky,
> Let growling surfs and surges give you mirth,
> Smile at Kirkcudbright, gaze across the Firth;
> The wave dash'd vessels from the tempests cry,
> Do all the good ye can, remain while earth
> Unsmelted will around her axle fly,
> Tho' still remember Skelly who am I.
> Whene'er a sailor from the offing hails,
> Your lofty lordships boldly answer lie,
> Come hither from the gale ye tar who sails,
> Along the wild bosom of the wrathful sea,

If for a shelter you incline to be,
Within our arms is one who never fails,
Through gurly hurricanes to form a lee,
Where pitching ceases, where no anchor trails,
Give Skelly's orders then when ocean rails.
Whoe'er can lie and snore upon the pillow,
And seamen weltering round in great distress,
Bawkling for mercy, struggling with the billow,
Will surely ne'er behold the land of bliss;
Contentment's lips they'll never, never kiss,
But will be scourged by some infernal fellow,
For such as these the devil cannot miss.
Oh help the weather-beaten sailor, will ye,
Is ever the sincere wish of Skipper Skelly.

May commerce futter up our lovely river,
And fright the grass from off the untrod street,
May spirit, sense, and worth forsake us never,
Let who are foes shake hands, and friendly meet,
That pride and spleen evaporate complete,
Who brews the venom, may that venom's fever,
Retort upon themselves with furious heat;
So we'll be look'd on borough bodies clever,
And I, an humble skipper, live for ever.

So now my land-marks, hear my last advice,
Let time's fell tusks scarce e'er your beauty tear,
Should distant ages disregard your price,
Shake shiver not nor stand aghast with fear–
When I must sink at last, through tear and wear,
Beneath the soil in death's cold arms of ice,
And my poor soul through foreign countries steer,
Be sure ay tell the worthy and the wise,
My simple efforts never to despise.

Scottish Gallovidian Encyclopedia by John Mactaggart (1824).

JAMES SKELLY thus honoured in prose and verse was born in Milnburn in 1760. The intention of his parents was to make him (an only son) a scholar, and he had begun the Latin, but his mother dying, and his father being in delicate health, the lad had to be taken from the school and was bound an apprentice to the trade of a heckler. He disliked the trade, and served as a mason and house carpenter; at that time the same workman used to be mason, slater and house carpenter. He afterwards worked at sawing wood for ship-carpenters, and then took to the ship-carpenter business itself:-he had a good head and good hands:- after working for a few years at the trade he learned to draft and prepare models of vessels.

Bailie Caleb Grayson, tanner, Milnburn, a well to do man, a Welshman, King of the Milnburn (then a primitive disconnected suburb of Kirkcudbright), Thomas Torbet, mariner, and James Skelly entered into an

agreement to build a sloop at the Creek leading from the Snuff-Mill Well –
now at the head of the first embankment. Torbet was to own two-eighths,
Grayson, three-eighths, and Skelly three-eighths. Skelly was to be master,
with a practical sailor for his assistant. The vessel was named the *Isabella,*
and was the finest and the favourite sloop of the Port. She was known by
a white stripe around her hull. Her principal trade was carrying lime then
greatly used for improving the land, and coals for Kirkcudbright and the
adjoining parishes.

The Tannery and dwelling house were on the site of the Almshouses
lately built by Edward Atkinson, Esquire, of London, retired manager of the
Provincial Bank of England, the 'peabody' of Kirkcudbright. Spalding of
Holm, who was wounded in a duel by Gordon of Kenmure was carried into
Grayson's house as being the nearest house to the place where the duel was
fought, being part of the old road leading from the Milnburn to Canada and
the Boreland farms. The spot is not far from the gate and style (at the top of
the Poor-house loaning) of the field for many years occupied by Bailie Hornel.

The Skipper was a great favourite with the Borgue farmers — they were
substantial men, influential and clannish. During a meal mob, no uncommon
occurrence at the time, Mr. Sproat, tenant of Brighouse, a grain dealer, was
on a Friday (market day), set upon by a mob of men and women, (the latter
being the ringleaders), dragged into the Ferry boat, which at that time plied
from the west side of the beach, and put over the side to which he held on.
They threatened to cut his hands. The Skipper came to his rescue, and got
his clothes almost torn off his back — thirty years afterwards he used to
show a checked shirt, badly torn, which he wore on the occasion — he kept
it in his sea chest as a relic. His conduct made him the greater favourite with
the Borgue customers, who at the time were almost all connected by blood
or marriage.

The Skipper made Grayson cashier or ship's-husband for the vessel,
paying over to him the free earnings of the concern.

About the year 1814 Skelly wished to have a settlement with Grayson, but
the latter refused or delayed to account. Grayson had then acquired Torbet's
shares. Matters came to a deadlock. Skelly was a first rate book-keeper. The
parties agreed to submit the matter to arbitration, and the arbiters appointed
were Samuel McKnight, merchant and shipowner, for Grayson, and John
Callie, mariner and shipowner for Skelly, but they could not agree. James
Douglas, merchant and shipowner was appointed oversman — he found
Grayson to be due to Skelly, on fair accounting, about £700. Grayson raised
a Suspension and Reduction in the Court of Session of the Decree Arbitral.
Lord Succouth gave a judgement in favour of Grayson – the case went into
the inner-house – Succouth's judgement was overturned — Skelly's books
were produced in the court and commended. Grayson appealed to the House
of Lords, and Cases were prepared – Brougham was Counsel for Skelly, and
Romilly for Grayson. In the meantime Grayson had to pay the sums awarded
and expenses, Skelly finding caution to refund, if he lost his case. Before the
appeal could be heard, Grayson died, (1819) leaving his affairs in confusion,
and two sons who were dissipated worthless young men. They agreed to a
compromise — that is to drop the appeal.

During the submission and law proceedings Skelly worked occasionally
as a ship-carpenter, he being an excellent workman. James Niven of
Glenarm, writer in Kirkcudbright, a good man and an able man of business,

was his country agent. He felt for Skelly, against whom was pitted a reputed wealthy, influential man, and a bailie in the Town Council. Mr. Niven stood by his client. Skelly had his difficulties in providing the expenses for the Edinburgh and London agents, but with the assistance of friends he managed to meet the remittances.

In the year 1816 the *Isabella* was sold by public roup, and bought by Skelly, David Caig, ship-carpenter, and William Armstrong, mariner. Armstrong sailed her as captain — he became dissipated, did no good as master, fell into bad health and died. A nephew of Caig succeeded him, and did no better. Skelly loved the old sloop dearly. After his death in 1828, she was sold to Mr. James Christal.

The elder of Grayson's two sons, Willie, was a character — see "Mactaggart's Gallovidian Encyclopedia." In winter 1813-14, he did what no man before or since ever did — he crossed on the ice of the River at Kirkcudbright on horseback. The horse was the well-known "Crop"— so named from having had his ears cropped. During the severe frost of last winter Mrs xxx told the milkman on his round, that she saw Wullie Grayson cross the river on the ice with his horse long ago;-the milkman being incredulous, John Bunewin (a character famous for drawing the long bow), when passing, overheard the dialogue and came to the rescue, saying, "Faith that's true – Wasn't I the very wee boy that sat in the gig with him!" To which the lady replied, "Toots, now John, that'll no do, for there was nae wee boy in the case – Wullie was on horse-back."

Mr. Skelly was a humane, public spirited man — he had ample experience of the dangers of the coast, and the difficulty of vessels seeking refuge in the Manxman's Lake. During stormy weather the coal vessels trading betwixt Cumberland and Ireland ran for the Lake, and many of them were wrecked in doing so, especially during the night. The Skipper got a memorial prepared containing a list and narrative of the wrecks and lives lost during a certain number of years, and made an appeal to shipowners and the public on both sides of the Firth, by which he raised funds sufficient to erect two beacons on the island of Little Ross, to guide mariners to the Manxman's Lake. When I was a lad at my apprenticeship, having a taste for drawing, I prepared by his direction a plan of the Beacons which I still possess, having found it amongst his papers. The foundation stone was laid on 14th August 1819, with Masonic honours. Mr. James Dyson, Grand Master, and others called on Mr. Skelly who lived in family with my father and mother (she was his only sister), to endeavour to get the event recorded in Mr. McDiarmid's *Dumfries Courier* of the Tuesday following. Their call took place on the Sunday, the day following the day of the ceremony. I was requested to try to write a paragraph and I did so — and wrote a letter sending it, which Mr. Dyson subscribed — the letter was sent by first post and on Tuesday I saw myself for the first time in print. Having lately got a Scrap Book I wrote to the *Courier,* and got a manuscript copy made of the paragraph. I had a singular feeling when after a lapse of sixty years I read the paragraph. I got Mr. James Nicholson to print it, and it forms the first of my scribblings extending over sixty years. It is as follows:-

"The foundation stones of two landmarks or beacons which the ship-owners of Kirkcudbright are now erecting, by subscription, on the Little Ross, a small island at the mouth of the River Dee, were laid in Masonic order by St Cuthbert's Lodge, on Saturday the 14th curt. At an early hour the river was covered with barges filled with freemasons and a number of other respectable individuals, including not a few of the fair sex. The whole proceeded down the river from the harbour of Kirkcudbright, attended with a band of music, whose notes, as the skiffs glided down the stream, had a very pleasing effect. They arrived at the island in a short time, and the freemasons went in procession to perform the ceremony, when the stones were laid with the honours attendant on such occasions. The whole was concluded with a most appropriate prayer by the Rev. David Haining, and in the evening the boats returned to the harbour of Kirkcudbright with the utmost regularity, without the slightest accident having happened."

James Skelly died a bachelor, in September 1828, aged 68, and his remains are interred in St Cuthbert's Church yard, at a distance of twenty paces north from the gate. Some of the old salts who blessed his memory said that they should have rested in the island of Little Ross, where he lived under canvas during the erection of his beacons.

John C. Mackenzie, Kirkcudbright, 30 November 1880.

The following extracts from the minute books of St. Cuthbert's Lodge, Kirkcudbright, presently in the care of the Stewartry Museum, bear out many of the facts in John C. Mackenzie's youthful account of the Masonic ceremony at Little Ross and also provide some details of the nature of at least one of the refreshments considered appropriate for such an occasion:

St. Cuthbert's Lodge 12th August 1819

When an apprentice Lodge was opened and the Master stated to the meeting that he had been applied to by the Committee appointed for erecting a landmark upon the Little Ross to call the Lodge together and state to them it was particularly wished that the foundation stone thereof should be laid in Masonic order.

The meeting therefore unanimously agree to comply with the above request and the lodge is directed from this meeting, to attend the office bearers at our Lodge room upon Saturday first at 7 o'clock in the morning when there will be a wherry prepared for the purpose of conveying them to the Ross and as that will cost a considerable expense and it will not be in the members' power to return before 5 o'clock, some refreshment will be necessary. The meeting order the Master to draw upon the Treasurer for Two Guineas and a half for the purpose of xxxxxxx defraying the above expenses.

St Cuthbert's Lodge, Kirkcudbright, 14th August 1819

When an apprentice Lodge was opened and the Brethren went in procession to the shore for the purpose of being conveyed down the river to the Little Ross for the purpose of laying the foundation stones of the two landmarks thereon which was done in true Masonic order after a suitable speech from the Master at the one and from the Depute Master at the other. The Rev. Mr. Haining delivered a very appropriate prayer upon the occasion, after which the Brethren sat down to some refreshment prepared for the occasion. They afterwards returned to the shore and proceeded to the

Lodge room and after receiving the thanks of the Master for their steady conduct as men and as masons, the Lodge was shut. Immediately thereafter the Committee of Management, attended with a number of gentlemen, invited the Lodge to drink shares of a gallon of whisky which was done in the greatest harmony when they returned thanks to the Lodge for their particular attention to such a laudable institution when they all parted in good order and much gratified.

James Dyson.

John C. Mackenzie's tribute to the skills and achievements of Captain James Skelly gives a valuable insight to his character, and to the events by which it was shaped. The last sentence of his tribute, in which he refers to the local opinion that his uncle's remains should have rested on Little Ross, is interesting. Firstly, because it highlights the extent of the general esteem in which James Skelly was held, and secondly, for the fact that his devotion to the proper completion of his project resulted in him living 'under canvas' on the island during construction of the beacons. This seems to provide circumstantial evidence that the little building of unknown purpose described in the previous chapter was not in a habitable condition in 1819. The beacons erected by James Skelly were not built in strict accordance with the drawing prepared by John C. Mackenzie and were sited much further apart than was originally planned.

James Skelly was evidently a person of intelligence with a will to succeed, who had the ambition to abandon a trade to which fate had made him an apprentice and the sense to adapt the skills he had learned during his apprenticeship to other grander purposes. He would be proud to know that the principle he established, of having a pair of leading marks on Little Ross, is still followed today, although it now seems that neither of the two beacons he erected has survived. Only one beacon now exists, the original southern one having been demolished in 1841 to permit the construction of the lighthouse. Two beacons are clearly shown on a Northern Lighthouse Board map of the island, which also includes the lighthouse and its ancillary buildings, but it must have become obvious that the original north beacon no longer served any useful purpose. The beacon, erected by Thomas Stevenson, now stands lower on the island's north-east side, and incorporates a solar-powered light utilising a technology that would have astounded and thrilled all those responsible for its original conception. The site of the original north beacon has been located, a little to the north of the western ends of the barn buildings; parts of its coping-stones have also been found on the island.

Today, the lighthouse and the north beacon, when brought into alignment with one another, continue to provide the leading marks advocated by James Skelly. These marks are still used by every competent mariner who either enters or leaves the channel of the River Dee at the mouth of Kirkcudbright Bay.

CHAPTER 3

The Case for a Lighthouse

In the early to mid-19th century, Great Britain was an extremely prosperous country, with a fleet of merchant ships that was among the largest in the world and was still expanding. Around the Irish Sea, foreign trade was generally carried out by large vessels which operated from coastal cities such as Liverpool and Glasgow, but some smaller vessels did manage to maintain foreign trading links directly from lesser ports, including many in the Solway Firth and northern parts of the Irish Sea. A large and growing fleet of coasting vessels, sloops, smacks, schooners, and brigs served most of the day-to-day needs of coastal towns, villages, hamlets, country houses, and farms. These were often owned, built, maintained, and operated by people who were local residents. Such vessels were immensely important to the economy of isolated communities at a time when roads were far from adequate for long distance travel and the growth of a rail network was still some years in the future. Any losses of local ships had a very dramatic effect not only on their homeports but also on the other local ports they served. When disasters occurred, families of masters and crewmen lost their relatives and breadwinners, owners and investors lost their capital, and it should be noted that in most cases, these investors included large numbers of local tradesmen, businessmen, and ordinary people from all walks of life who had modest shares in the ownership of particular vessels. Lastly, customers lost the cargoes they had either dispatched or expected to receive, with devastating effects on their businesses.

The first recorded suggestion that a lighthouse at Little Ross might be desirable appears in *The Statistical Account of Scotland*, published in 1792. It was written by the Rev. Dr. Robert Muter, a distinguished minister of the Parish Church of Kirkcudbright, which was then sited on the Moat Brae, overlooking Kirkcudbright harbour. Robert Muter had a keen interest in the harbour and its trade and was probably recording the views of prominent mariners of his day:

> In stormy weather, when vessels can neither keep the sea, nor clear the land, this harbour is the best in the South coast of Scotland for shelter, and on that account is much frequented in winter. But the entrance into it being narrow,

a strong tide setting right across, and no light-house to direct them, it is dangerous to run for it in the dark, and engage with a lee shore. Many fatal accidents happen by ships missing the harbour, and being driven, either into Wigtown Bay, or on the banks of the Solway Firth. The island of Little Ross affords an excellent situation for a light-house. One might be erected there at a small expense and kept up on moderate terms. It would be of the utmost utility to all shipping, and particularly to strangers, in the hour of danger. Were government apprised of the great benefit that would result from this, it is to be hoped they would think the matter worthy of their attention, and cause a light-house to be erected at the public expense.

Robert Muter's clear and concise case for a lighthouse was never bettered, but there is no record of it having prompted either debate or action. Twenty-one years later, in describing Little Ross Island in his *Topographical Dictionary of Scotland: and of the islands in the British Seas,* published in 1813, Nicholas Carlisle quoted most of Robert Muter's case for the construction of a lighthouse, bringing it to potentially wider public attention.

It now seems rather odd that such a well-argued case for a lighthouse was made some years before Captain James Skelly achieved success with his beacons. Captain Skelly was almost certainly one of the mariners that would have advised Robert Muter, but it seems probable that James Skelly chose to proceed with his beacons, knowing that their completion could be achieved within his own practical power.

The success of James Skelly's campaign to erect beacons on Little Ross Island was an inspiration to the many people who had supported him, and proved that a well-fought campaign for a sensible cause could ultimately succeed. It also illustrated that a great deal of time, perseverance, and money was necessary to make such things happen. Moreover, it also demonstrated that some political skill was essential to persuade influential people not conversant with nautical matters to support the best measures for the protection of lives, cargoes, trade, and shipping from the many hazards faced by mariners. James Skelly's beacons achieved what he had set out do: provide leading marks, the use of which, in daylight hours, enabled vessels that had arrived safely in the bay to proceed up the River Dee to the harbour and port of Kirkcudbright. A demand was now arising to further improve the safety of shipping in the whole of the north Irish Sea and to enhance Kirkcudbright's position as a port, by the provision of a lighthouse on Little Ross Island. The purpose of such a light was to help mariners to determine their position when in the north Irish Sea, and to thereby enhance the safety of themselves, their crews, their, ships and their cargoes, thus benefitting all the communities on the shores of the north Irish Sea and Solway Firth.

Captain James Skelly, ably advised and assisted by Kirkcudbright writer Mr. James Niven, put together an impressive document in the form of a 'Memorial and Petition to the Commissioners for Northern Lights'. The document, now in the collection of the Stewartry Museum, clearly outlines the case for a lighthouse and bears the signatures of ship owners, merchants, and other traffickers within the limits of the port of Kirkcudbright, and also those of freeholders, justices of the peace, commissioners of supply, and landholders in the Stewartry of Kirkcudbright. The collector and the comptroller of customs at Kirkcudbright supported the memorial and petition in their official capacities, as did the merchants and ship owners of Maryport, and the ship owners of Workington, in a generous display of cross-border solidarity. Perhaps most importantly of all, Sir John Reid, Captain of His Majesty's Revenue Cutter *Prince Edward* gave strong and well-reasoned support for the initiative, based on his long experience of patrolling the north Irish Sea and North Channel. Lastly, Mr. Edward McClune of Kirkcudbright, who had been a pilot and tacksman at the port of Kirkcudbright for over 30 years, gave a deposition which detailed the extent of use of Kirkcudbright Bay by shipping, including vessels which were neither bound for nor departing from the town of Kirkcudbright. The many vessels that came into this latter category were generally using Kirkcudbright Bay as a port of refuge in adverse weather, or during inconvenient tidal conditions. His deposition was signed on 8 December 1820:

> Unto the Honourable The Commissioners for Northern Lights,
>
> The Memorial and Petition of the Subscribers all Ship Owners, Merchants and other Traffickers within the limits of the Port of Kirkcudbright Humbly Sheweth
>
> That Torrs Lake commonly called Manxman's Lake in the River Dee near Kirkcudbright affords safe and commodious Anchorage for vessels of any burden and it is the only safe and commodious Anchorage in the South of Scotland-
>
> That there is also an excellent Roadstead under the Island of Little Ross at the mouth of the River, where Vessels of all descriptions may ride in safety, till there be a sufficiency of water to carry them up to the Lake-
>
> That these facts are well known to every mariner navigating in the Solway Frith [sic] and the Irish Sea who often avail themselves of the aforesaid Roadstead and Anchorage ground, there being none so commodious either for ingress or egress in the Counties of Lancaster, Westmoreland and Cumberland in England or in the Counties of Dumfries, Kirkcudbright and Wigtown in Scotland, excepting Loch Ryan in Wigtownshire near to the mouth of the Frith [sic] of Clyde, which being so far to the North West, affords no accommodation to vessels navigating the Solway Frith [sic] or that part of the Irish Sea connecting with it-
>
> That the mouth of the River Dee below the Anchorage ground at Torrs Lake is guarded by a Bar or Sand Bank, which not only prevents Vessels from getting up to the Lake at low water, but renders it difficult or rather impossible for Strangers to navigate up to the Lake even at high water-
>
> That of late years two Towers have been erected by private subscription on the island of Little Ross, which have been found of great utility in guiding Mariners into the River in the day time but these Towers afford little or no advantage to navigation in the night time; so that a Light House is still very much wanted on the Island of Little Ross for the safety and preservation of the lives and property of those engaged in Commerce and Navigation in these seas-

That the Scottish Shore for more than twenty miles on the East side, and also on the West side of the mouth of the River Dee is bold and rocky and extremely dangerous to mariners, especially in the night time, when for want of a light on the Island of Little Ross, they are incapable of knowing where they are, and therefore dare not attempt to approach the Roadstead, or enter the River–

That in these circumstances, many valuable lives have been lost, and much property has been destroyed within the limits of the Port of Kirkcudbright in the course of the last thirty years, as well as will appear from the following statement–

In the year 1790, the brig *Fame* (Ardal, Master) from Petersburgh to Dumfries, laden with tallow and hemp, was wrecked about one mile West of the mouth of the River Dee, and very much damaged.

In 1791 the brig *Morning Star,* a collier (Shepherd, Master) was wrecked about one mile West of the mouth of the River Dee, and totally lost, and one man drowned.

In 1793 the brig *Thomas,* a collier was wrecked about one mile West of the mouth of the River Dee and totally lost, and seven men drowned.

In 1795, the brig *Greyhound* from Baltimore was wrecked about seven miles East of the mouth of the River Dee, and totally lost

In the same year, the brig------- a collier (McMillan, Master) was wrecked on the Island of Little Ross, and totally lost, and five men drowned.

In the same year, the ship *Lydia* (Dawson, Master) with a cargo of tallow and hemp from Petersburgh to Whitehaven, was wrecked about six miles East of the mouth of the River Dee, and totally lost.

In the same year the sloop *Mally and Sally* of Preston, laden with corn, was wrecked about one quarter of a mile West of the mouth of the River Dee, and totally lost and two men drowned.

In 1796, the sloop *Carlisle,* with a general cargo from Liverpool to Annan, was wrecked about twelve miles East of the mouth of the River Dee, and totally lost and four men drowned.

In 1797, the ship *Adventure* of New York (Zacharia Swain, Master) laden with flaxseed and fruit was wrecked about five miles West of the mouth of the River Dee and the cargo destroyed.

In the same year the brig *William* of Dublin bound for Jamaica was wrecked about twelve miles East of the mouth of the River Dee and totally lost.

In the same year the sloop *Diana* of Kirkcudbright (James Carter, Master) laden with coals, was wrecked about one quarter mile West of the mouth of the River Dee and totally lost.

In 1799, the sloop *Betty* of Greenock, laden with beef and butter was wrecked about one quarter of a mile West of the mouth of the River Dee and totally lost; the cargo was partly destroyed and four men drowned.

In the same year a sloop from the Isle of Man (name unknown) was lost on the Island of Little Ross and all hands drowned.

In 1800, the sloop *Experiment* of Garlieston was wrecked about eight miles East of the mouth of the River Dee, and totally lost.

In the same year, the brig-------- a collier (Steel, Master) was wrecked about half a mile West of the mouth of the River Dee and totally lost.

In 1801 the sloop *May* of Kirkcudbright (McGeorge, Master) was wrecked about five miles West of the mouth of the River Dee and very much damaged.

In the same year the brig *Betsy* of Whitehaven (Branthet, Master) was wrecked about four miles East of the mouth of the River Dee and very much damaged.

In the same year a sloop from Stornoway (name unknown) laden with kelp for Liverpool, was wrecked on the Island of Little Ross. Both vessel and cargo were lost and seven men drowned.

In the same year the ship *Middleton* of Maryport (Murdoch McLeod, Master) laden with timber from America was wrecked about half a mile West of the mouth of the River Dee and totally lost.

In 1803 the brig *Singleton* (Harper, Master) from Ireland to Whitehaven was wrecked about four miles East of the mouth of the River Dee and totally lost.

In 1805 the sloop *Catherine* of Kirkcudbright (Stitt, Master) laden with corn was wrecked about two miles East of the mouth of the River Dee, and the sloop and cargo totally lost.

In the same year two other sloops having general cargoes from Liverpool to the Clyde were wrecked about seven miles East of the mouth of the River Dee. Both of the sloops were totally lost and one man belonging to each drowned.

In 1806 the ship *Favourite* from Jamaica for Whitehaven, laden with rum and sugar, was wrecked about five miles East of the mouth of the River Dee. The ship was totally lost but part of the cargo saved.

In the same year the ship *Atlas* from Jamaica to Whitehaven laden with rum and sugar was wrecked about twelve miles East of the mouth of the River Dee. The ship and almost the whole of the cargo destroyed, and all hands on board consisting of twenty-four persons were drowned.

In 1807 the brig *Favourite* of Maryport (Sheridan, Master) was wrecked about two miles West of the mouth of the River Dee, and totally lost, and five men drowned.

In 1808 the sloop *Brothers* of Dumfries (Garmory, Master) was wrecked about six miles East of the mouth of the River Dee and totally lost.

In 1812 the sloop *Brothers* of Dumfries (Kirk, Master) was wrecked about one quarter of a mile West of the mouth of the River Dee and totally lost.

In the same year the brig *Mermaid,* a collier (Boyd, Master) was wrecked about one mile West of the mouth of the River Dee and totally lost.

In 1814 the sloop *Anna* of Garlieston (McMichan, Master) laden with coals was wrecked about twelve miles West of the mouth of the River Dee, and totally lost.

In the same year, the sloop *Mary* (Gibson, Master) laden with salt from Liverpool was wrecked about seven miles West of the mouth of the River Dee, and totally lost.

In 1815, the brig *Good Intent* of Maryport, a collier (Hewat, Master) was wrecked about two miles East of the mouth of the River Dee and totally lost and three men drowned.

In 1816, the sloop *Ellen and Agnes* of Wigtown (Hill, Master) laden with beef and butter was wrecked immediately on the East side of the mouth of the River Dee, and the sloop and cargo were totally lost and three of the crew drowned.

In the same year, a sloop from Ireland (name unknown) was wrecked about twelve miles East of the mouth of the River Dee and totally lost.

In 1818, the sloop *Industry* of Garlieston (Hannay, Master) laden with coals was wrecked about five miles West of the mouth of the River Dee, and totally lost, and all hands drowned.

In the same year, the schooner *Friendship* of Preston, laden with corn was wrecked on the Island of Little Ross, and totally lost and one man drowned.

In 1819 the brig *Diana* of Dumfries (Martin, Master) laden with timber from America was wrecked about twelve miles East of the mouth of the River Dee and greatly damaged.

In the same tear the sloop *Mary* of Kirkcudbright (Gordon, Master) laden with coals was wrecked about three miles West of the mouth of the River Dee and totally lost.

In 1820, The brig *Port of Sunderland* from America to Kirkcudbright (Brough, Master) laden with timber was wrecked about twelve miles West of the mouth of the River Dee, and totally lost. Part of the cargo was also lost.

And in the same year, the sloop *Joan* (Ewart, Master) from Whitehaven to Dumfries with a general cargo, was wrecked about thirteen miles East of the mouth of the River Dee, and totally lost. Almost the whole of the cargo was also lost.

That all these accidents happened in the night time, when for want of a Light on the island of Little Ross it was impossible to distinguish that Island or the mouth of the River Dee from the rest of the Coast, and there is every reason to believe that few or none of the accidents would have happened, had there been a Light on the Island of Little Ross for the information of Mariners and to guide them to a place of safety.

That besides the great number of accidents before enumerated, there were also many others, some of comparatively less importance, and others that cannot now be distinctly stated; but the Memorialists refrain from troubling your Honours with a detailed statement of these, not doubting that the many instances of distress already enumerated will be sufficient to convince your Honours of the expediency and necessity of erecting a Light House on the Island of Little Ross within the limits of the Port of Kirkcudbright.

May it therefore please your Honours to take the premises into consideration, and to grant authority for erecting and maintaining a Light House on the Island of Little Ross in all time coming.

And your Petitioners shall ever pray etc.

G. Wishart	Andw. McClure	John Kissock
Thomas McClune	John Grant	David Cowan
Wm. McClymont	Thos. Morrison	David Caig
Saml. Rae	William Mouncy	James Cavan
Archd. McLellan	Samuel McCaul	Thomas Sproat
Peter Gourlay	Rob. Cochrane Jr.	Samuel McKnight
John Cristal	John McCartney	James Douglas
John Nicolson	Thomas Burnie	Jas. Waugh
John Clarke	John McClure	John Callie
James Williamson	William Johnston	John Williamson
John Stevenson	James Douglas	James Rankine
David Arnot	Willm. McKinnell	Alexr. Rae
John McIntyre	Robert Erskine	Robt. Carson
John Brydson	Thos. McLellan	Edwd. McClune
W Ad. Roddan	John McCleave	
James Skelly	David Morrison	

We the Subscribers all Freeholders, Justices of the Peace, Commissioners of Supply and Landholders in the Stewartry of Kirkcudbright Do Certify that the facts stated in the Memorial and Petition written on the ten preceding pages are just and true to the best of our knowledge and belief, and we recommend the said Memorial and Petition to the consideration of the Honorable [sic] The Commissioners for Northern Lights as a matter of great public importance.

John S. Shand Provost of Burgh of Kirkcudbright
Thomas McMillan Bailie of Burgh of Kirkcudbright
David Blair of B. Craig
Alexr. Melville of Barquar, Collector of Landtax etc.etc.
David Blair of Borgue
D. Maxwell J.P. of Cardoness
Ja. Burnie Bailie of the Burgh of Kirkcudbright
Will. Mure J.P.
Robt. Coltart of Bluehill
David Halliday of Chapmanton
E. Drew of Auchenhay
Jas. M. Gordon Captn. R.N.
Alexr. Gordon Steward Depute of Kirkcudbright
John Napier of Mollance
Robt. Hannay J.P. of Rusco
William Ireland of Barbey J.P.
Jas. Niven of Glenarn
William Bell
Wm. Beck of Newton
Ad. Thomson Mure of Muncraig

Alexr Craig J.P. and also for
Alexr. Murray of Broughton
Hugh Stewart J.P.
David Maitland of Barcaple
D. McCulloch of Torhousekie
John Heron J.P. of Ingleston
Samuel Douglas of Netherlaw.

We the Collector and Comptroller of His Majesty's Customs at the Port of Kirkcudbright also certify the verity of the facts stated in the foregoing Petition and that the erection of a light House on the Island of Little Ross at the mouth of the River Dee, here, will be of great utility to the Public.

Signed
D. M. Jolly, Collr. Of Customs
Da. McLellan, Comptr.

We the undersigned Merchants, Ship Owners etc. of Maryport having been applied to for our opinion with respect to a Sea Light being kept on the Little Ross, at the mouth of the River Dee, for the benefit of Shipping hereby express our approbation of the same. 12th December 1820.

William Robinson	William Pearson	Jos. Wheelwright
William Thomson	James Gardiner	John Peat Junr.
Josh. Skelton	Peter Straughton	Wilkinson Ostle
Adam Russel	JohnPairr	Gustavus Richmond
Henry Tickle	John Ritson	Henry Richmond
Thomas Tolson	Jonh. Wilson	Edwd. Tyson
Wm. Fletcher	John Wharton	John Penny
Hugh Brown	Henry Christian	James Pitcairn
Jas. Todd	John Parrot	Eagld. Ashley
Robert Fearon	William Walker	Thos. Jackson
Richd. Scott	Samuel Wilson	John Bowman
Jona. Nicholson	John Robinson	Robert Smith
John Metcalf	Myles Briggs	Joseph Seymour
John Scott	John Walker	Thos. Braithwaite
Joseph Millsion	John Sealby	John Hodgson
John Walker	Sealby Fearon	Robert Glaister
Wilson Walker	Jas. Inman	John Simond
John Harrison	Jos. Robinson	
John Bigland	John Lewthwaite	

We the undersigned, being Ship Owners in the Port of Workington, do agree with our friends at Maryport in expressing our hearty wishes for a Sea Light on the Little Ross, at the entrance of the River Dee as described in the annexed Letter from Mr. McCaul:

David Fletcher	Andr. Little	Richard Thompson
Wm. Plasket	John Hodgson	Nich. Falcon
Wm. Fisher	Edward Millwall	Isaac Scott
T. Harding	Wm.Wilson	James Scott
John Moordaff	Wm. Gilles	Peter Hurd
William Douglas	Robert Wallace	John Falcon
Thomas Cragg	Wm Casson	John Carlisle
Helsick Wood	Allison Foster	John Thompson
John Irwing	John Smith	Joseph Tickle

Copy letter – Sir John Reid Commander, of His Majesty's Revenue Cutter *Prince Edward*.

To the Magistrates and Shipowners of Kirkcudbright Manxman's Lake, 28th October 1820

I have read your Memorial to the Commissioners for Northern Lights on the subject of erecting a Light House on the Little Ross at the entrance of its Roadstead, and am of the opinion if such takes place, it will be a very great benefit to trade on this dangerous coast, and be the means of saving many valuable lives, as well as vast property. Having been now cruising in the Channel more than twenty years I can say that many losses that have happened in that time would not have taken place, had there been a light on the Little Ross to enable them to have taken this place; and in particular the two fine Jamaica Ships drove from off Whitehaven, as they intended when blown off that Port to have run for this Roadstead, but for want of making proper allowance for the tide and indraft of the Solway Frith, were lost to the Eastward, which a light on the Little Ross would have prevented.

Should the Commissioners for the Northern Lights be disposed to listen to your Memorial, I shall at any time meet their Engineer, and render such information as comes within my knowledge – I am etc. (signed) J. Reid

Deposition by Edward McClune of Kirkcudbright:

I, Edward McClune residing in Kirkcudbright, Tacksman of the Anchorage Dues belonging to the town of Kirkcudbright, Manxman's Lake South of Grange Burn, do Certify that I was born at Manxman's Lake, and resided there till Whitsunday 1815 when I was forty seven years of age and that although I have resided in the town of Kirkcudbright since Whitsunday 1815 I have been at Manxman's Lake very frequently and sometimes twice or thrice in a day since that date. For these thirty years past and upwards I have acted as a pilot and assisted to navigate Vessels up and down the River Dee from the Roadstead at Little Ross to Manxman's Lake, and from Manxman's Lake to sea, and also from the Roadstead at Little Ross up to the Harbour at Kirkcudbright, and from the Harbour at Kirkcudbright down the River and out to sea.

During the same period I have very frequently been employed to collect the Anchorage Dues aforesaid, partly on my own account, and partly on account of others who were also occasionally tacksmen of these dues. And I do further Certify that in stormy weather and variable winds, I have frequently seen and counted from Twenty to Thirty Sail of Vessels take shelter in Manxman's Lake in Harvest and also in Winter, and on one occasion I saw and counted thirty-six vessels all at anchor in that Lake – Witness my hand at Kirkcudbright the seventh day of December in the year One thousand eight hundred and twenty (signed) Edward McClune.

Edward McClune residing in Kirkcudbright being solemnly sworn and interrogated Depones that the facts stated in the Certificate written on the preceding page are just and true to the best of his knowledge and judgement. And further Depones that by far the greater part of the Vessels that took shelter in Manxman's Lake as mentioned in the Certificate were Vessels trading from Cumberland to Ireland Liverpool and elsewhere, and vessels trading from Ireland to Cumberland and Lancashire and elsewhere And that all this is truth as he shall answer to God (signed) Edward McClune Kirkcudbright 8th December 1820 Sworn before (signed) Wm. Ireland, Steward Substitute.

Memorial and Petition to the Commissioners for Northern Lights, (1820) in the collection of the Stewartry Museum

The largest and busiest port in the general area of the Solway Firth and north Irish Sea is Whitehaven, and it is therefore surprising that none of the dignitaries, mariners, and merchants of that town were signatories to the petition. Considerable correspondence had taken place on the subject of the proposed lighthouse between the petitioners in Kirkcudbright and Captain Robinson, a prominent and trusted Cumberland mariner who was well known in Kirkcudbright and had been asked by the petitioners to act as an agent for them. Captain Robinson readily found support in Workington and Maryport, but encountered some cynicism in Whitehaven, where there was cautious support for the idea of a lighthouse, but also an overriding concern about who was going to be asked to contribute to funding.

In a letter addressed to Captain Robinson, now in the collection of the Stewartry Museum, the petitioners tried to provide reassurance:

Kirkcudbright, 27th December 1820

The proposed light on Little Ross must of course be established and supported on the same principle as the Manx lights and by the same means, namely a small duty per ton on all vessels navigating within the Solway Frith and that part of the Irish Sea connecting with it from Holyhead and Houth [sic] Head in the South to Donaghadee and Portpatrick in the North. These are the limits defined in the Act of Parliament establishing the Manx lights; and it is the general opinion here that the same limits should be defined in the Act of Parliament to be obtained for establishing a light on Little Ross.

There are no monies in the hands of the Commissioners for Northern Lights; but as soon as an Act of Parliament is obtained to authorise the proposed establishment and to levy a tonnage duty on the shipping money will be borrowed to defray the expence [sic] in the meantime till the accumulation of the tonnage duties shall be sufficient to discharge it.

I understand that all the other Northern Lights are established and supported on the same principle and it is certainly very fair that every shipowner benefited by a light shall contribute towards the expence [sic] of it.

I hope that this explanation will satisfy the shipowners in Cumberland and will be glad to hear from you again at your earliest convenience. In the meantime be so good as send me the letters of concurrence you have obtained at Maryport and Workington.

I am, Dear Sir,
Yours .....

A further letter to Captain Robinson, dated 4 January 1821, advised him that a new lighthouse would not result in an increased duty rate per ton of cargo, and pressed him for a rapid response, as the Commissioners were due to meet on 13 January to consider the matter. No record has been found of a response from Captain Robinson, so it is assumed that in the few days available, he was unsuccessful in persuading Whitehaven's mariners to give their written support.

The following copy of an unsigned letter in the collection of the Stewartry Museum demonstrates that those in support of the memorial to the Commissioners for Northern Lights understood the value of lobbying prominent people to gain support for their cause. Even in small places remote from capital cities, there are still connections to such people and ways of exploiting them to advantage:

Copy letter to Mr. Mure: dated 8th January 1821, Kirkcudbright

Dear Sirs,

I am told that Lady Selkirk is to set out for Edinburgh tomorrow and I think it highly probable that you will see her Ladyship before she sets out.

The Commissioners for Northern Lights meet at Edinburgh on Saturday next, the 13th current and if you find an opportunity of speaking with Lady Selkirk before she proceeds on her journey be so good as mention to her the application for the establishment of a lighthouse on Little Ross and request her Ladyship to interest her brother the Solicitor General to support the application at the meeting of the Commissioners on Saturday.

I am convinced that Mr. Maitland has done and will do all that he can to forward the application but still Lady Selkirk's interference with the Solicitor General may be of importance.

I am
Yours sincerely
(unsigned)

Unfortunately, due to a combination of bereavement, misfortune, and blunders, the necessary papers were not put before the Commissioners on 13 January 1821 as had been hoped, to the frustration and disappointment of all concerned. Somehow, despite the considerable efforts of James Skelly and so many others, the campaign for a lighthouse then seemed to lose impetus, and no evidence has been found of any further moves to bring the matter to the top of the Commissioners' priorities.

In the meantime, nothing more could be done to protect either the passing ships or their men. A dreadful gale in March 1822 gave dramatic evidence of this when five vessels and many of their crews were lost in Kirkcudbright Bay. The brigs *Joshua, Mary Isabella, Falcon,* and *Dido,* and the sloop *Wellington,* are all understood to have been at anchor in the lee of Little Ross Island, sheltering from a sudden and unexpected southerly gale. Their anchors failed to hold and they were all swept northwards until they struck the bar. Damaged by the initial impact, they were then carried further up the bay, where they were variously dismasted, capsized, sunk, and finally wrecked on Milton Sands and on the shores of St Mary's Isle Point. The *Joshua* was lost with all hands, Captain Ormonby, or Ormsby of the *Mary Isabella* was lost with seven of his crew, and two of the crew of the *Falcon* were also lost, including the ship's boy, who was brought ashore alive but sadly died a few hours later. Only the crews of the *Dido* and the *Wellington* survived intact.

Captain Ormonby seems to have been a very highly respected and popular young man, and his loss, combined with that of the young cabin boy, caused widespread grief among the general public. The wealthier and more influential members of this society were occasionally guilty of turning blind eyes to the deprivations faced by the poor sailors, fishermen, coal miners, and labourers on whom their prosperity depended. John Mactaggart's *Scottish Gallovidian Encyclopedia* of 1824 gives an emotional and informative account of the foregoing events in verse that is perhaps naïve, but heartfelt and moving:

> About two years ago, five ships were torn from their moorings there [Little Ross] by an awful gale, and dashed to pieces on the Bar; one of these was commanded by a young man belonging to Cumberland, of the best disposition and manners; his loss was so deeply lamented both in England and Scotland, that the following *true* song was produced on the subject:

> Captain Ormonby

> Sweet maidens fair in Cumberland, what griefs have I to tell,
> The dear young Captain Ormonby, who loved ye all so well,
> Is over-whelmed with the storm, is sunk beneath the wave,
> In the wild deep, there he doth sleep, there is his watery grave.

> He left your shores for Dublin-bay with a deep laden bark,
> The day was fine, the wind was fair, and sweetly sang the lark,
> But ere the sun stood north and south, the sky was all o'ercast,
> And by *Blackcoomb,* with awful boom, came roaring on the blast.

> The surges o'er the head-lands rose, and buried every mool,
> The Isle of Man they seem'd to sink, and break out o'er *Barool;*
> What ship could stand such billows vast, she must run for a lee,
> With naked masts, before the blasts, forlorn she on must flee?

So on did steer young Ormonby before the furious wind,
The tide being out along the shores, no harbour could he find;
The little *Ross* no shelter was, the anchors would not hold,
So our noble tar, upon the Bar, among the foam was roll'd.

Up high the brig was heaved whiles by the tremendous sea,
Then down again, with thundering sound, upon the sands of Dee;
But soon she stove, and soon she sunk, the sailors stood aghast,
Then, for the live did climb and strive to save't upon the mast.

As on the maintop they did cling, and gazing all around,
Four other ships, besides themselves, were on the stormy ground;
"What shall we do?" a sailor cried, "lo, yonder's one upset,"
"Altho' dry land be near at hand, to it we'll never get."

"The tide will flow by six o'clock "(the captain then did say),
"And down will fall our only hope, this mast here will give way;
There's not a chance that we'll be saved, no, not a chance for one,
No boat can live, none help can give, we're drowned every man."

"O! let us, since we see our fate, to the Almighty pray,
Implore him for to save our souls, and not cast them away;
For soon my brother sufferers dear before him they will be,
For death doth ride upon the tide, this awful night we see."

But scarcely had good Ormonby sooth'd his despairing crew,
When down the mast with crashing fell, the surges o'er them flew;
Their shrieks were stifled with the storm, the waters mad did roar,
And dashed them down, to gasp and drown, and never to rise more.

Poor Bill, 'ere this an hardy tar, who had sail'd many a sea
A hunting whales among the ice, and slaves by hot Goree;
Reach'd the fore-mast with trouble great, and saw the horrid fate
Which did befal [sic] his mess-mates all, for him but to relate.

And while poor Bill did tell the tale, with sorrow he did weep,
"my kind young captain," he did cry "is buried in the deep;
Tis thirty years now, since a boy, I first did sail the sea,
And I've never had, such a good lad, a master over me."

Lament then for this worthy youth all who have hearts can feel,
His sweetheart's breast is wounded deep, we fear 'twill never heal;
On Whitehaven Quay she parted that morn with her true love,
No more to see nor with him be till she's in heaven above.

Well mayst thou moan thou Ocean now, upon the Milton sand,
For Ormonby thou hast devoured, what can thy wrath withstand?
The tall black rocks around thy shores, even totter with thy rage,
So how then can, the art of man, with thee in war engage?

> O! sing this song, my sailors all, when you're in mournful mood,
> And think on the distresses great, your brethren whiles have stood;
> Be still prepared to meet the storm, be still prepared to drown,
> So then will ye, like Ormonby, gain an eternal crown.

The loss of the popular Captain Ormonby and 14 crew members of the *Mary Isabella, Joshua, Falcon, Dido,* and *Wellington* seems to have galvanised the community into renewed efforts to improve the safety of the port of Kirkcudbright, and these efforts focused sharply on to the perceived need for a lighthouse on Little Ross Island. Ironically, the presence of a lighthouse on Little Ross would have had no bearing on the losses that occurred in the foregoing incident, but that was not the issue for the good citizens who were now dedicated to improving the lot of mariners and the local shipping industry any way they could.

Despite the best efforts of the community in providing the Commissioners for Northern Lights with a full statement of their case, supported by well-informed and influential people and backed-up by a comprehensive list of the vessels that had come to grief in the vicinity, nothing happened as quickly as the petitioners had expected, and indeed it seemed that nothing happened at all as the years drifted past.

Following a 'numerous and respectable meeting of merchants, shipowners and shipmasters of the town and port of Kirkcudbright', Provost William McKinnell wrote to the Commissioners on 29 December 1823, pressing them to further consider the matter of a lighthouse on Little Ross at their meeting on Friday, 2 January. James Skelly never gave up in his quest and continued to do everything in his power to advance matters, writing on 13 April 1824 to the National Institution for the Preservation of Life from Shipwrecks seeking their support.

James Skelly died in September 1828, aged 68. His place in Kirkcudbright's history had already been earned and secured, but he must have been disappointed that he never lived to hear of any commitment to the planning and construction of a lighthouse by the Commissioners for Northern Lights. For the campaign to build a lighthouse on Little Ross to now succeed, it was vital that a new leader should be found to take on Captain Skelly's mantle. Ideally, such a person might have been recruited from Kirkcudbright's many seafarers and ship owners, but by the very nature of their businesses, many such people were away from the town for months on end. It is also perhaps fair to say that most local seafarers were tough and practical people who, although astute, did not necessarily possess the political skills of which Captain Skelly had made such effective use. It seems that for a while, no new leader emerged, and the campaign faltered accordingly. Five years later however, in 1833, a new and extremely persuasive advocate of the case for a lighthouse at Little Ross emerged in the person of John C. Mackenzie, nephew of James Skelly. John C. Mackenzie had been born in Kirkcudbright in 1800, educated at Kirkcudbright Academy, and had served a legal apprenticeship with Bailie Burnie in Kirkcudbright. He then worked for about 12 years in Edinburgh before his return to Kirkcudbright in 1833 as a partner of William Mure (Writers and Agents). He quickly became a popular figure in the town, being young, clever, enthusiastic, and an able public speaker. Prompted by information he had been given in Edinburgh, he began to make enquiries as to what was delaying consideration of the case for a lighthouse at Little Ross Island and to gently but determinedly agitate for its urgent resolution.

Portrait of John C. Mackenzie, courtesy of Broughton House, and the National Trust for Scotland

It did not take long for John C. Mackenzie's enquiries to produce a result. The following letter from Robert Stevenson, Engineer to the Commissioners for Northern Lights, makes it very clear that financial and probably other unstated concerns had meant that a lighthouse on Little Ross was not high among the Commissioners' priorities:

Edinburgh 12th April 1833

To Alexr. Wood Esq.
Sheriff Depute

Dear Sir,

In answer to your enquiries regarding the Light House long proposed on the coast of Wigton [sic] – I beg to acquaint you that the subject is still in the view of the Light House Board – but for the present its progress has been somewhat checked by a call from the Treasury for the payment of an advance made long since, — which was not calculated upon being required otherwise than in the form of interest.

There are still two or three pressing points on the Coast to be attended to which are now at a stand. Seeing no immediate prospect of doing anything on the Kirkcudbright or Wigton [sic] Coast I have never completed my survey of that beyond the Little Ross Island – but in due time I shall attend to this as I have indeed stated severally to Sir R. Abercromby and Mr. Gordon, who with you, take a warm interest in this matter.

I have the honour to be, Dear Sir,
Your most obedient servant,
Robert Stevenson

From a copy of the original letter in the collection of the Stewartry Museum.

Robert Stevenson's reference to his intention to deal with the matter 'in due time' would have done little to reassure Sheriff Depute Wood that a lighthouse at Little Ross was under active consideration. This response was clearly a very great blow to the hopes and aspirations of the petitioners and their supporters. Thirteen years after their submission had been made to the Commissioners for Northern Lights, nothing had happened, and both the tone and content of Robert Stevenson's letter indicated that nothing was likely to happen for some considerable time. The fact that Robert Stevenson seemed unsure of the location of Little Ross, and did not spell Wigtown correctly may also perhaps not have gone unnoticed.

Many signatories of the petition, though persuaded of the worthiness of its cause, were not sufficiently familiar with nautical matters to be able to balance local needs against national needs. They doubtless interpreted Robert Stevenson's letter as a terse and high-handed reply by a mere engineer and an inappropriate response to their plea to the Commissioners.

Robert Stevenson was of course no mere engineer. As the founder of the dynasty of Stevenson family engineers responsible for the design and supervision of construction of many of the finest lighthouses in the world, he was not a man to underestimate. His rise to prominence followed shortly after his completion of the stunning Bell Rock Lighthouse, a seemingly impossible task due to its location on a semi-submerged rock, 11 miles south of Arbroath. In successfully completing this unbelievably challenging project, he eclipsed the no less distinguished engineer John Rennie, who had prepared the original design for the Bell Rock Lighthouse, and Robert Stevenson went on to design and build the following ten Scottish lighthouses for the Commissioners for Northern Lights between 1821 and 1833:

Sumburgh Head, Shetland, 1821
Rinns of Islay, Inner Hebrides, 1825
Buchan Ness, Aberdeenshire, 1827
Cape Wrath, Sutherland, 1828
Tarbat Ness, near Portmahomach 1830
Mull of Galloway, Wigtownshire, 1830
Dunnet Head, Caithness, 1831
Girdle Ness Aberdeenshire, 1833
Barra Head, Outer Hebrides, 1833
Eilan Musdile, Lismore, 1833

In addition to coping with the staggering workload generated by bringing all the above projects to successful completion, Robert Stevenson had been Engineer to the Convention of Scottish Burghs since 1813, resulting in his involvement in a huge range of other public works such as roads, bridges, harbours, and canals.

Consultants in specialist subjects such as engineering are by their very nature head and shoulders above most other people in their understanding of extremely complicated technical matters, and do not always find it easy, or even necessary, to explain or to justify their opinions, conclusions, and actions. Robert Stevenson was a practical and dedicated engineer at the very peak of a profession that was much in the public eye, but he was by no means an academic or intellectual figure. He was driven chiefly by the satisfaction of overcoming technical problems, consolidating the reputation of his family's firm, and ensuring its successful development in the hands of his sons.

Despite the zeal and enthusiasm of the petitioners who advocated for a lighthouse on Little Ross, it is hard to argue that the case for such a lighthouse, viewed nationally, should have taken precedence over that of any other of the lighthouses listed above. Robert Stevenson had used his understanding of specialised matters such as navigation, meteorology, safety at sea, trade routes, and shipping generally, to wisely guide the Commissioners for Northern Lights in establishing priorities.

Colonel James Gordon of Balcary House, on the coast near Auchencairn, caused some agitation among the petitioners when he wrote to them via Kirkcudbright writer David Niven on 8 July 1834. Colonel Gordon was an advocate, a judge of the Commissary Court of Edinburgh, and an officer of the Kirkcudbrightshire Yeomen Cavalry. He had become aware – following direct correspondence with the Commissioners for Northern Lights – that they would regard any lighthouses built on either Hestan Island or Little Ross Island as merely minor, or harbour, lights, and he seems to have considered this to be an unacceptable loss of status. His proposed solution is outlined in the following (rather muddled) paragraph extracted from his letter:

> The mariners who are often forced to take shelter in this bay [Balcary Bay] have all told me that a lighthouse at Abbey Head would answer much better for either the mouth of the Dee or the entrance to the River Urr to show a lighthouse at each River, as too many lights confuse them, and that Abbey Head is the first land which they make in storms from the current of the tide and usual point from which the wind blows in stormy weather.

> From a copy of the original letter in the care of the Stewartry Museum.

John C. Mackenzie, having set his mind to advancing the case made by his uncle, James Skelly, and having already garnered such a strong measure of local support, was not going to readily give way to the views of a dissident minority. His mind and the minds of the petitioners were by this point fully occupied with what seemed likely to become an increasingly bitter wrangle with the powerful

Commissioners for Northern Lights and their engineer Robert Stevenson. Firm action was needed to re-focus public attention onto promoting the case for a lighthouse on Little Ross Island.

Events spurred him on to take the issue to a higher level, and the fact that he was a local solicitor gave him the necessary knowledge and experience. Mr. Mackenzie was probably aware that there was some concern being raised in Parliament at this time regarding the efficiency of the various lighthouse services in England, Scotland, and Ireland, and that a movement was afoot to replace the three separate authorities responsible with a new single authority. A Parliamentary Report on Lighthouses, published 8 August 1834, had been critical of all three authorities to varying degrees, but had not gone so far as to favour the creation of a single authority. Trinity House came out worst from the Parliamentary Report, but the matter was far from resolved. A further dramatic shipwreck provided Mr. Mackenzie with the cue he needed to pursue his case, and prompted the following letter to the editor of the *Dumfries and Galloway Courier*:

17th March 1835

Sir, - In your paper of the 4th March current, I observe a report of the loss of the brigantine "Grace" of Workington, near the mouth of the River Dee, all hands having perished. I never see the account of a shipwreck in that part of the coast without lamenting the late ineffectual efforts of the shipowners of Kirkcudbright to procure the erection of a Light-house on the Little Ross, to serve, in the words of your paper, as a beacon to guide the mariner in cases of a storm to a haven of safety in the Manxman's Lake. At this stirring time I am unwilling to ask a corner of your paper for the purpose of calling the attention not only of the merchants and shipowners of Galloway and the opposite coast, but also of every humane person in the neighbourhood of so many shipwrecks, to the propriety of exerting themselves to obtain what is so imperiously called for to prevent a constant recurrence of the loss of lives and destruction of property. The shipwreck of the "Grace" is another addition to the long and heart rending catalogue of losses which were embodied several years ago in a Memorial by the late Mr. James Skelly, shipowner and master mariner, and part owner of the Sloop "Isabella" which traded betwixt Galloway and Cumberland for nearly thirty years, who until his dying day, strained every nerve to procure so important an object. That individual succeeded in getting erected, by private subscription, beacons to serve as a guide during day light, but it pleased the Commissioners of Northern Light-houses to lend a deaf ear to the application for a Light-house, although if the number of shipwrecks which have occurred in the quarter in question, and the bold nature of the coast, could warrant the erection of such a building, few places could have made out a better claim. I remember my impression on reading the memorial. The tales of suffering there recounted, independent altogether of the loss of property were heart-rending in the extreme. I do not think that after the applications which have already been made to the Commissioners, it would serve any good purpose to try another, but there is a quarter where an application, if properly made would in all likelihood have effect – I mean in the House of Commons. I see that Lieut. Denham, R.N., is likely to make a Government Survey of the coast, and the present appears to me as particularly fitting for making the attempt. If the influential proprietory [sic] of the new steamer which is also to ply betwixt Liverpool and Galloway were to put their shoulder to the wheel, I would fondly anticipate a favourable result. The Members for the South of Scotland I am sure would be inclined to support our claim. If Parliament should not interfere in this particular case, might the appeal not have the effect of opening the eyes of the country to the necessity of putting the management of Light-houses into the hands of others than the Commissioners. Assuredly it will ultimately come to this and the sooner the better. I understand that the only objection to the erection of the Light-house was the want of trade in the district. I grant that the shipowners of the Port of Kirkcudbright have no reason to demand a Light-house on the ground of the extent of their trade, but he who views the matter thus, views it in a wrong light, for vessels which would derive most benefit from it would be those never enter the Port of Kirkcudbright, but which in trading betwixt England and Ireland are frequently overtaken during night by storms, and know not whither to fly for shelter, being encircled on all hands by an iron-bound coast. We may rest assured that unless we adopt the Great D----- plan and agitate, we shall never obtain the desired object. We have knocked at the door of the Commissioners quite long enough. Let us therefore now make our plaint [sic] at the bar of the House of Commons before the Government Survey is made, and if Lieut. Denham reports in our favour, perhaps his report may carry as much weight with it as the report of the Commissioners' Inspector. – I am sir, your obedient servt., - McK.

This letter accurately summed up the general situation and whipped up local grief and frustration at the loss of yet another ship and her crew. Perhaps more importantly, it cleverly raised the threat of a move to oust control of at least one Scottish lighthouse, and possibly others, from the hands of the Commissioners for Northern Lights and transfer that power to another, unspecified, authority. The relationship between Trinity House and the Commissioners for Northern Lights was not always comfortable, and the prospect of friction arising over navigational aids in the Solway Firth and north Irish Sea at the very interface between the two authorities was certain to generate heated political debate. A few days later, Mr. Mackenzie wrote to his MP, Robert Cutlar Fergusson of Craigdarroch and Orroland, in terms that were even more specific:

Kirkcudbright, 23rd March,1835

Sir, - I understand that Colonel James Gordon of Balcarry [sic] is at present in correspondence with you regarding the erection of a Light-house on the Little Ross, at the mouth of the River Dee, and as I feel much interest in the subject, I use the freedom of sending you a copy of a Memorial to the Commissioners of Northern Lights. The memorial is alluded to in a letter which I got inserted in the "Dumfries Courier" of 18th March current, in the hope of calling the attention of the public to the subject. I also send you a copy of a letter to the Secretary of the National Institution for the preservation of life from shipwreck. That letter contains a continuation of the losses from the date of the memorial until 1824. Since 1824 there have been many shipwrecks in the same quarter, a narrative of which I would have little difficulty (although I was not resident in Kirkcudbright betwixt 1824 and 1834) in making out. I may mention that in 1826 a vessel belonging to Kirkcudbright, the crew all being natives of this town and well acquainted with the coast, was wrecked to the west of Little Ross, having during the night mistaken part of the Borgue shore for the entrance to the river, and two men perished. We thought of petitioning the House of Commons on the subject of light-houses generally or to put the coast from the Mull of Galloway to the Port of Carlisle under the Trinity Board, in the hope that they would listen to our application which the Commissioners had refused; but as we observe that the whole subject of light-houses is to be brought under the notice of the House of Commons by Mr. Hume and that there is a likelihood of Government bringing forward a measure on the subject, we deem it unnecessary at present to present a petition. These papers I beg to send you, however, in the hope that you may find in them a proof of the partiality of the Commissioners, and may be disposed to support any measure for the purpose of putting light-houses into the hands of a different Board. I will feel obliged by you presenting the papers, as in all likelihood the shipowners of Kirkcudbright may, so soon as a new Board of Management is appointed, memorialise them on the subject of a light-house, and they may use the freedom of begging your support on the occasion, which they confidently rely upon when they take into consideration that in your parliamentary career you have gained for yourself a name throughout the world as the advocate of humanity. Should you succeed in procuring for us a light-house you will lay the inhabitants of this district under a lasting obligation to you, and your name will be held dear to the mariner and go down to posterity as having accomplished that which had long been anxiously sought for — though sought for in vain.

I shall be glad to furnish you with any information on the subject which you may require, and I have the honor [sic] to be, etc.

J. C. Mackenzie

From a copy of the original letter in the collection of the Stewartry Museum.

Robert Cutlar Fergusson's reply was a credit to the speed and efficiency of the horse-drawn mail system, and to himself for his prompt attention to the matter:

London, 38 Portman Square, 25th March, 1835.

Sir, - I have been favoured with your letter of the 23rd instant with its enclosures, under two covers, respecting the necessity of a change in the general system of management of Light-houses; and directing my attention particularly to the urgency of having a Light-house erected on Little Ross. From a careful perusal of the documents sent to me, as well as from a former consideration which I gave to the subject (followed by an unsuccessful application to the Board of Northern Lights) I am quite satisfied that the object is of the greatest importance as well as urgency; and as such no exertion on my part, that can be considered useful shall be spared to promote its attainment.

You may be assured that I will give my best attention as well to the general subject, when it comes to be discussed in Parliament, as to the particular grievance of which there is so much reason to complain.

I remain, Sir, your obedt. Humble servant,
R. Cutlar Fergusson

From a copy of the original letter in the collection of the Stewartry Museum.

Robert Cutlar Fergusson was born in Craigdarroch, near Moniaive, in 1768. After publishing *The Proposed Reform of the Counties of Scotland* in 1792, he studied English law, entered The Honourable Society of Lincoln's Inn, and was called to the Bar on 4 July 1797. After a fracas at the end of a trial for high treason in Maidstone in 1798, he and others were accused of impeding Bow Street runners in their efforts to re-arrest a prisoner for whom he was defence counsel, and who the court had just found to be not guilty. The evidence against Mr. Fergusson was of dubious quality but he was nevertheless found guilty, fined heavily, and sentenced to one year's imprisonment. After his release, he emigrated to Calcutta, where he practised as a barrister for 20 years and became Attorney General of Bengal. In 1826 he returned to Scotland a wealthy man, and in addition to Craigdarroch, had a home at Orroland House, on the coast near Auchencairn in Kirkcudbrightshire. He was elected to Parliament as the Liberal member for the Stewartry of Kirkcudbright, later becoming Judge Advocate General and a Privy Counsellor. He was generally regarded as energetic, accomplished, and an eloquent supporter of liberal causes. He was a director of the East India Company 1830–1835.

Mr. Fergusson pressed forward the case exactly as he had promised, and on 26 March 1835, the *London Morning Chronicle* gave the following report of his speech in Parliament:

> Mr. Cutlar Fergusson was favourable to the establishment of a Central Board for the management of all the light-houses in the kingdom. The inhabitants of that part of Scotland with which he was connected were not at all satisfied with the administration of the Board of Northern Lights. He believed that the gentlemen of whom the Board was composed were men of the highest honor [sic], but in point of fact they were ignorant of nautical affairs and in consequence left the whole management of the lights to their engineer, who had often a personal interest in erecting them in places where they were not as much required as in others. The honorable [sic] gentleman proceeded to complain of the want of proper lights in the Solway Firth, which with the exception of the Red Sea (and he, Mr. Fergusson, would not even make that an exception) was acknowledged to be the most dangerous navigation in the world. He had for many years endeavoured to induce the Board of Northern Lights to establish a proper light in the Firth, but his exertions had hitherto been unsuccessful, and many shipwrecks, accompanied with great loss of life

and property had in consequence occurred almost in sight of Kirkcudbright, the principal town of the county which he had the honour to represent. In a maritime country like England [sic], no expense should be spared in the erection of proper lights on every part of the coast. He thought that the whole of the Light-house establishment should be a national establishment (hear) and that dues should be imposed upon vessels for the particular lights they might be compelled to pass. The establishment should be national, the expense national. If the title of private individuals to particular lights could be proved to be good, they ought undoubtedly to receive compensation, but if the their titles were not good they should no longer be allowed to continue so great and abuse.

The *Morning Chronicle* was the extremely popular radical London newspaper that employed Charles Dickens to write short stories under the pseudonym 'Boz'. Mr. Fergusson's points were well made in his speech, and his use of a considerable degree of hyperbole in comparing the relative dangers of the Solway Firth and the Red Sea would have perhaps helped him to gain the attention of quite a few members of the House who, like the Commissioners of whom he was so critical, had neither direct knowledge nor understanding of nautical matters.

For the first time since their petition and memorial had been drawn up 15 years earlier, the interested parties in Kirkcudbright had the comfort of knowing that their request had been eloquently and directly expressed to people who carried even more power and authority than the Commissioners for Northern Lights. Their gratitude to their diligent representative in Parliament was speedily recorded in the following letter and enclosed minute:

Kirkcudbright, 30th March, 1835.

Sir, - As Chairman for a Meeting of the Shipowners, Mariners, Merchants, and other traffickers of the town and Port of Kirkcudbright, held here this day, I beg leave to enclose a Copy of the Minute, containing a vote of thanks to you for the manner in which you have brought under the notice of Parliament the necessity of erecting a Light-house in this neighbourhood, and to express a hope that you will be pleased to continue your valuable exertions to promote the attainment of so humane an object.

The opinion expressed by Sir John Reid, alluded to in the Minutes, you will find contained in a communication lately made to you by Mr. John C. Mackenzie of this place.

I have the honor [sic] to be, Sir, your obedt. Humble servant,
William Johnston

Minute of Meeting of the Shipowners, Mariners, Merchants, and other traffickers of the Town and Port of Kirkcudbright.

Kirkcudbright 30th March, 1835.

At a Meeting of the Shipowners, Mariners, Merchants, and other traffickers of the Town and Port of Kirkcudbright, held here this day,

Mr. William Johnston, merchant and shipowner, in the Chair,

The attention of the meeting was called to the "Morning Chronicle" of 26th March, 1835, containing the Report of a Speech of the Right Honourable Robert Cutlar Fergusson of Craigdarroch and Orroland, Representative in Parliament for the Stewartry of Kirkcudbright, upon the Motion brought forward in the House of Commons by Joseph Hume, Esquire, upon the subject of Light-houses. The Meeting taking into consideration the able manner in which Mr. Fergusson had directed the attention of Parliament to the subject of Light-houses generally and to the particular grievance of the want of a Light-house in the neighbourhood of Kirkcudbright, deem it their duty to take the earliest opportunity of expressing their deep sense of their obligation to the Right Honourable Gentleman for his marked attention to the subject at present, as well as his former exertions in the same humane cause.

The meeting request the Preses to convey their thanks to Mr. Fergusson, and to express a hope that he will continue his valuable exertions towards the attainment of the object in view; and at same time, to call Mr. Fergusson's attention to the necessity of the Light-house being erected on the Little Ross, at the mouth of the River Dee, this being allowed by all mariners and persons skilled in nautical affairs to be the most suitable for such a building, and particularly recommended as such to the Commissioners of Northern Lights by the late Sir John Reid, Commander of his Majesty's Revenue Cutter *Prince Edward,* who cruized [sic] for nearly half a century in the Solway Firth, and whose opinions as to the particular locality, from his great experience and professional knowledge, is entitled to the greatest weight.

From a copy of the original letter in the collection of the Stewartry Museum.

It is hard to believe that there were any experienced mariners who did not support the case for a lighthouse on Little Ross Island, but some parties were still drawing Robert Cutlar Fergusson's attention towards the possibility that Abbey Head, three and a half miles to the east southeast of Little Ross might be a better location. As a conscientious Member of Parliament, Mr. Fergusson would must have considered such a possibility, but without expert knowledge, it would have been difficult for him to determine the relative merits of the two locations. Local politics are often influenced by rivalry between people in different small communities, and there were doubtless landowners, businessmen, and ordinary people who resented anything being done and any money being spent on a community other than their own. The fact that Mr. Fergusson had a substantial seaside home at Orroland, in the vicinity of Abbey Head, would have made it even more difficult for him not to take seriously the suggestion that there was an alternative, or even a better, location for the proposed lighthouse than Little Ross Island:

Petition of the Magistrates and Council of the Royal Burgh of Kirkcudbright to the Honourable the Commissioners of Supply for the Stewartry of Kirkcudbright.

Unto the Honourable the Commissioners of Supply for the Stewartry of Kirkcudbright.

The Petition of the Magistrates and Council of the Royal Burgh of Kirkcudbright.

Humbly Sheweth,

That the want of proper Light on the Island of Little Ross at the mouth of the River Dee has been long and severely felt and complained of, and repeated applications have been made to the Board of the Commissioners of Northern Light-Houses for the erection of a Light-House on that island.

That these applications were signed by many of your number and by others, Freeholders, Justices of the Peace, Commissioners of Supply, and Landowners in the Stewartry, by the Magistrates and Council of the Burgh for the time, and the Shipowners, Merchants and other Traffickers within the limits of the Port of Kirkcudbright, by the Collector and Comptroller, and by numerous Shipowners on the English coast.

That the applications however did not meet with that attention from the Board, to which the Petitioners considered they were undoubtedly entitled, but the petitioners have lately been gratified to observe that the Right Honourable Robert Cutlar Fergusson, Member for the County being deeply impressed with the fact that an indispensable necessity exists for the immediate erection of a Light-house on the Island of Little Ross, has oftener than once brought the subject under the notice of the House of Commons, and from a letter to the Provost of Kirkcudbright, herewith produced, it appears he is continuing to exert himself for the attainment of the object in view.

That while the petitioners would rejoice to see Lights erected on every part of the coast wherever they might be useful, they regret to observe that of late Mr Fergusson's attention has been attempted to be directed to another locality, as being preferable to that of the Island of Little Ross, for the erection of a Light-house.

That the petitioners are satisfied the locality in question, Abbey-head cannot be compared to that of the Little Ross, which public opinion for upwards of half a century has pronounced to be a spot as being from many circumstances by far the most suitable for the erection of the Light on this coast.

That the petitioners are unwilling to take up your Honour's time in specifying the various circumstances entitling the Island of Little Ross to a priority in the erection of a Light-house. They may state however, that at no great distance from the Island there are two harbours, one of which, the Manxman's Lake, affords the only safe and commodious anchorage in the South of Scotland, and under the Island itself there is an excellent roadstead, where vessels of all descriptions may ride in safety till there be a sufficiency of water to carry them up to the Lake.

The superiority of the said roadstead and anchorage ground to any in the Counties of Lancaster, Westmoreland and Cumberland in England, or in the Counties of Dumfries, Kirkcudbright and Wigtown, for vessels navigating the Solway Firth or that part of the Irish sea connected with it, is well known to mariners.

That Sir John Reid, Commander of His Majesty's Revenue Cutter *Prince Edward,* who had cruised in the Channel for more that twenty years, recommended the Island of Little Ross as being a most suitable locality for the proposed Light.

That Mr. Fergusson's exertions have all been directed towards the erection of the Lights in that quarter, but from his letter he appears to fear that the recent difference of opinion as to the best locality may interfere with his exertions, for he says that it would be most desirable that the several parties who differ in respect to the choice of a spot the most proper for the erection of a Light-house would come to an understanding, in order that some specific proposal approved of by them might be submitted to the Commissioners of Northern Lights, and if successful that the matter might be brought before the Government or the House of Commons.

That the petitioners are most anxious to adopt Mr. Fergusson's valuable suggestions, for they are convinced that success is to be obtained only by all parties on this coast agreeing in directing his efforts to one point, instead of distracting his attention by starting from time to time new localities.

That the locality of Abbeyhead is inferior to Little Ross in many respects, and in particular that a Light there would not be visible to vessels navigating on the West side of the mouth of the River Dee, although at no great distance from the light. In fact the petitioners have heard it maintained that a Light on the Abbeyhead would be worse than useless, inasmuch as it might lead vessels bearing up for it into the most dangerous navigation to the east of it, occasioned both by the nature of the coast and the numerous sandbanks in that quarter.

May it please your Honours to recommend to Mr. Fergusson to continue his valuable exertions towards the procuring of a Light-house on the Island of Little Ross.

And the petitioners as in duty bound will ever pray, etc.

from a copy of the original in the collection of the Stewartry Museum.

The Commissioners of Supply for the Stewartry of Kirkcudbright were responsible for the assessment of land tax, and it is not immediately clear why the petitioners thought it appropriate to try to secure their support for their cause. There were however several prominent Commissioners of Supply who were signatories to the original petition to the Commissioners for Northern Lights and at least one dissenter, James Gordon of Balcary. Perhaps the intention was to prompt a dialogue which would hopefully result in a majority favouring a clear recommendation to Robert Cutlar Fergusson to continue to pursue the Little Ross location with undiluted energy. Several years later, the Commissioners of Supply did send their own petition in support of a lighthouse on Little Ross Island to the Northern Lighthouse Board.

John C. Mackenzie provides a detailed account of a special visit to Little Ross made by Mr. Fergusson and other interested parties at about this time. They were conveyed to the island on board the first paddle steamer to bear the name *Countess of Galloway,* that substantial new vessel having been chartered by the Magistrates and Town Council of Kirkcudbright for the occasion. Though no date is given for this event, it must have taken place between 1835 and 1838, as the first steamer bearing that name was built in 1835, and Robert Cutlar Fergusson died in November 1838.

> Mr. Fergusson, during the course of his endeavours to promote the erection of the lighthouse visited the Bay and Ross in the first *Countess of Galloway* steamer. The Magistrates and Council provided the vessel. Several gentlemen favourable to the project were invited to be present. I was of their number. We embarked at the Lake and were carried on sailors' backs to the small boat to convey us to the steamer. The sea especially in going out of the bay was lumpy, and I was very sick, and so were Provost McKinnel [sic], a very bilious looking man, and many others. When safely anchored on our return to the harbour, there was a *feed* — a sort of cold one with lots of warm toddy, and healths and toasts. The memory of Skipper Skelly was given and I responded, saying that the Light-house had been the subject of his day and night dreams for many years.
>
> From John C. Mackenzie's Tribute to James Skelly (1880).

Mr. Mackenzie wrote the foregoing account in the eightieth year of his life, and it is likely that he meant to refer to Mr. McKinnell as ex-Provost rather than Provost, as Provost McKinnell only held office 1823–1829 and 1831–1833, before the steamer *Countess of Galloway* had been built. In the same publication, Mr. Mackenzie summarised a few of the key events in his campaign for the lighthouse:

> On the eve of my leaving Edinburgh, in 1833, to commence business here, as a writer, in partnership with Mr William Mure, junior, my friend Mr. David Doud, of the Dean of Guild's Office, Edinburgh, advised me to take up the matter of a Light-house on the Little Ross, for which uncle Skelly had agitated for years, but to which the Commissioners of Northern Lights gave a deaf ear, influenced by Mr. Robert Stevenson, the elder, their engineer, who declared that the Light would be only a Harbour Light, and as such did not fall under their province. I acted upon my friend's suggestion, and made two copies of my uncle's memorial, the one I sent to that noble man Mr. Robert Cutlar Fergusson, Esq., M.P for the Stewartry, and the other to General Sharp, M.P. for the burghs (whose object in getting into Parliament was to obtain a regiment). Mr. Fergusson in a day or two brought the matter before Parliament, and wrote to me sending an extract from *Hansard* of his speech. I got up a meeting of the ship-owners, mariners, traffickers, etc., of the town, and having a Petition cut and dry to Parliament, they signed it and I sent it to Mr. Fergusson. General Sharpe did not so much as acknowledge receipt of my despatch. Uncle's memorial was afterwards printed by, or for, the Commissioners and Parliament.

General Matthew Sharpe was a Dumfriesshire man, born in 1774 at Hoddom Castle, who in 1832 became a Member of Parliament for the Dumfries Burghs. Prior to his political career, he had served in the British army with the 28th Light Dragoons until they were disbanded in 1802, by which time he had attained the rank of Lieutenant Colonel. He was later appointed to the army's general staff, and was promoted to Lieutenant General in 1825. Following his retirement in 1841, he was awarded the brevet rank of General. Brevet rank was generally awarded in recognition of the fact that outstanding service had been given, but carried neither the higher power nor the increased pay that the new status implied:

To General Sharpe, M.P. for the Dumfries District of Burghs.

Kirkcudbright, 13th June, 1835.

Sir, I think it not unlikely that you are aware that the want of a Light-house on the island of Little Ross at the mouth of the River Dee, in this neighbourhood, has long been a subject of complaint in this and the opposite coast. Some time previous to Mr. Hume's motion on the subject of Light-houses generally, I took the opportunity of reminding Mr. Fergusson, the Member for the County, of our particular grievance, by sending him a copy of the Memorial now enclosed. Mr. Fergusson had for many years used his influence to procure the erection of a Light-house on the Little Ross, and at that time I did not think of troubling you with a copy of the documents now sent. As it is of importance that the Member for this district should be fully informed on the subject, I use the freedom of sending you copies of the papers regarding the proposed Light-House, from a perusal of which I confidently anticipate that you will be satisfied that the Commissioners of Northern Lights have hitherto given the go by to the application upon anything but fair grounds, in fact Mr. Fergusson in his speech in Parliament on the subject did not hesitate to point out clearly where the blame lay.

I fear that until Light-houses are put under a new Board there is little chance of our getting the proposed Light-house. The engineer for the Northern Lights was here for a second time last autumn, and we have not yet learned the determination of the Board upon the subject. If you have any influence with the Commissioners, your writing to them enquiring as to the results of the application might benefit the cause, for it would prove to them that the matter was likely to fall into the hands of persons who would see that the application should be decided upon its merits.

Captain Henderson of the Royal Engineers, is about to make a Government Survey of the Solway Firth, Government having been memorialised upon the subject by a body of gentlemen in Carlisle. It has occurred to me that it might be of advantage if Captain Henderson's attention could be called to the locality of Little Ross as the site of an intended Light-House. There is every possibility I learn of Light-Houses being put under a London Board. If Captain Henderson were in possession of the documents now sent, he could without any additional trouble direct his attention to the subject, and reference might afterwards be made to him, but you yourself will judge of the propriety of communicating to him the papers sent, my object in sending them to you being to inform you on a subject which is of great local interest, in the hope of securing your valuable influence, leaving it to yourself to use that influence in the manner which you may deem the most likely to further the cause.

I am, etc., J. C. Mackenzie

From a copy of the original letter in the collection of the Stewartry Museum.

By the time Mr. Hume's Bill went before Parliament, it had been modified greatly from the sweeping purge that he and many others had originally believed to be necessary. Even Mr. Hume had come to realise that the commissioning and management of lighthouses was a rather more complicated matter than it had first appeared to be. The Parliamentary Select Committee chaired by him in 1834 had made rather more criticisms of Trinity House than it had of the Scottish and Irish authorities, so the plan to increase the power and authority of Trinity House and to reduce that of the Scottish and Irish Authorities had discreetly been shelved. Mr. Hume's Bill sought mainly to ensure that all lighthouses in England, and other specified aids to navigation, be brought under the control of a restructured Trinity House, bringing to an end the situation in which many English lighthouses were under private ownership and control:

> Mr. Hume rose to move for leave to bring in a Bill for vesting Light-houses on the coast of England in the Trinity-house of Deptford Strand. In 1834, a Committee sat a long time to inquire into the subject of the light-houses of England, Scotland, and Ireland, and made a report thereon. As chairman of that Committee he was instructed to bring in a Bill with a view to consolidate those three important branches under one Board in London. He did so, but the Bill met with considerable opposition. In the first place, his hon. Friend the hon. and learned Member for Dublin, and the Irish Members generally, objected to their light-houses being transferred to the Trinity-house, which was the course recommended by a majority of the Committee. The Members for Scotland also did not think the Trinity-house the most proper Board to place their light-houses under; and he must candidly say, that such was his own opinion. He could wish the subject to be taken up as a Government question, and that there should be a separate Board under which these three great branches should be placed, with a view of establishing one uniform regulation among the whole, instead of there being as now, conducted under three different sets of regulations. The rate of charge for ships, it was well known, differed greatly in the three countries; and it was most extraordinary that a naval nation like this should have arrived at its present state of greatness without any Government authority having been established for managing and carrying on these lighthouses.
>
> Hansard Ref. Lighthouses on the coast of England. HC Deb 08 February 1836 vol 31 cc166-76, 166-167.

Joseph Hume MP had been born in Montrose in 1777; the son of a shipmaster, he had studied at Montrose Academy and the University of Edinburgh. He went to India, becoming an assistant surgeon with the East India Company and later served with the Bengal Medical Establishment between 1799 and 1808. After his return to Britain, he purchased a seat in Parliament in 1812, representing Weymouth and Melcombe Regis. He was elected as a Member of Parliament for Aberdeen Burghs in 1818, later representing the Middlesex, Kilkenny, and Montrose Burghs. He attended the House of Commons with such regularity that he became regarded almost as a fixture, always occupying the same seat. He was greatly mocked for his physical appearance, being cruelly described as portly, bull-necked, comely, and even 'stupid-looking', and was further criticised for being perverse, irritating, conceited, and boring. Perhaps worst of all, he spoke with a strong east Scotland accent, was alleged to have had a minimal understanding of grammar, and was deemed to be incapable of constructing easily intelligible sentences.

Portrait of Joseph Hume, courtesy of the Wellcome Library, London.

Despite all of the foregoing, and his propensity for numerous blunders, he was widely accepted as being earnest and industrious, making over 4,000 speeches, interventions, motions for papers, and presentations of petitions between 1820 and 1832. During his political career, he specialised in exposing misuses of public money, Trinity House being but one of many targets in his pursuit of that cause. He died in 1855.

In the Stewartry of Kirkcudbright, far from the headquarters of the Commissioners for Northern Lights in Edinburgh, and even further from the bars, coffee houses, and debating chambers of Westminster, patience was in short supply. Sixteen years had now elapsed since the original petition requesting provision of a lighthouse had been lodged, without any progress being made. An unsigned copy of a letter to Robert Cutlar Fergusson in June 1836, from the ship owners, merchants, and traffickers of Kirkcudbright lacks a copy of the minute referred to therein, but nevertheless displays evidence of rising anger in Kirkcudbright:

Kirkcudbright June 1836

As instructed by a meeting of the Shipowners, Merchants, and other Traffickers of this port held here this day, I take the liberty of sending the enclosed minute and in name of that meeting, I have to thank you for your attention and useful exertions in the cause to which the minute refers and to implore you to use your best endeavours in contradicting and exposing the absurd assertions made by the Engineer to the Commissioners for Northern Lights regarding the roadstead at Little Ross and the anchorage in the immediate neighbourhood.

I am etc.,
Your most obedient humble servant…

Quoted from a copy in the collection of the Stewartry Museum.

Mr. Fergusson's response was swift, and in a forceful speech in the House of Commons on 16 June 1836, he presented the petitioners' case, summarising its content, criticising the Commissioners for Northern Lights, and undermining the basis of adverse opinions apparently expressed by the Commissioners' engineer regarding the qualities of the anchorages in Kirkcudbright Bay. He attempted to prompt debate on the matter, but contravened Parliamentary procedure and was obliged to withdraw the petition due to the fact that the new Lighthouses Bill was already under consideration:

Mr. Cutlar Fergusson rose to present Petitions from the landholders and commissioners of supply of the stewartry, and from the merchants, shipowners, and mariners of the port of Kirkcudbright, complaining of the want of lighthouses on the Scotch [sic] side of the Solway Frith, whereby numerous shipwrecks and great loss of life were frequently occasioned on that coast. The matter complained of was a great and crying grievance in that part of the country. There was only a single lighthouse from the Mull of Cantyre [sic] to the coast of Dumfries, and the whole of that navigation was of the most perilous description, being along a rocky shore, upon which shipwrecks were extremely frequent. For the last thirty-five years those who were interested in the stewartry had endeavoured to obtain the erection of a lighthouse on the island of Little Ross, and since he had come into Parliament, he had made representations for that purpose to the Commissioners of Northern Lights, on grounds that he conceived it impossible to resist. They were resisted, however, and on grounds that it appeared to him impossible to sustain. The Commissioners took great credit to themselves for having established a lighthouse at the Mull of Galloway, but in consequence of an intervening headland, that light was not of any use to vessels navigating along the coast of Kirkcudbright. During the last year four vessels had been lost there, two of them with all hands on board, and of the crews of the other two a considerable portion were drowned. If there had been a light on Little Ross Island, this loss of life would not have occurred. There had been sixty-six vessels altogether lost on that part of the coast during the last thirty years, and he could state, on the best authority, that the establishment of a lighthouse on the spot he had named might have averted to a great extent, if not entirely, such a destruction of life and property. A lighthouse could be constructed there for £1,400 which was scarcely one-tenth of the amount of the cargoes of some of the ships lost there. He did not desire to cast any reflections on the Commissioners of the Northern Lights—they were all most respectable gentlemen; but he must question the constitution of that Board. Of course the House supposed that it was mainly composed of scientific persons and of mariners. There was not, however, a single individual of either class upon it. It was composed of Edinburgh lawyers, and of the sheriffs of certain maritime counties in Scotland, and the Commissioners were entirely led by the judgment of their engineer. That gentleman had not done his duty towards the county which he (Mr. Fergusson) represented. From 1820 up to the present time his constituents had never been able to obtain an answer to their request that a lighthouse should be established on Little Ross Island. The reply to them now was, that the harbour there had been surveyed by the engineer of the Board, and that he had reported that it was dry at low water. Now what was the fact? In this very harbour King William rode for several days, with all his fleet, on his way to raise the siege of Drogheda. Hundreds of vessels have been seen riding there in safety, and if the engineer had consulted any manner on the spot, he would have told him that at the lowest ebb there were from three and a half to four fathoms water in the harbour. He had been informed by a most respectable resident in Kirkcudbright, that the engineer arrived there on a Sunday, went to Little Ross Island, merely looked at the harbour, and without asking a question of a single mariner there, and without taking soundings, left the place. The harbour was, in fact, one where vessels coasting from Ireland to Cumberland, Dumfries, and Kirkcudbrightshire, could ride with perfect safety, and the light was asked for it as a harbour of refuge. He might be asked what could the House do? It could legislate on the subject, and by a Bill compel the Commissioners to do their duty. The Speaker interrupted the right hon. Gentleman, and reminded him that it was one of the regulations of the House not to go into a discussion on a Petition relating to a matter that had been, or would be, made the subject of a specific motion. Mr. Cutlar Fergusson said, that in that respect the regulations of the House were changed since he had come into it. He still thought that petitioners had a right to have their case stated, though they might not have a right to have a debate upon it. He now gave notice, that on Thursday next he would present these petitions, and move for papers on the subject.

The Speaker said, that he was bound in duty to enforce that which had been laid down as the general understanding of the House.

Petition withdrawn.

Hansard Ref. Lighthouses (Scotland) HC Deb 16 June 1836 vol. 34 cc 558-60.

When the speech quoted above was reported in the press, Robert Stevenson took offence at the part of its content that referred to him having arrived in Kirkcudbright on a Sunday and visited Little Ross Island. The following extract is taken from his letter to Robert Cutlar Fergusson, dated 25 June 1836:

I would not be understood to complain of any remarks on my professional conduct which is of course open to public opinion, but the statement of which I complain is injurious to my character as the father of a family and as an Elder of the Church of Scotland as well as to the Board for which I act.

Business Records of Robert Stevenson and sons, civil engineers, National Library of Scotland.

By today's standards, it seems quite extraordinary that Robert Stevenson should be so upset about a perception that he stood accused of failure to observe the Sabbath, rather than the clear suggestion that his survey was neither thorough nor accurate. In a terse note in reply, dated 29 June 1836 Mr. Fergusson wrote:

I never used the word 'Sunday' in the discussion to which you refer and I have stated to the house that the report in that respect was incorrect.

Business Records of Robert Stevenson and sons, civil engineers, National Library of Scotland.

The Lighthouses Bill that eventually went before Parliament during 1836, did not propose the setting up of a new central authority to control lighthouses and buoys throughout the United Kingdom, but did seek to make improvements in how each of the three authorities already established was to be structured and administered. Perhaps needless to say, the measures that were proposed fell short of what Mr. Fergusson and others had advocated, and on 12 July 1836, when a House of Commons Committee met to discuss details of the proposed Lighthouses Bill, he used the opportunity both to make further specific criticisms of the Northern Lighthouse Board and to restate his grievance at their failure to commit to supporting the principle of a lighthouse being established at Little Ross Island:

Mr. Cutlar Fergusson was understood to say, that as to the Board of Northern Lights, there never was a more irresponsible body; it was composed chiefly of lawyers of Edinburgh, men who, from the very nature of their profession, were, and must be, incompetent to carry on the important trust committed to their charge, though he believed they had generally acted with great zeal, and with the most perfect disinterestedness. They had, however, never once called to their Councils, any of the Sheriffs of the maritime counties. The petition which he had presented on a former occasion prayed, that every Sheriff of the maritime counties should be a member of this Board. The hon. and learned Member stated the fact that, along the coast of Kirkcudbright, there had been lost, in the course of the last thirty years, no less than sixty-six ships, many of them with the crews, he believed almost in every case for want of a lighthouse on the island of Little Ross. On the whole coast, there was one harbour of refuge to the mouth of the Dee. There was a roadstead, (and he vouched for the truth of his statement), sufficient for fifty or sixty vessels to ride at anchor at low water, and wait for the tide, and sail up to the bay of Kirkcudbright. All these petitioners asked was, that a lighthouse should be erected, which would not cost more than £1,200. He approved of the general principle of this Bill, but thought that the Scotch [sic] Board required revision.

Hansard Ref. Lighthouses (Scotland) HC Deb 12 July 1836 vol. 35 cc139–49.

Within two weeks of Mr. Fergusson's speech in Parliament, the Engineer to the Commissioners of the Northern Lights made an updated report on the qualities of the anchorages at Little Ross Island and Kirkcudbright Bay generally in which, to the shock of the petitioners, he reaffirmed the highly critical comments he had previously made regarding the characteristics of the anchorages within Kirkcudbright Bay:

> Excerpt from Report by Engineer to the Commissioners of the Northern Light Houses dated 31st December 1836.
>
> Kirkcudbright
>
> The Reporter visited Kirkcudbright Bay in the latter end of July last and made farther observations on this much contested ground; but with the same result as formerly in as much as he finds that it wants depth of water in all places where vessels can anchor in safety and have shelter with inshore winds; such anchorage being dry at low water. With regard therefore to the establishment of a light upon the Ross Island at the entrance of Kirkcudbright this proposition stands in a very different predicament from that of the island of Devar [sic] leading to Campbelton [sic] Loch where any ship may enter and ride afloat at all times of tide. It is no doubt true that a lighthouse on this coast would be useful to the Trade of the District including more particularly Kirkcudbright, Dumfries, and the small ports on the northern side of the Solway Firth, but the question recurs regarding the willingness of the Trade to pay for the light, and adequacy of these Ports to maintain the Establishment, at the rate of a halfpenny per ton per voyage.
>
> In the month of October last the Reporter had the honour of an interview with Mr. Fergusson the Member for Kirkcudbright when he stated to him generally this Opinion. Something upon a much less and more manageable Scale than a light on the island of Ross might answer the shipping of Kirkcudbright which port is chiefly interested in the erection of a Harbour Light. The general purposes of the Navigation of the Solway seem to be already answered by the sea lights of St. Bees Head in Cumberland, the Point of Ayre in the Isle of Man, and the light on the Mull of Galloway.
>
> From a copy of the original in the collection of the Stewartry Museum.

This report, dated 31 December 1836, inaccurate in certain important respects, and rather scathing generally in its appraisal of Kirkcudbright Bay's usefulness as a port of refuge, gives no indication of any weakening in Robert Stevenson's opposition to the provision of a lighthouse at Little Ross Island. It does however provide a possible clue as to the reason for his lack of enthusiasm. In comparison with Campbeltown, or indeed most other ports on the Firth of Clyde, Kirkcudbright Bay undoubtedly offers only relatively shallow water at even its best anchorages. It is also used by a much less impressive volume of shipping than most ports with which the

Stevensons would have been involved, being far from any main shipping lanes and remote from the principal grounds for the herring fishing fleet. Mr. Stevenson, on behalf of the Commissioners of Northern Lights, was concerned therefore that there would be neither sufficient tonnage of shipping nor sufficient volume to generate the income necessary to fund the construction and maintenance of a lighthouse. The Commissioners seem to have made no allowance for the fact that firstly, Kirkcudbright is the only significant port on the south-facing coast of Scotland to offer refuge of any kind from the prevailing southerly wind, and secondly, that the vast majority of ships seeking such shelter were small vessels of shallow draft, in recognition of the particular local conditions that prevailed in the Solway Firth and north Irish Sea. The local case being fought so ably by John C. Mackenzie and many others took for granted that local mariners, who risk their lives in carrying local cargoes, are as entitled to every bit as much assistance in achieving safe trading conditions as those in larger, wealthier communities. It is unclear exactly when news of this further report, or leaked information regarding its content, reached Kirkcudbright, but its arrival would certainly have brought about both extreme disappointment and some irritation at the fact that it merely reinforced a view previously expressed: that a 'harbour light' was all that was required at Little Ross.

Despite his undoubted talent and his worldwide recognition as one of Scotland's most distinguished engineers, Robert Stevenson had not impressed the petitioners who sought a lighthouse on Little Ross. It is not possible to determine whether this was due to poor briefing, an inaccurate survey, a clash of personalities or a combination of all three. Sadly, local hero Captain James Skelly seems to have been particularly upset by the attitude displayed by Robert Stevenson:

> James Skelly was the man who first agitated for the lighthouse — he never mentioned the name of the elder Mr. Stevenson without a feeling of displeasure — he felt no more respect for him than he did for the very poor Court of Session Judge Lord Succoth, who had decided the case against him [See Chapter II].

Tribute to the Memory of James Skelly, John C. Mackenzie, (1880).

Robert Cutlar Fergusson died of a consumptive illness in Paris on 16 November 1838, at a time when the case to which he had devoted so much energy to promoting was all but won. The precise reason for the ultimate success of the long campaign is not clear, but it could be simply that some form of lighthouse at Little Ross had eventually come to the top of the list of priorities of the Commissioners for Northern Lights. That however does not explain why the Commissioners for Northern Lights seem to have eventually ignored the denial by Robert Stevenson of the existence of a useful anchorage at Little Ross, and his insistence that a mere harbour light was all that was required there. The threat to bring the Scottish lighthouses and buoys under the control of a single United Kingdom authority with even more powers than Trinity House would undoubtedly have made the Commissioners very sensitive to criticism of their efficiency and may have obliged them to reconsider their position. Perhaps most importantly, Captain C. G. Robinson RN FGS, had surveyed Kirkcudbright Bay in 1838. The Hydrographic Office did not publish the resulting chart of Kirkcudbright Bay until 1850, and by that date it had been amended to include details of Little Ross lighthouse. This excellent chart remained in use, with minor corrections, until 1960, and clearly showed an anchorage to the north east of Little Ross Island in a minimum depth of between three and three and a half fathoms of water. The carrying out of this survey would have been a matter of great local interest. Its preliminary findings would almost certainly have been recognised as confirming the case made by the petitioners, and contradicting the findings in the two reports by Robert Stevenson, engineer to the Northern Lighthouse Board.

Writing in 1880, John C. Mackenzie recorded that Mr. Fergusson had all but gained his point before he died. His successor as Member of Parliament representing the Stewartry of Kirkcudbright, Mr. Murray of Broughton, had however continued to pursue the matter. The campaigners finally won their long battle in early January of 1840, and the *Caledonian Mercury* of 25 January published the following gleeful account of their triumph:

LIGHTHOUSE ON THE LITTLE ROSS

We rejoice to learn (says the Dumfries Times) that this humane contrivance to save life and guide the storm-tossed mariner to a safe haven is now certain to be erected, as our readers will see from the following communication. The late Judge-Advocate, Mr. Fergusson, deserved the best thanks of the county for his exertions in this cause; but it is mainly to the exertions and high influence of Mr. Murray of Broughton, The Lord Advocate, and the friends who worked with them, that the lighthouse on the Little Ross has been obtained. The thanks of the Stewartry, and of all the sea-ports in Wigtownshire, the Stewartry, and along the coasts of the Solway, are due to Mr. Murray for his good services in this good cause.

"Kirkcudbright, 18th January – it is with much pleasure that I inform you, the lighthouse on Little Ross, so long and so anxiously wished for by our merchants and mariners on this coast, is now in a fair way of being soon erected, as you will learn from the following copy of a letter, from the secretary of the Northern Lighthouses, to Mr. Niven, Clerk of Supply. This lighthouse will be a most appropriate monument to the memory of our lamented Member, Mr. Cutlar Fergusson, who many a night, fought the battles of the bewildered seamen in the House of Commons, and to whose exertions we are indebted for this great benefit. Many a brave and hardy sailor will hail with joy the Little Ross light:-

Northern Lights Office
Edinburgh, 13th January 1840

Sir, – I have to acquaint you, that the Commissioners of the Northern Lighthouses having, at a general meeting held here on the 11th inst. Had under their consideration the report of a deputation of their number who visited the island of Little Ross, in the view of considering its eligibility as a station for a lighthouse, have come to the resolution of erecting a light on that island, as soon as the work can be undertaken by the boards; and have remitted to the engineer to report as to the nature of the light which ought to be exhibited, the requisite buildings, and the probable expense.

I am etc. C. Cunningham, Secretary.

Clerk to the Commissioners of Supply, Kirkcudbright."

Reproduced, courtesy of The British Library, 96 Euston Rd., London NW1 2DB.

The news of the decision to proceed with all haste to build the lighthouse was quickly conveyed to the Provost of Kirkcudbright and is recorded in the Town Council minutes, but no records have been uncovered which describe any celebrations that took place either on Little Ross Island or in the town. It nevertheless must have been a matter of the greatest satisfaction, not only to all the people in the area who had been so tenacious in the furtherance of their case, but also to all the mariners in the north Irish Sea and Solway Firth who stood to benefit so greatly from the presence of a new lighthouse. John C. Mackenzie must have been particularly delighted by the success of the two campaigns in which he and his uncle, Captain James Skelly, had played such significant parts, However, he may perhaps have been a little put out regarding the fact that that so much glory was given to members of parliament, dignitaries, and people of great social standing, rather than the local part-time campaigners who had worked so hard for so long.

The following extract from the *Report from the Select Committee on Lighthouses,* published on 1 August 1845, sheds light on the sequence of events which led up to the granting of approval to build a lighthouse at Little Ross. It provides confirmation of Robert Stevenson's lack of support for the Little Ross option, and evidence of the importance of the roles played by Captain Robinson RN, the Lord Advocate, and Trinity House in overcoming his resistance.

> Return showing list of persons who have applied for or pointed out different stations for the Erection of Lighthouses since 1834, distinguishing which of them have been surveyed, and on which (if any) Lighthouses have been erected.
>
> Lighthouse at Little Ross or Abbey Head
>
> **8th January 1834:** Application from Mr. James Gordon, Balcarry [sic], for lighthouse on either of these places.
>
> **14th February 1835:** Engineer reported that it was not of much general importance, and preferred Abbey Head. Note – Copies of the above applications, with many previous, and report by engineer have been already presented to Parliament.

14th January 1837: Engineer again reports.

13th January 1838: Petition from Magistrates and Council of Kirkcudbright.

24th January 1838: Committee delayed consideration of matter.

22nd March 1838: Letter from Provost of Kirkcudbright for an answer to the petition.

To answer that it is delayed.

21st May 1839: Letter from Trinity House, 10th April 1839, with representation as to light, and report from Captain Robertson [sic] R.N.; letter from Lord Advocate, Mr. Murray M.P., and other communications.

Engineer to correspond with Captain Robertson [sic].

10th June 1839: Petition from Commissioners of Supply and Landholders of Kirkcudbright; letter from Lord Advocate, enclosing Petition from shipowners, shipmasters, and others interested in the navigation of the Solway Frith with 398 signatures.

Answer delayed; in consequence of no reply from Captain Robertson [sic].

9th January 1840: Report by deputation of Commissioners. Committee approve of report, and recommend to general meeting to build.

11th January 1840: General meeting approve, so soon as work can be undertaken.

3rd February 1840: Letter from Trinity House, concurring in erection of lighthouse.

28th October 1840: Report by Engineer; survey completed.

Lighthouse built; lighted **1st January 1843**.

The moment on New Year's Day 1843 when the light at Little Ross began to shine and its beam to radiate for over 18 miles must have been thrilling, and the eloquent Mr. Mackenzie is not likely to have failed to record his thoughts on that great occasion. Sadly however, although he lived to be 92, the manner in which he and his fellow petitioners celebrated their victory must now be left to one's imagination, as no records have been found despite a rigorous search.

CHAPTER 4

Design, The Building Contract, and Construction

In little rural towns like Kirkcudbright, the arrival of strangers in suits rarely goes unnoticed, however inconspicuous such strangers may think themselves to be. The sudden appearance of Robert Stevenson and his son Thomas, with either a theodolite or a dumpy level, surveying staff, and rods would therefore have been a significant event that would have aroused public interest, prompted speculation, and probably generated much spreading of ill-founded rumour. When the Stevensons boarded a vessel bound for Little Ross Island there would have been widespread belief that the long-awaited commencement of construction of Little Ross lighthouse had begun. The following letter addressed to Robert Stevenson on 5 October 1840 by Mr. Alexander Murray MP of Cally, near Gatehouse of Fleet, illustrates how quickly and effectively news travelled:

> Having heard from the Lord Advocate that you were to be at Kirkcudbright about this time, and being extremely anxious about our lighthouse upon the Little Ross I should be very glad to have some conversation with you upon the subject before your departure from the County. Tomorrow I am particularly engaged but the next day Wednesday it would give me much pleasure if you would favour me with your company at dinner at 6 o'clock.

Robert Stevenson replied the next day by adding the following note to Mr. Murray's letter of invitation:

> I have received your obliging note of yesterday from Provost McBain [the Provost of Kirkcudbright] and I regret that it will not be in my power to have the honour of waiting upon you tomorrow — but if you are to be at home on Thursday morning I would drive to Cally to breakfast along with my son who is at the Little Ross on the survey.

> From a copy of the original letter in the collection of the Stewartry Museum.

It did not take long for newspapers to report that the first indications of the long anticipated signs of activity in construction of a lighthouse on Little Ross Island had been observed:

> The erection of a lighthouse on the Little Ross has at last commenced. Mr. Stevenson, engineer to the Commissioners of the Northern Lighthouses, accompanied by his son, arrived at Kirkcudbright on Tuesday week, and next day proceeded to the island; and after a patient and minute search for a proper foundation, which was at last satisfactorily found, the site of the lighthouse, and other necessary buildings, was marked according to the directions of Mr. Stevenson.

Cumberland Pacquet (Naval Chronicle in The Nautical Magazine, 1840).

The Stevensons would have set out the proposed buildings on the ground in accordance with their intended plans and would have taken levels and dimensions of the chosen site at all critical points to enable them to return to Edinburgh and to commence the lengthy process of preparing detailed construction drawings. These would then be sent out to selected potential tenderers. There would have been great excitement in Kirkcudbright and the surrounding district at the prospect of imminent construction, and the *Cumberland Pacquet's* report illustrates that this enthusiasm was matched in Workington, Maryport, and Whitehaven despite the many years that had passed since the case for construction of a lighthouse at Little Ross was first made. The following fuller and more flowery press report was published a few days later in the most prominent Dumfries newspaper, and if the Stevensons had been wounded in any way by the activities of Robert Cutlar Fergusson on behalf of the petitioners who sought a lighthouse, this report would have added salt to those wounds:

> Robert Stevenson esq., engineer to the Commissioners of Northern Lights, has surveyed the Ross within the last few days; and although he has now left Kirkcudbright, his son, who remains behind, is busily engaged in making the necessary designs and calculations for the erection of a lighthouse. The works will be commenced in spring, and in twelve months or so a Pharos will exhibit its welcome lights, much to the relief of the mariners on both sides of the Solway. On no portion of our iron-bound coast is a beacon more imperiously required; the vessels trading between England and Ireland frequently fly for shelter in the Manxman's Lake, by no means the most secure portion of the estuary of the Dee; and when a light enables them to round the prominent island at the mouth of the river, they will be enabled to ride out without detriment the severest gales that blow. During the last twenty years more accidents have occurred to coasters seeking entrance to the Dee, than over the whole coast of Galloway, and details exist in our files sufficient to fill a little volume, embracing all the varying horror of storm and wreck. For long all seafaring men have been most anxious for a beacon on the Little Ross; but from whatever cause obstacles were interposed, which the late member for the Stewartry, R. C. Fergusson Esq., had the honour of removing at the Trinity Board, London. Mr. Murray followed zealously in the wake of his predecessor, until victory at length has crowned his efforts;

and the sea-faring public and others, far and near, owe a tribute of gratitude to the memory of the one, and an enthusiastic cup of thanks to the other.

Dumfries Courier, (13 October 1840).

Robert Stevenson, the head of the family firm, bore the title of Engineer to the Commissioners of Northern Lights, and was therefore the person who carried overall responsibility for the design and construction of the new lighthouse station. But he was however very close to retirement age when Little Ross lighthouse was designed and built, so he was already delegating considerable responsibility to his son, Alan. The detailed design of Little Ross lighthouse shows evidence of the hand of Alan, who had a unique ability to work in accordance with his father's rigid practical dictates and yet introduce quite playful aesthetic references derived from his enthusiastic study of the classics. Other assistants and apprentices in the Stevensons' Edinburgh office would also have been involved in the preparation of plans, sections, and elevations of all the proposed buildings and engineering works at Little Ross, together with drawings of architectural detailing that would have been adapted from the family's archives of tried and tested designs. Robert Stevenson's youngest son, Thomas, carried out most of the survey and investigative work on site and went on to supervise construction throughout the building process. The date of Robert's retirement in November 1842 coincided with the practical completion of Little Ross lighthouse, making it among the last projects in his long and illustrious career. Alan was Clerk of Works to the Commissioners for Northern Lights during the construction work at Little Ross, but was appointed Engineer in succession to his father.

Before any construction work could commence, agreement must have been reached with Lord Selkirk, whose extensive estate included the island and much of the land which surrounded Kirkcudbright Bay. During 1841, the Sheriff of Aberdeenshire, representing the Northern Lighthouse Board, visited Little Ross Island accompanied by Robert Stevenson. A settlement was reached with Lord Selkirk thereafter regarding two separate tacks (lease or rental agreements). The first tack was for one acre (Scots) of land to be rented for 999 years at a rate of £5 per acre, commencing at Whitsunday (15 May) for the preceding year. The second tack was for the remainder of the island, to be rented for 14 years from Whitsunday 1841 at a rent of £45. The beginning of the rental period was then recorded as being Martinmas (11 November).

One of the earliest references to work being carried out at Little Ross is in the form of an initial progress report by the engineer (Robert Stevenson) in which he refers to the need for

Alan Stevenson, sketch portrait, courtesy of the Northern Lighthouse Board

Cross-section through Little Ross lighthouse tower and houses, courtesy of the Northern Lighthouse Board

a beacon to be removed at a cost of £25–£30. The lighthouse tower would eventually supersede James Skelly's original south beacon, which is presumed to have been sited very close to where the lighthouse tower now stands.

On 22 March 1841, at a committee meeting of the Northern Lighthouse Board, Robert Stevenson reported that he had circulated the plans and specifications of the proposed buildings at Little Ross Island among different 'builders of respectability' and had received the following tenders for the construction works proposed:

R. Hume Gatehouse	£3977/1/1
Smith and Watson Leith	£4145/4/5
Thomson Neilson Carlisle	£4920
Alexander Rae Edinburgh	£3712
Thomson McEachie Dumfries	£4767/8
R. Geddes Whitehaven	£4605/4
Brebner and Neilson Perth	£4613/11/7

Robert Hume of Girthon, Gatehouse of Fleet, was the successful tenderer for the works at Little Ross Island, despite the fact that when taken at face value, his offer was not the lowest. It frequently happens that tenders for construction works, once checked, are found to have either arithmetical errors or items that have not been properly covered, and correction of these matters can alter the final tender figure. It is also possible that the Northern Lighthouse Board may have considered the programme for the construction works proposed by a lower tenderer to be less favourable than that offered by Robert Hume. No records have been found that give any evidence of the criteria that were used to make a final decision.

One might reasonably imagine that work such as the construction of lighthouses is so specialised and demanding that tenders for it would only have been considered from firms known to have experience in such matters and to be of proven ability to attain the exacting standards required by the Stevenson family. Robert Hume, based in the very small town of Gatehouse of Fleet, had a good reputation and had successfully carried out work for the prominent owners of several large estates and houses in the vicinity. These gentlemen may well have provided references both to the Stevensons and to individual members of the Northern Lighthouse Board which influenced them in their choice. The presence of a local contractor on the tender list would be very welcome to the Board, as it could provide an opportunity for them to receive a tender that showed substantial savings in travelling costs, and probable benefits in procurement of both local tradesmen and materials for the project. It does however seem that a risk was being taken in awarding an important contract to a young man, aged only a little over 30, who had no previous experience of lighthouse work. Someone must have either spoken very convincingly of his talents and abilities, or drawn attention to particularly impressive examples of his previous work. The new portico at the building now known as the Cally Palace Hotel, then a private house owned by Alexander Murray, was a prestigious project on which Robert Hume was employed as a stonemason in the 1830s.

Robert Hume in the course of a long career has been variously described as a stonemason, building contractor, architect/builder, monumental sculptor, brick maker, lessee of the local gas-works, elder of the church, and inspector of the poor. His technical skill, ambition, versatility, and dynamism would all be severely tested at Little Ross.

On being awarded the contract, Robert Hume would have had to consider the requirements of each essential trade, decide how many men would be needed in each trade, and determine the order in which they would need to be deployed. Some trades might have had to be sub-contracted, and he would have needed to reach agreement with the principals of the relevant firms. Unlike the situation on most other construction contracts, he would also have had to agree, in conjunction with the Stevenson family and the Northern Lighthouse Board, where these men were to be accommodated, how they and the necessary building materials were to be brought to the island, and how food and water were to be made available to the workforce for the duration of the works. Prolonged winter gales could easily have precluded landings on Little Ross Island for several days at a time, so large stocks of basic foodstuffs and fuel would need to have been stored on the island and made secure from predators.

Despite the cordial relationship that seemed to be developing between the Stevensons and Mr. Alexander Murray MP, there was still a residue of ill-feeling between them and the late Mr. Fergusson, who had been so critical of their prolonged opposition to the cause he had supported so vigorously. The following letter from Thomas Stevenson to his father refers to a planned foundation stone-laying ceremony:

Kirkcudbright 16th April 1841

You will observe from the papers that our lighthouse is to be made a mere political tool of. I shall certainly do nothing to xxxxxxx the abominable Masonic display which is intended. It is really despicable to think of the thing being made a 'bauble of' in order to suit political parties.

The lighthouse buildings are all laid off and the sod taken off. Tomorrow I intend should the weather be anything favourable to lay off the line of the road. The contractor seemed to understand the laying out of the works perfectly....

....There is a quarry on the Eastern side of the island from which we have got some good blocks. I expect to be home on Saturday.

Business Records of Robert Stevenson and sons, civil engineers, National Library of Scotland

The following press report, which might have been the one that generated Thomas Stevenson's wrath, originated in the *Liverpool Albion,* and was later published in the *Westmoreland Gazette* on 24 April 1841. Whilst it seems to be an accurate account of the situation, the Northern Lighthouse Board and the Stevensons, may have been understandably irritated at being excluded from the 'friends of humanity'.

LIGHTHOUSE ON LITTLE ROSS

The shipowners connected with the Cumberland coast, and also those in and near Kirkcudbright have long been anxious to have a lighthouse erected on the Little Ross, a small island about six miles southwest of the town of Kirkcudbright; but their applications to the Commissioners of the Northern Lights proved unavailing. The applicants have at length been successful, and great praise is due to Alexander Murray, Esq., M.P. for The Stewartry, and also to the different members connected with the county and towns in Cumberland, for their unwearied exertions in bringing about what is so much desired by the friends of humanity. A short time ago the whole of the buildings were contracted for, and reports state that the foundation stone is to be laid on the 1st of May next, when it is confidently expected a large assemblance of personages will witness the interesting proceedings. Mr. Robert Hume, mason, of Gatehouse, is the contractor; the whole of the buildings are to be finished by the middle of July 1842; and in the immediate time there will be regular work for a number of masons, quarrymen, joiners etc. The 1st of May is looked forward to with lively interest, and the completion of the work will diffuse general satisfaction.

Courtesy of the British Library, 96 Euston Rd., London NW1 2DB.

No records have been found which provide any details of the foundation stone-laying ceremony planned for 1 May, and no press reports have been found either of the form the ceremony took, or by whom it was attended. The Masonic minute book which covers the year of 1841 is sadly not among those in the care of the Stewartry Museum in Kirkcudbright, and no evidence of its existence has been found elsewhere.

Robert Stevenson had appointed his youngest son, Thomas, to be the engineer in charge of all operations on site at Little Ross. Thomas, although only 23, had experience of assisting his elder brother Alan in a similar role at the rock station of Skerryvore. The following letter from Thomas to his father gives an early indication that he was already well able to assert himself:

> Inverary, 10th July 1841
>
> I am so far on my way home from Skerryvore. You have certainly kept me much in the dark about Little Ross. I trust that I am in good time.
>
> *Business Records of Robert Stevenson and sons, civil engineers,* National Library of Scotland.

On his eventual arrival at Little Ross, Thomas Stevenson took charge of the supervision of all construction work on the island and assumed responsibility for administration of the contract with Robert Hume. He lived initially in lodgings at Ross Bay (then known as Balmangan), and he must have travelled daily between the mainland and the island by small boat. The role of the client's sole representative on site, especially a site as remote as Little Ross, was bound to be difficult. To earn his rate of pay of ten shillings and sixpence a day, young Thomas would be expected to have the answer to every question raised by Robert Hume, and the instant solution to every unforeseen problem that arose on site. To fail to promptly provide the contractor with the information he needed to advance the works without delay would result in both loss of face and extra expense. To provide wrong answers would add to any delay, incur the wrath of his father, and could easily jeopardise the all-important relationship between himself and Robert Hume. In the absence of telephones, he would have had to think on his feet and exercise considerable tact and diplomacy, in addition to great technical skill. On his arrival at Little Ross, Thomas had been understandably disconcerted to find that construction was already progressing rapidly, and wrote somewhat testily to his father, expressing some of his concerns:

> Kirkcudbright 19th July 1841
>
> I have just now read your letter from Stirling and have but two or three minutes to write to you. In a future letter I hope entirely to reverse, by reference to my journal, the charge of not writing.
>
> The buildings are at level of basement. How you did not give me some notion of this I confess I know not. The rubble backing I object to and today I am to select suitable stones and go over the storehouse and the barns.
>
> I am at present oppressed with heaps of furniture which the xxxx has got and which with the exception of what I use myself must lie for a year good in the town of Kirkcudbright.
>
> Whenever I am a little at leisure from the works, I shall write out the bills as indicated.

> The bible and flag I send to the town as it would be quite out of the question to oppose the minister of Borgue. It would in my estimation be making a job of the thing.

Business Records of Robert Stevenson and sons, civil engineers, National Library of Scotland.

The last sentence of the foregoing letter is difficult to interpret, but it may refer to items related to the previously mentioned possible foundation stone-laying ceremony. No records of any such ceremony have been located, but if such a ceremony did take place, the minister of the Parish of Borgue could have been in attendance, as the island is in that Parish. The minister of the Parish of Kirkcudbright however would also be likely to have been involved because of the importance of the lighthouse to the status of the port. Some tact and diplomacy may have had to be exercised.

One month later, in a progress report to his father, Thomas gave a detailed account of the ways in which he had dealt with a technical problem, an uncooperative foreman, and a request from the local Member of Parliament. He also vented his frustration regarding the quality of stationery with which he had been supplied and gave a fascinating but all too brief account of his own domestic arrangements. Despite his youth and relative lack of experience, he seems to have dealt with all these complicated and diverse matters with some skill and confidence:

Little Ross, 19th August 1841

> I have had a good deal of trouble I should rather say a vast of trouble with the drain which runs under the tower but having written home about that before, I need not say more of it excepting this that in no future lighthouse should that drain be carried under the tower. While it lasted I was in the foundation pit from seven till seven and dined at half past eight — breakfasting at six. I assisted at the laying of most of the stones and saw every backing the size of a five-shilling piece laid. There is not a stronger piece of rubble in the three kingdoms.
>
> I was obliged to take it entirely into my own hands, the foreman not being willing to do as I wished him. Hume was in Liverpool at the time.
>
> Mr. Alexander Murray M.P. requests me to consider the best way of forming a refuge harbour at the Ross.
>
> The stationery sent contains no blotting paper that most essential of all things. The paper indeed is wrapped up in a single sheet which is all broken and cut to pieces.
>
> The pewter ink-bottle sent exerted a chemical action on the ink by which ink is at one night's time converted into a species of snuff house water. I have had to coat the bottle or cup with sealing wax.
>
> The back wall of the dwelling houses from ashpit to ashpit has been brought up to the level of the window-sills which are laid. The centre wall has got all the jambs set and is progressing.
>
> I have got a housekeeper of 24 years age [Thomas was still only 23 years of age at this time]. She is younger than I wanted but bears a respectable character.
>
> My house is about ready – I expect to be in it tonight or tomorrow. I mean to charge my lodging at Balmangan. It converts to two pounds and five

shillings for five weeks.

We caught a rat last night which the night before kept me awake till two in the morning, I have got a young bitch which however is terrified out of its wits for them.

Business Records of Robert Stevenson and sons, civil engineers, National Library of Scotland.

One of the post-automation tenants of the houses at Little Ross, Douglas Molyneux, who has lived on Little Ross Island for longer than anyone else in its known history, has extensive knowledge of many aspects of the maintenance of the island's buildings and comments on the foregoing letter from Thomas as follows:

I wholly sympathise with Thomas Stevenson on his opinion of the drain which passes below the lighthouse tower base! While excavating for our own drains we encountered the two stone culverts which carried both the overflow from the rainwater collection tanks beneath the perimeter pavement in the courtyard and the effluent from the two ash pits located at the north and south ends of the cottages. These culverts also collected rainwater from two grids located centrally in the cobbled courtyards. The culverts were beautifully constructed in dressed stone and laid to a shallow fall under the courtyard but then were combined and plunged down several feet so as to pass below the tower base and subsequently reappear on the eastern slope of the island to discharge into a form of tank. The single drain so formed could be seen under the central column in the lighthouse tower, as I discovered when doing some repair work on the column for the Northern Lighthouse Board.

I had to lay drain pipes for our own sewers through the original culverts while maintaining their passageway, ensuring our own pipes would not crack in any settlement and still have adequate gradient to function.

A considerable gap in surviving correspondence means that little is known about further details of the progress of construction work, and many aspects are difficult to explain without undue resort to conjecture. In the spring of 1842, Thomas wrote to his father providing feedback on the abilities and performance of a Mr. Smith. As Thomas also refers to his own return to Little Ross, it is possible that Mr. Smith was carrying out supervision work in Thomas's absence, either on holiday or whilst engaged in other duties:

Little Ross lighthouse works, 10th May 1842.

Mr. Smith has requested me to write to you regarding the state in which the works are.

I have in accordance with his request to state that on my return I found the works in a satisfactory state and have good reason to believe that Mr. Smith is thoroughly acquainted with masonry and joiner work in all their details.

If Mr. Syme comes he should bring a sextant. Be so good as tell Mr. Murdoch that the sooner we have the copper foots for the water pipes of the parapet wall the better.

Business Records of Robert Stevenson and sons, civil engineers, National Library of Scotland.

The Mr. Syme referred to above was perhaps Mr. J. T. Syme, civil engineer, referred to by Thomas Stevenson in Chapter 1. Construction of the various ancillary buildings on little Ross Island, such as the stores, cart-houses, barns, byres, smithy and pigsties was in accordance with traditional building techniques used all over Scotland. Reference to traditional techniques does not imply that the standards required in these buildings would be in any way inferior to those required in the lighthouse tower and dwelling houses, but is made simply to explain that Robert Hume and his men would have found this work familiar and well within the scope of their experience.

The construction of the lighthouse tower and houses was rather more sophisticated and probably much more challenging. Although the tower and houses appear to be built entirely of stone, the external walls actually consist of both natural stone and brickwork, and the internal walls and partitions are mainly of brickwork. This is a little surprising when one considers the amount of whinstone that was available at Little Ross. However, the incorporation of a cavity wall was essential to achieve the standard of weatherproofing required by the Stevensons, but its inner leaf could be built much more economically as a thin skin of brick of manufactured thickness than as the essentially more substantial wall that would result from the use of random rubble. The quarrying and dressing of the whinstone was probably one of the most time-consuming and expensive operations on site. The exact source of the bricks used in construction on the island is difficult to determine with certainty; then again, the bricks must have been shipped to the island, probably from either Kirkcudbright or from Port Macadam in Gatehouse of Fleet. A brickworks was in existence in Kirkcudbright in 1850 and possibly earlier, so could have been an easy source, but Robert Hume produced his own bricks in Gatehouse of Fleet in the 1850s, and if his brickworks was functioning before that date, he could have gained a considerable financial advantage in manufacturing and supplying his own products. Robert Hume's brickworks was adjacent to his home in Gatehouse of Fleet, and only a few hundred yards from Port Macadam. A sample brick, recovered after minor alteration work at Little Ross lighthouse cottages, appears to exactly match the bricks made in Gatehouse of Fleet that were used in construction of the terraced houses in Birtwhistle Street in that town. These bricks are quite distinctive, being of smaller dimensions than other locally manufactured items.

The walls of the keepers' cottages have an outer leaf of whinstone, dressed, squared, and built in level courses. The inner leaves of the walls are of brickwork and the stone and brick leaves are separated by a cavity, permitting any water which penetrates through the outer leaf to drain to the bottom, where a lead tray collects it and channels it safely to the outside. Although this system of construction was in use in Europe in the 19th century, its use was not widespread in Britain until the 1920s, so the Stevenson family's engineers were at least 80 years ahead of most Scottish mainstream designers and builders of their day.

The walls of the lighthouse tower are also built of two leaves. The outer leaf is of whinstone, the external face of which is battered from the vertical by an inch and a half in four feet. At its base, the external wall is five feet wide and tapers to a width of two feet and nine inches below the level of the gallery. The inner leaf of the wall is vertical, consisting of a thin skin of brickwork, separated from the inner stone face by a cavity, as in the cottages. The building of a round and tapering tower to the standards of accuracy and workmanship required by the Stevensons would be no easy task today, but a much more difficult one in the early 1840s, armed only with the most basic of surveying instruments and protected by a minimum of safety equipment. A hollow core of brickwork rises through the centre of the tower, supporting the spiral staircase and providing a duct in which the weight that powered the clockwork mechanism could rise and fall. The bricks which form this core are curved to a suitable radius and were presumably made specially by Robert Hume.

View down the central brick core, courtesy of Graeme Macdonald and the Northern Lighthouse Board

The central brick core which supports the staircase and houses the weight for the clockwork mechanism, courtesy of Graeme Macdonald and the Northern Lighthouse Board

In June 1842, busy as he must have been, Thomas Stevenson still found time to undertake some minor consultancy work at the request of Mr. McLellan, the clerk of the Prison Board for Kirkcudbright. Alterations were about to be made to the town's jail, adjacent to what was until 2015 the Sheriff Court House in High Street, and Thomas was asked to comment on the competence of local tradesmen to carry out the proposed work and on the practicality of some of the proposed alterations. In his lengthy report, sent from 'Little Ross Lighthouse Works', Thomas diplomatically stated that 'judging from my own experience in this district I cannot question the competency of some at least of the Master Tradesmen to execute the work'. The greater part of his report is concerned with making impressive and meticulously detailed directions as to how the work should be undertaken. The complete report, probably written in very spartan accommodation on Little Ross Island, is a fine illustration of the depth of knowledge possessed by even this very young member of the Stevenson family team. Thomas sent the following covering letter with his report:

Little Ross Works 17th June 1842

To W. H. McLellan Esq., Kirkcudbright

Dear Sir,

You will herewith receive the Plans and Documents relating to the proposed alterations on the gaol together with my report or rather specification. I intended having sent it sooner but owing to my father's late visit my time has been much occupied.

I remain, Dear Sir, Yours very truly, Thomas Stevenson

P.S. I cannot procure thread for stitching up the specification in this out-of-the-way quarter and judge it best not to lose time in getting it from the town but to send it as it is. T.S.

From a copy of the original letter in the collection of the Stewartry Museum.

By early autumn 1842, Thomas Stevenson was finding his task of supervising the rapidly advancing construction at Little Ross both demanding and frustrating. His worries spilled over in a letter to his brother, David, in which he admitted to a near calamity, at least partly caused by a lapse in supervision. Perhaps he may not have been quite so candid had he chosen to write to his father on the subject. He also sought indirect help from Alan Stevenson on one particular issue, and was highly critical of their father's repeated failure to answer his urgent requests for information:

Little Ross, 26th September 1842

We have this morning succeeded in getting our dome fairly in its place for which I am very thankful as it was rather a critical business. Lewis rather shyed taking a lift so that the whole devolved upon myself. The fact is that after we had the shears [shearlegs] up I went into the house to write a letter and Brodie let down the shears to the angle but letting them come too far the guys became inoperative and hearing a cry I came out and saw the shears quickly descending and everybody getting out of the way. Smack they went and had it not been for the railing catching them they would have come down and spread destruction in the court below. After this terribly awkward business he rather sang dumb. I think I have written five or six letters to my father and had a long letter from Elgin the other day without an answer to any of my queries — such as about the boatman's allowance and whether the men get anything on the dome going on. Now the dome is on and the men dissatisfied and I have no authority can give nothing — again I wish to know what Alan pays at stations where he lives as I know not what to pay Ritson. I really must insist upon my correspondence being answered in a business-like way as it places me in a stupid–awkward like box.

I have had no answer to my letter about the corner stones for the new beacon which I should really like to commence.
Business Records of Robert Stevenson and sons, civil engineers, National Library of Scotland

Despite everything, good progress was being made with the building work, and attention was being turned to dealing with the usual mass of minor matters that frustrate the achievement of completion of most construction projects. The reference in the last sentence of the foregoing letter is the sole scrap of evidence that points to the conclusion that Captain Skelly's original north beacon was to be replaced. A surviving notebook kept by Thomas Stevenson records that the corner stones that were ultimately used in the new beacon were of 'Barlocco' stone, dressed on all exposed faces, and flush with the face of the walls (Barlocco stone is presumed to have been quarried from the shore of Barlocco Island, at the Isles of Fleet). It is possible that Thomas had sought authority for a more decorative solution which might have been considered an unnecessary expense.

As the work neared completion, Thomas Stevenson was probably exhausted and perhaps a little bored with his isolation from friends, relatives, and a social life in Edinburgh. He was aware that official procedures had to be followed punctiliously in order that the new lighthouse could be brought into service on schedule, and he became anxious from past experience that any delays in dealing with correspondence might force him to extend his stay on the island:

Little Ross, 13th October 1842:

I am anxious that the light should be advertised forthwith as it will be the 1st December before it can be lighted as it must I understand be six weeks previously advertised. I beg that no time will be lost in advertising therefore as I have no wish to be tied down here after the 1st December, It will of course be necessary that I see the advertisement before it is put in the newspapers.

I have been very busy of late with one thing and another. I dined and spent the day last Sunday with Mr. Murray at Cally and thereafter went with him in his carriage to Kirkcudbright calling for Mr. Maitland of Dundrennan about a new quay at Tongueland. I have attended two of the County meetings and explained my plan which is in a different place from what was intended. It [will] go on next summer. Length 100 feet.

Business Records of Robert Stevenson and sons, civil engineers, National Library of Scotland.

Thomas Stevenson's work at Little Ross Island was nearly done, and in between tidying up the few loose ends, he had found time to undertake some more minor consultancy work, this time for Mr. Murray and Mr. Maitland, two influential local gentlemen whose presence in his circle of friends and business acquaintances would do his career and reputation no harm. Thomas however had ambitions beyond the construction of a minor quay at the tiny port of Tongueland (now known as Tongland but still pronounced in accordance with the original spelling), and was now doubtless relishing the prospect of escaping from the confines of life on Little Ross and returning to Edinburgh. Mr. Thomas Ritson, the first principal keeper at Little Ross, commenced his duties in June 1842, and was doubtless engaged in advance of the lighthouse's completion date to enable him to have a full understanding of all its workings before it went into commission. There was also a Mr. James Ritson, a trusted and long-serving employee in the Stevensons' Edinburgh office who may have had a role in the latter stages of completing the new lighthouse. Thomas's last letter sent from Little Ross to his father was dated 28 October 1842:

> Little Ross, Friday 28th October 1842
>
> As I have completed the work and had the house several times lighted, I do not intend spending the following months of November and December here to see some dry dykes built and the like. These can be done at the sight of Mr. Ritson. I purpose preparing for my departure after Mr. Murdoch and Mr. Kennedy come.
>
> *Business Records of Robert Stevenson and sons, civil engineers,* National Library of Scotland.

The *Accounts and Papers of the Commissioners of Northern Lights,* dated 28 January 1843, included the following undated progress report:

> The works of the Little Ross Lighthouse, in the Stewartry of Kirkcudbright were commenced, and the lighthouse tower and storehouse were brought to the level of the surface of the ground, while the walls of the light keepers' houses were carried nearly to their full height. The preparation of the dioptric apparatus for this station was also commenced at the works of Messrs Isaac Cookson and Company of Newcastle-on-Tyne.

By the time the above progress report was published with the accounts, the building work at Little Ross had been completed and the lighthouse was in use. Frances Groome's *Ordnance Gazetteer of Scotland* for 1882 records that the cost of the lighthouse station at Little Ross was £8,478, which represents a considerable increase over the tender figure, and an even greater increase over the figure of £1,200 rather rashly first estimated by Robert Cutlar Fergusson in 1836. No details are now available of either the breakdown of the tender figure, or of the reported final cost, so it is not known how many of the island's buildings, slipways, jetties, wells, walls, and quays are included in any of these figures.

The completed buildings at Little Ross are a great credit, not only to their distinguished designers, but also to their little-known builder and his men. Despite being exposed to severe winds, salt spray, frost, and snow for over 173 years, none of the masonry is cracked or eroded, and the arrises are as sharp as they were on the day they were cut. Although alterations have been made to modernise the interiors of the houses over the years, only minor changes have been made to the exterior. As a result, much of the design and construction work remains as envisaged by the Stevensons and as implemented by Robert Hume.

The plaque over the entrance to the tower, courtesy of Graeme Macdonald and the Northern Lighthouse Board

In 1844, work began in the village of Twynholm on the construction of a new school. Twynholm is only five miles from Gatehouse of Fleet, and the design of its new school is attributed to a Robert Hume in the current online *Dictionary of Scottish Architects*. At that time, it was not unusual for experienced and successful builders to be generally regarded as architects, so it seems highly likely that lighthouse builder Robert Hume, despite a lack of any formal training in design, progressed to designing and building Twynholm School.

The Northern Lighthouse Board members must certainly have been impressed by the performance of Robert Hume, as his firm was added to the list of potential contractors for one of their subsequent projects, Ardnamurchan Lighthouse. There could be no doubt as to his capabilities as a builder, but the submission of a tender for work so far from his home base and so remote from sources of men and materials must have presented Robert Hume with an extremely demanding task. He would know that he was going to be in competition with larger and more experienced firms and that his tender would need to be very keenly priced if it was going to have any chance of success. He did however have one great advantage over his competitors, in that the design of the two houses at the base of the tower at Ardnamurchan was virtually identical to those he had already completed at Little Ross. His records of the time and resources necessary to complete the works at Little Ross must have stood him in good stead, as he was successful in securing the contract for the new lighthouse station at Ardnamurchan and work commenced there during 1846. By late 1848 however, Robert Hume was experiencing serious financial difficulties.

An unprecedented general increase in wages of about 25–30% took place immediately after Robert Hume's tender was accepted, raising his costs by an unforeseen £900. In a tragic accident, a falling block of stone killed one of his workmen, a valuable horse died having 'fallen from a precipice', and during 1847 an outbreak of scurvy among his workforce left them debilitated for a period of four months. Unfortunately, it could be difficult to provide proper nourishment for a large workforce based in an area in which fresh food was not easily available. Robert Hume made an impassioned plea to the Northern Lighthouse Board, seeking some recognition that the difficulties he was labouring under were not of his own making and requesting additional payment. Despite Alan Stevenson's general acceptance of the facts presented by Robert Hume, the Board members were not immediately inclined to take any such action and instead wrote to the various prominent persons in Gatehouse of Fleet who had provided sureties on behalf of Robert Hume, requesting that they consider putting up some of the money that was necessary to enable him to finish his contract.

These backers were William Neilson, Thomas Campbell, David Credie, John Brown, and Robert Hannay. William Neilson was a Kirkcudbrightshire man who had been a successful businessman in Canada. On his return to Scotland, he came to live in Gatehouse of Fleet, and invested in several properties there. Thomas Campbell was a grocer in the town. David Credie was a nurseryman at Cally Estate and held the position of Provost of Gatehouse of Fleet. John Brown was a Justice of the Peace, and Robert Hannay of Rusko was a local landowner.

Robert Hume's backers acted honourably and promptly provided a further £100 to enable him to advance the works. They also asked the Commissioners to make early payment to Mr. Hume for works he had carried out which were additional to the original contract, and suggested a schedule of staged payments for the further works necessary to complete the contract. This sensible proposal was eventually agreed to, enabling the work to be completed to the satisfaction of all parties. Ardnamurchan lighthouse was completed in 1849 and was automated in 1988. The lighthouse cottages and outbuildings are now operated as Ardnamurchan Visitors Centre, allowing the general public to visit and learn about the lighthouse station, its construction, and the lives of the men who lived and worked there.

On completion of Ardnamurchan Lighthouse however, Robert Hume was on the brink of ruin, heavily in debt, and with a wife, sister, and eight children to support. Despite everything, he and his firm survived, recovered, and even prospered in a long and successful career in Kirkcudbrightshire. Perhaps his appointment late in life as an inspector of the poor indicates that his own experience of extreme financial hardship had given him the motive to help others to recover from similar difficulties. Very few building contractors in rural areas can have such magnificent monuments to their enterprise and ability, as Robert Hume has at the lighthouses of Little Ross and Ardnamurchan.

CHAPTER 5

Shipwrecks near to Little Ross Island

Many shipwrecks that occurred near Little Ross Island between 1790 and 1822 have already been recorded in Chapter 3. Despite the lengthy and ultimately successful campaigns to erect firstly beacon towers and secondly a lighthouse on Little Ross Island, shipwrecks continued to occur regularly in the vicinity for several decades after the lighthouse was built for many reasons. First, there was the geography of the south-west coast of Scotland. In southerly winds, the section of coast between the upper reaches of the Solway Firth and the southern tip of the Mull of Galloway is exposed to seas building up over the full length of the Irish Sea, but offers no safe deep-water harbours.

There was also a general lack of dependable and universally understood navigational aids at that time, such as lighthouses, buoys, and other markers. The purpose of most lighthouses is not so much to warn of hazards, but to assist mariners in determining the exact positions of their vessels by day or night. If the master of a vessel is unsure of his position, his vessel and his crew are in danger and at night, or in conditions of poor visibility, that danger is greatly heightened.

Many mishaps occurred at sea prior to the early 20th century because of the relative inefficiency of the sailing vessels of the day at sailing against the wind. Most mariners, particularly in the days of sail, were all too well aware of the dangers of their positions with regard to rocks, shoals, and lee shores, yet were on occasions unable to take any evasive action due to the strength and direction of wind and tide. This was particularly relevant at ports such as Kirkcudbright, which have extreme tidal ranges and rapidly flowing tidal streams.

Moreover, a considerable number of vessels in the large fleet of merchant sailing ships of that time were coming to the end of their working lives, and their owners had neither the money nor the confidence in their future to repair, maintain, and equip them properly. The age of steam and many other new technologies had dawned and was increasing public demands for higher standards of efficiency and safety. Sadly, despite the efforts of Samuel Plimsoll and others to improve standards, many ships that were plying their trade in coastal waters during the second half of the 19th century and first few years of the 20th century were variously elderly, rotten, ill-equipped, overloaded, and undermanned. A significant number of them suffered from a combination of several, or even all of these conditions.

Communications at that time were restricted to signals visible in daylight, such as storm cones, flags, beacons, and semaphore, so from the time a vessel left its home port until it passed a lighthouse, or until it arrived off the port to which it was bound, its master had no information whatsoever about weather forecasts other than that which was derived from his own experience, local knowledge, and intuition.

The following list provides brief details of some selected conspicuous incidents that occurred either on the shores of Little Ross Island, or within sight of the island, between 1822 and 1956:

> **1822** –The smack *Ross*, of Whitehaven, was anchored at Ross Roads in Kirkcudbright Bay on 18 June with a cargo of bottles when a fire broke out in the galley and got out of control, forcing her crew to abandon ship. They were picked up by local Customs and Excise men and brought safely ashore, leaving their vessel to burn to the waterline and sink.

> **1826** – The *Castle of Harrington* was returning from Belfast to Whitehaven when she was wrecked on Little Ross Island in November. Captain John Bough and his crew lowered themselves from the bowsprit to the rocks and came ashore safely. The mate returned to the ship to attempt to save a woman passenger, but both were lost.

> **1828** – The sloop *Nelly and Margaret,* from Harrington, Cumberland, sailed from Kirkcudbright on 19 March under the command of Captain Martin. She struck rocks between St Mary's Isle Point and Torrs Point and was wrecked.

> **1830** – The 161 ton brig *Mary* was on passage from Donaghadee to Harrington under the command of Captain Ditchbridge when she put in to Kirkcudbright Bay on 20 November, seeking shelter from a south/south-westerly gale. Her master attempted to anchor to the north of Little Ross Island, but his vessel drifted onto the rocks on the north side of Ross Bay. Two crew members and three passengers came ashore safely but nine people and 86 head of cattle were drowned.

> **1840** – The schooner *Mary and Francis*, of Maryport, was anchored in Kirkcudbright Bay on 20 November while on passage from Dublin to Dumfries with a cargo of seed potatoes. Her anchor cable broke during a gale, causing her to come ashore near Little Ross Island and to break up. All the crew came ashore safely.

> **1846** – The *Rosalinda*, of Belfast, sank near Little Ross Island at the mouth of the River Dee on 27 November.

1849 – The sloop *Lancaster Rose*, of Fleetwood, was on passage from Liverpool to Leith with a cargo of rosewood and general goods when she had to seek shelter in Kirkcudbright Bay on 18 January. She struck the Frenchman rocks on the west side of the bay and was holed below the waterline, causing the crew to abandon her and take to the ship's boat. They all came ashore safely and the wreckage of their vessel drifted to the Nunmill shore.

1850 – The schooner *Novelty*, of Larne, was driven upon the north-west shore of Little Ross Island on 19 January.

1855 – The brig *Phillipa*, under the command of Captain McTier of Belfast, was on passage from Workington with a cargo of coals. She grounded on Milton Sands on 18 December and was broken to pieces. One crewman was drowned.

1858 – The sloop *Raeberry Castle* dragged her anchor at the Manxman's Lake on 14 December and drifted onto St Mary's Isle Point where she broke up.

1861 – The *Parrsboro* was bound from Maryport to Belfast under the command of Captain McCully when she struck the bottom in the Manxman's Lake on 25 November and was driven ashore. She was driven further on shore on 12 December and then filled with the tide.

1865 – The schooner *Maggie Lauder*, owned by Mr. Duff of Whithorn, was lost in Ross Bay during severe weather on 21 November.

1866 – The Wigtown sloop *Jennie*, commanded by Captain Tweed, was carrying coals from Workington when she was holed rocks at Ross Bay on 8 January and was subsequently filled by the flooding tide. Her crew was saved.

1866 – The schooner *Mary*, under the command of Captain Kerrosh from Douglas, Isle of Man, was bound for Workington in ballast. She came ashore at Senwick on 7 March having burst her chains and was feared to be wrecked. Her crew was saved.

1867 – The schooner *Shirleywitch*, under the command of Captain Beaty, was bound from Carrickfergus to Maryport in ballast. She was driven ashore on rocks and stranded near Kirkcudbright on 5 April. The crew was saved but the vessel was filled by the flooding tide.

1868 – The *Elizabeth* was on passage from Whitehaven to Ireland with a cargo of coals and had reached the Mull of Galloway when a westerly gale forced her to turn back. She ran for shelter in Kirkcudbright Bay, but on 20 February her anchors failed to hold and she ran aground, losing 16-year-old crewman John Collins in the process. Next morning, the remainder of the crew came ashore safely, leaving the *Elizabeth* with only the top of her mast showing above the water.

1868 – The smack *Nancy and Jenny* was on passage from Kirkcudbright to Belfast in ballast when she was struck by a squall and went on to the rocks at Little Ross Island on 1 June. Captain McIlroy and his crew survived.

1868 – The Belfast schooner *William Henry* was bound from Belfast to Maryport under the command of Captain Milliken, but she parted her chains in Kirkcudbright Bay and came ashore on rocks off St Mary's Isle on 1 December. Kirkcudbright lifeboat was called out and her crew succeeded in rescuing the crew of the stricken vessel.

1868 – The schooner *William*, belonging to the Isle of Man and under the command of Captain Radcliff, was on passage from Liverpool to Douglas but came on shore on the north side of Ross Bay in a gale on 10 December. James Finlay of Borgue put out in an open boat and rescued Captain Radcliff and the crew, for which he received a well-deserved award.

1870 – The schooner *Zenobie,* of and from Nantes and under the command of Captain Jestin, arrived in Kirkcudbright Bay on 29 January with a cargo of linseed cake and flour. She anchored in Ross Roads but broke the chain of one anchor and dragged another. She went on to the rocks in Ross Bay, yet her crew reached safety in their own boat. The *Zenobie* broke up a few days later.

1870 – The *Bloomer* was bound from Maryport to Abbey Burnfoot with a cargo of coal under the command of Captain Davies, when she came ashore at Meikle Ross on 23 October. Her keel was damaged and carpenters were sent for to attempt to repair her and enable her to be re-floated. Her cargo was later discharged and it was thought that she would become a wreck.

1871 – The schooner *Rising Sun*, while on passage from Liverpool to Dublin, was driven into the Manxman's Lake in Kirkcudbright Bay in a sinking condition during November. One of her crew, Mr. Timothy O'Dare, aged about 50, collapsed at the pumps and was taken ashore, where he later died.

1872 – The wherry *Briton,* bound from Fleetwood for White Abbey, Belfast, with a cargo of coals was run ashore on 19 October while leaking badly at Manxman's Lake and was expected to become a total loss.

1873 – The smack *Robert Irving*, of Douglas, was bound from Maryport to Douglas with a cargo of 50 tons of coal when she drifted into Kirkcudbright Bay in a sinking condition in the first week of March. She sank during the early morning, just outside the bar and Captain Kennan and his two crewmen came ashore safely but with great difficulty in high seas. The smack and her cargo were lost.

1879 – The smack *Sir Sidney* was on passage from Liverpool to Peel when she was caught in a southerly gale. She entered Kirkcudbright Bay on 29 September but was driven ashore in Ross Bay. Captain Maley and crewmen Owen and Jackson swam safely to the shore but their vessel and her cargo were lost.

1882 – The 65 ton brigantine *Camel* was on passage from Maryport to Bangor with a cargo of coal when she struck the bar on 7 November during a force 9 gale from the south/south-east. Captain G. Sloan and his crew of three men were saved.

1884 – The barque *Madras,* of Liverpool, arrived off Whitehaven on 22 January, laden with a cargo of pitch pine which she had carried from Pensacola in the United States of America. Unable to enter Whitehaven because of tidal conditions, she was driven towards the Scottish coast by a severe storm, forcing Captain Robert Whiteford to seek shelter in the lee of Little Ross Island. On entering Kirkcudbright Bay, she struck the bar and was soon dismasted and began to break up. Basil Mackenzie, a local fisherman, raised the alarm and all 14 crewmen were rescued and safely put ashore near St Mary's Isle.

1886 – A vessel named *Naiad* was reported to have been lost in Kirkcudbright Bay on 1 January. No further details are known.

1887 – The 45 ton schooner *Janet Hunter,* under the command of Captain A. Stitt and owned by J. Williamson of Kirkcudbright, was carrying a cargo of lime when she went on fire in Manxman's Lake on 14 September and was destroyed. Her captain and crew of three men were saved.

1888 – The *Effa Bella* was on passage from Annalong in Ireland to Whitehaven with a cargo of granite setts and was anchored in the lee of Little Ross Island on 24 August. After slipping her anchor cable, she went ashore on the island, resulting in a serious leak. Her fate is not recorded.

1891 – The 37 ton smack *Lady Bulkeley (or Buckley)* sprang a leak while on passage from Bangor to Silloth with a cargo of slates. On 4 October, Captain William Roberts, beached her on Little Ross Island. Captain Roberts and his crew came ashore safely and the cargo was later salvaged but the smack was a total loss.

1891 – The Belfast-based brigantine *Jane* was observed to be in distress near Little Ross Island on 13 October. Kirkcudbright lifeboat was called out and assisted in bringing her and her crew safely to the harbour.

1894 – In November, distress signals relayed from Little Ross lighthouse resulted in Kirkcudbright lifeboat being launched. On reaching Little Ross Island, the lifeboat crew found the smack *Aerial,* of Caernarvon, in ballast, lying to the north of the island, having lost her anchor. Some of the lifeboat crew were put aboard to assist the *Aerial's* crew, and she was escorted safely to Kirkcudbright harbour.

1895 – The smack *Jane McMillan* was bound for Portaferry with a cargo of coals when she struck rocks off the Meikle Ross during heavy snow in February. The crew came ashore safely but the vessel sank.

1895 – The barque *Nordstjernen,* of Christiansand, was bringing a cargo of beans from Morocco to J. A. Cavan of Kirkcudbright; on 6 November she dragged her anchor while her captain was waiting at the mouth of the bay for favourable tide and ran aground on the bar. The keepers at Little Ross raised the alarm by firing signal rockets and the crew was saved by Kirkcudbright lifeboat. The vessel broke up on the bar and her wreckage was sold to Captain Stitt of Kirkcudbright for £13.

1896 – The 50-year-old smack *Hematite*, of Dumfries, Master and owner J. Hekset of Allonby in Cumberland, was on passage from Maryport to Kirkandrews when she collided with the *Daisy* of Whitehaven then sank in Ross Bay on 3rd February.

1897 – The 155 ton Belfast schooner *Happy-go-Lucky* was destroyed by fire in Manxman's Lake on 13 March. She was under the command of Captain J. Starkey and her owner was R. McConky. She was formerly the *Garland*, built in 1847.

1899 – The 37 ton schooner *Jessie Rae*, of Belfast, was on passage from Maryport to Strangford when she developed a leak during severe weather and was forced to seek refuge in Kirkcudbright Bay. On 10 December she struck the bar, after which Captain H. McNamara and his crew of two men abandoned their sinking vessel and came ashore safely in the ship's boat.

1900 – In November, the schooner *Monreith* was on passage from County Down to Silloth with a cargo of granite kerbstones. Her skipper put in to Kirkcudbright Bay, probably to await favourable tidal conditions to proceed to Silloth, but struck the bar and was driven over Milton Sands where the vessel broke up. Her crew all came ashore safely and the wreck of the *Monreith* still lies in Dhoon Bay.

1902 – The brigantine *Prospect*, of Campbeltown, was on passage from Campbeltown to Whitehaven in ballast, and had taken shelter in Ross Roads from a south/south-westerly gale. On 15 October she dragged her anchors and eventually came ashore near the fish house on the west bank of the River Dee. The wreck of the vessel was sold at public auction a month later for £41.

1905 – The 52 ton ketch *Windward* was bound from Whitehaven to Gatehouse of Fleet with a cargo of coal; however, on 14 January Captain James McDowall was forced by adverse weather to anchor in Ross Roads. The vessel was overwhelmed by heavy seas while at anchor and sank. Her crew all reached safety in the ship's boat.

1905 – While on passage from Dalbeattie to Belfast with a cargo of crushed granite, the 41 ton steamship *Bonito* was wrecked on the east shore of Little Ross Island on 29 November. Three crewmen came ashore safely in their own ship's boat but the fourth crewman drowned.

1908 – In December, the 160 ton schooner *Kate*, of Barrow-in-Furness, while on passage from Annan to Liverpool, anchored in the lee of Little Ross Island, as Captain David Duke of Dalbeattie tried to find shelter from a blizzard. The keepers at Little Ross lighthouse, Robert Brown and John H. McLeod, became concerned for the safety of her crew when they observed waves breaking over the schooner's deck, and raised the alarm. Kirkcudbright lifeboat was launched on four occasions in the next few days to assist the vessel; the crew eventually left in the ship's own boat and came ashore safely.

1916 – The 38 ton topsail schooner *Charles*, of Gatehouse of Fleet, was stranded on the east side of Little Ross Island on 28 January while carrying coals from Whitehaven to Gatehouse of Fleet. The crew of two came ashore safely on the island and were looked after by the lighthouse keepers.

1918 – The 33 ton ketch *Day Star*, of Belfast, was loaded with coals and on passage from Whitehaven to Ballywater. On 6 October, she was anchored in Ross Roads in a strong south/south-westerly gale. Kirkcudbright lifeboat was called out by the lighthouse keepers on Little Ross Island when seas could be seen breaking over the vessel. The lighthouse keepers at that time were William Begg and George Mackie. Captain John Martin and crewmen Hugh Adair and James Beattie were taken off safely, but the vessel broke up and sank off Little Ross Island. Her mizzen mast was used as a flagpole on the Moat Brae in the centre of Kirkcudbright for many years.

1918 – The schooner *Resolution*, carrying a cargo of bricks, was found to be leaking and she eventually sank outside Little Ross Island on 18 November. The weather was good and Captain Harrison and his crew landed safely at Kirkcudbright, presumably in the ship's boat.

1920 – The 140 ton schooner *Venus*, of Port St Mary, Isle of Man, was bound from Whitehaven to Kinsale with a cargo of coals, but on 12 March she was reported to be in difficulty in Kirkcudbright Bay. Kirkcudbright lifeboat stood by her as she drifted in heavy seas and a very strong and squally wind from the west/northwest, between Little Ross Island and the east side of the bay. Eventually however, her master had no alternative but to request that he and his crew be taken off their stricken vessel.

The 'Venus' and the 'Marten', beached for maintenance at Kirkcudbright, circa 1900

1944 – The three-masted, 227 ton topsail schooner *Mary B. Mitchell* was on passage from Dublin to Silloth with a cargo of burnt ore when most of her sails were blown out by a gale. On 15 December, with only one engine functioning, she grounded on the bar at the mouth of Kirkcudbright Bay. The alarm was raised by the keepers at Little Ross lighthouse, and Captain Brennan and his crew of eight were safely taken off by Kirkcudbright lifeboat. The lighthouse keepers at that time were Robert M. Pearson and Charles J. F. Gifford. At first light next day, the vessel was found to have been driven across the bay onto the rocky shore at Senwick, where her remains can still be seen. Charles Gifford's eye witness account of the incident is given in Chapter 11, and gives rise to some speculation regarding the circumstances of the loss of this famous vessel. The *Mary B. Mitchell* was one of the very last few commercial sailing vessels to come to Kirkcudbright Bay.

1956 – The 813 G.R.T. coastal tanker *B.P. Marketer* was leaving Kirkcudbright harbour on 28 December but slowed down off St Mary's Isle Point in order to let the pilot, George Poland, be taken off the vessel before sea conditions worsened during a south-easterly gale. As a result, the *B.P. Marketer,* having lost way, was driven aground onto the west shore of the bay. Kirkcudbright lifeboat stood by until the tide receded, and the *B.P. Marketer* was successfully re-floated a few days later with the assistance of the tug *Solway.* There was no serious damage, no pollution, and no loss of life.

At the end of 1842, on the eve of Little Ross lighthouse coming into service, the most influential group of people in Kirkcudbright let it be known to the Northern Lighthouse Board that they had not yet finished their work in pursuit of improved measures to protect their port, its trade, its men, and its ships. Captain James Skelly would have been as proud of them as they had been of him:

Memorial to the Commissioners of Northern Lights, 17th December 1842.
To erect Beacons and place Buoys in the Firth

Unto the Honourable the Commissioners of Northern Light-houses

The Memorial of the Magistrates, Councillors, Shipowners,
Merchants and Traders of the Royal Burgh of Kirkcudbright,

Respectfully Sheweth,

That the Memorialists view with extreme gratification the establishment of a Light-house on the Island of Little Ross, at the mouth of the River Dee, in the neighbourhood of the Burgh, and are satisfied that it will be the means of saving many useful lives, and much valuable property.

That there is only wanting to complete the good work, the erection of suitable Beacons on certain points of the coast of the Solway Firth, and the placing of certain Buoys on certain dangerous sands and rocks in the locality.

That the Memorialists need not here dilate upon the excellency of the Roadstead of Little Ross and of the Harbour at Manxman's Lake, as places of refuge for vessels overtaken by storms, — this having been made known to your Honours in former memorials. Suffice it to say, that Beacons and Buoys in proper places would form most valuable adjuncts to the Light-house, and prove of great service to vessels navigating the Solway Firth.

May it therefore please your Honours, upon considering the facts before stated, to cause to be erected and placed Beacons and Buoys as above petitioned.

And your Memorialists, as in duty bound, will ever pray, etc.

From a copy of the original in the collection of the Stewartry Museum.

No evidence has been found of any response to the petitioners' request, and at Kirkcudbright, the ancient system of marking the channel by perches and withies remained in use for over 100 more years. During that long period, the ageing fleet of sailing vessels was gradually replaced by new steamships; at the same time, the expansion of the country's road and rail network brought about a major decline in the coastal shipping trade. The numbers of shipwrecks began to reduce accordingly.

Up until the Second World War, steamships were not infrequent visitors to Kirkcudbright, carrying cement, fertilisers, and other products for use in agriculture. After the war however, the harbour became almost completely disused until 1956, when coastal tankers began to deliver oil for distribution from a newly-built Scottish Oils and Shell-Mex depot. This important new use of the harbour generated a fresh and urgent need for greatly improved buoyage to define the tortuous channel that follows the course of the River Dee. The port of Kirkcudbright was at that time controlled by the Town Council of the Royal Burgh of Kirkcudbright, who shouldered an unforeseen responsibility and established an excellent new system of buoyage. In 1982, coastal tankers stopped berthing at Kirkcudbright and the Shell Mex depot was closed. By this time however, a thriving fishing industry had developed and growing numbers of visiting yachts and other pleasure craft were calling at Kirkcudbright, so the harbour continued to be heavily used and the new buoys continued to be maintained.

All modern coasting cargo vessels, fishing vessels, and most pleasure craft are now equipped with navigational equipment and communications so sophisticated that there is little excuse for any mariner not accurately knowing his position at sea. Whilst this almost entirely removes one of the main causes of shipwrecks, accidents can still happen due to the failure of mechanical and electrical equipment and human error. Fortunately, when accidents happen today, modern communications systems enable early contact to be made with other vessels in the vicinity and coastguards are usually able to summon lifeboats or helicopters as necessary. Tragically, there have been some losses of ships and men from Kirkcudbright's fishing fleet in recent years, but no losses that approach the scale of those that occurred in the early 19th century.

CHAPTER 6

The Lighthouse Station

Almost 20 years after the petition in support of a lighthouse on Little Ross Island was submitted to the Commissioners for Northern Lights in Edinburgh, the following Notice to Mariners was issued:

NOTICE TO MARINERS
LITTLE ROSS ISLAND LIGHTHOUSE

Edinburgh, 16th November, 1842.

The Commissioners of Northern Light Houses hereby give notice that a Light House has been erected upon the summit of the Little Ross Island, in the Stewartry of Kirkcudbright, the light of which will be exhibited on the night of the 1st day of January 1843, and every night thereafter from sun-set till sun-rise.

The following is a Specification of the Position of the Light House, and the Appearance of the Light, by Mr. Stevenson, Engineer:

The Little Ross Island lies off the entrance of Kirkcudbright Bay and Harbour, in lat. 54 deg. 46 minutes North, and long. 4 deg. 5 minutes West.

By compass the Light House bears from Burrow Head, in Wigtownshire, E., distant 12 miles; from the Point of Ayre Light House, in the Isle of Man, N.E. ¾ E., distant 23 miles; from St. Bee's Head Light House, in Cumberland, N.N.W. ¼ N., distant 23 miles; from Abbey Head, Kirkcudbrightshire, W.N.W., distant 3 ½ miles.

The Little Ross Light will be known to Mariners as a revolving light, producing a bright flash of light, of the natural appearance, once in every 5 seconds of time, or 12 flashes a minute.

The lantern, which is open from N. b. E. round to N.W. b. W. southerly, is elevated 175 feet above the level of the sea. In clear weather the flashes will be seen at the distance of 6 leagues, and at lesser distances according to the state of the atmosphere; and, in favourable circumstances, the light will not wholly disappear between the flashes at lesser distances.

And the Commissioners hereby further give notice, that by virtue of a warrant from the Queen in Council, of date the 2nd day of November instant, the following tolls will be levied, in respect of this light, from all vessels navigating the Solway Frith [sic] to and from ports or places to the Eastward of St Bee's Head and the Mull of Galloway, viz., for every vessel belonging to the United Kingdom of Great Britain and Ireland (the same not belonging to her Majesty or being navigated wholly in ballast), and for every Foreign vessel privileged as British the same not being navigated wholly in ballast, the toll of one halfpenny per ton of the burden of every such vessel, and for every Foreign vessel, not so privileged, the toll of one penny per ton.

By order of the Commissioners of the Northern Light Houses,

C. CUNINGHAM,
ALEX. CUNINGHAM,
Joint Secretaries

Local reactions to the new lighthouse, particularly from those from Whitehaven, the busy Cumberland port at the mouth of the Solway Firth, were swift and very positive:

NEW LIGHTHOUSE

The new lighthouse erected on the Little Ross Island, at the entrance to Kirkcudbright, was lighted for the very first time on Sunday night last, and proved a very conspicuous object from Whitehaven piers and the high ground on each side of that harbour. This beacon, the want of which has long been complained of, must prove of incalculable benefit to mariners navigating the dangerous waters of the Solway Frith [sic].

Carlisle Journal, Saturday 7th January 1843

Courtesy of The British Library, 96 Euston Rd., London NW1 2DB.

The following press report of an incident which occurred very shortly after Little Ross lighthouse went into service, and the gratitude expressed therein by the master of the vessel concerned, must have delighted all those who had worked so hard campaigning for and building the lighthouse:

THE LITTLE ROSS LIGHTHOUSE.

The commissioners of Northern Lighthouses have just completed a lighthouse on Little Ross Island, situated at the entrance of the anchorage of Kirkcudbright, the light of which was exhibited on the 1st of January. The master of a schooner, about 200 tons burthen, bound from Whitehaven to Belfast, which had sprung a leak at sea, has just got safely to the anchorage, and reports the water had reached the cabin, and that, unless he had got sight of the Little Ross light, which enabled him speedily to take shelter at Kirkcudbright, the vessel must have gone down, and all on board perished. The utility of this light has thus been very soon made apparent.

From *The Glasgow Argus,* published in the *Belfast Banner of Ulster* on 3 February 1843.

Further good publicity for the new lighthouse followed a few months later in a Carlisle newspaper:

LITTLE ROSS LIGHTHOUSE.

Little Ross is a small island in the Solway Frith, at the entrance of Kirkcudbright Bay, or roadstead. A lighthouse has lately been put on it; and in the squally and foggy weather which often prevails in the Solway, vessels now run with confidence to the roadstead for shelter.

Carlisle Patriot, 3 June 1843.

John C. Mackenzie, who had been involved so heavily throughout the campaign for the new lighthouse, recorded the following brief remarks in 1880:

The Lighthouse has been a blessing. Wrecks are now almost *nil*. Vessels at night can take the Bay and Manxman's Lake with comparative safety.

Tribute to the memory of James Skelly, John C. Mackenzie (1880).

In the first full year of Little Ross lighthouse's operation, duties were paid by the masters of 6,832 coasting vessels, of a total tonnage of 477,861. Duties were also paid by the masters of 61 foreign vessels of a total tonnage of 13,715. These duties amounted to a grand total of £1,024, two shillings, and four pence in 1843. It seems

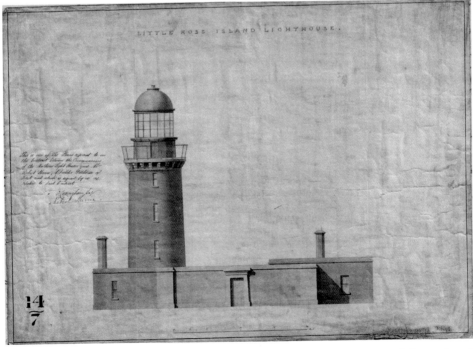

Elevation of lighthouse tower at Little Ross Island, courtesy of the Northern Lighthouse Board

that the Stevensons had been unduly pessimistic about the potential income that could be generated by a lighthouse on Little Ross, as the foregoing figures compare favourably with those of many other Scottish lighthouses during the same period.

The lighthouse station at Little Ross Island consists of a lighthouse tower, two groups of buildings on different sites on the island, and a few smaller and entirely separate building and engineering works. The dominant man–made feature on the island is of course the lighthouse tower, which is visible from all surrounding areas of land and sea both night and day, subject only to conditions such as fog, driving rain, and snow. The lighthouse is the focal point of many of the most attractive views from the shores of Kirkcudbright Bay, and is a welcome first glimpse of the approach to the port of Kirkcudbright for the masters and crews of both local and visiting vessels. On the island, it acts as a magnet for visitors, and regardless of how many previous visits to the island have been made, few people can resist the temptation to walk to its modest summit to enjoy the panoramic views it affords.

The tower rises to a height of 65 ft. and is accessed from a stone-paved, cobbled, and walled courtyard by an imposing pedimented doorway on its western face. A semi-circular single-storey building wraps round the base of the tower and provides storerooms to the north and south of the tower at courtyard level, and a lamp room store/workshop at ground floor level. The two storerooms are accessed directly from the courtyard, and the lamp room store/workshop from the staircase inside the tower. Until relatively recently, the lamp room store/workshop had a small fireplace.

This single-storey section of the tower building has two separate chimney stacks, yet only one fireplace has been located, the purpose of which has not been established with certainty. A possible explanation for the presence of a fireplace in the lamp room/workshop is that in extremely cold weather, a fire could be lit there to warm the lighthouse tower and to prevent the oil thickening in both the lamps and the clockwork mechanism, which would have impaired their efficiency. In any weather other than the most extreme cold, the use of this fire would have been discouraged, as the resulting smoke and soot would have had a detrimental effect on the cleanliness of the all–important lens at the top of the tower. The comfort of the keepers while on duty does not seem to have been a concern; there may have been sufficient heat emitted by the lamp to provide some relief from the cold night air. Apart from on the rare occasions on which a fire was lit, a chimney and a fireplace opening would have helped to provide ventilation and to avoid an accumulation of fumes from the paraffin which was in constant use. It is also possible however that the three rooms at the base of the tower were temporarily the 'house' referred to by Thomas Stevenson in Chapter 4 and were occupied for a short time by Thomas and his housekeeper during construction of the station. The second chimney stack could then have served a second fireplace dating from that temporary usage, or it could have been built merely to give symmetry to the external appearance of the east elevation.

Cellar at Little Ross lighthouse, courtesy of Graeme Macdonald and the Northern Lighthouse Board

Beneath the lamp room store is a small vaulted cellar which was originally used as the paraffin store. The tower's interior contains a spiral staircase, which winds clockwise round a brick core from the cellar until it reaches the level of the sill of the highest window in the tower. The core is hollow from the ground floor upwards and was used to house the weight which provided the energy to activate the clockwork mechanism necessary to drive and to govern the revolutions of the lamp. At the top of the spiral staircase, a metal ladder permits access to a further level, from which a door leads outwards to a cantilevered stone-flagged balcony partially supported by a course of magnificent stone corbels. This balcony and its cast-iron balustrade circle the tower and the lamp room above it, permitting relatively safe cleaning and maintenance of the external face of its glazing, as well as providing a spectacular viewpoint from which the keepers once surveyed their domain. From the balcony, a small and permanently-mounted metal ladder rises vertically up the external face of the lamp room wall and then follows the curve of the domed roof to its peak. To ascend that little ladder is quite a thrilling experience, although not originally in accordance with modern health and safety requirements. The ever-thoughtful Stevenson family provided a little distraction for anyone who made this perilous ascent by incorporating bizarre reptilian forms, sculpted and cast into components of the iron structure. From the balcony level, a metal ladder inside the lighthouse gives access to the lamp room. The lamp room is glazed almost all the way round and has minimal cast-iron glazing bars, which also support the domed metal roof structure.

The paved and cobbled courtyard at the base of the tower is rectangular in shape, 84 ft. 9 in. in length, and 32 ft. 9 in. in width. At its shorter sides, to north and south, are gated openings, and its west side is bounded by the east wall of the two light keepers' cottages. The courtyard wall, 3 ft. 7 in. in height, is built of whinstone, with a shallow pitched stone coping. It was originally of the same height as the cottages (11 ft. 9 in.), and incorporated a pedimented doorway, similar to that of the lighthouse tower, in its north face and a less imposing opening on the south face. This wall had been designed to provide shelter from the wind and weather that the keepers and their families would have had to endure in their daily comings and goings from the houses and the tower. A similar wall at another lighthouse station, Covesea Skerries, was reduced in height in 1907 after it was found to have caused strong whirlwinds within the courtyard. It was also considered to be hindering the keepers' abilities to keep a good lookout. Difficulties were also experienced at Little Ross, and at an unknown date the courtyard walls were duly reduced in height, the coping stones being set aside and re-used at the new lower level. The surplus of the dressed whinstone was tipped over the steep south-eastern side of the island, below the lighthouse tower, where its presence has caused some subsequent puzzlement to those who were unaware of the history of the courtyard wall.

The two flat-roofed cottages for the keepers and their families were built to a seemingly standard Stevenson design, which had varied slightly over the years to suit changing requirements and to meet local conditions as necessary. The houses were built to a very high quality of design, specification, and workmanship, offering simple, well-planned, and practical accommodation sturdy enough to withstand not only extreme weather conditions, but also the wear and tear generated by a considerable number of different occupants, many with large families. Despite their form strictly following functional requirements, the houses are also elegant in both proportion and detailed design. Parapet walls with dressed stone copes and string-courses, projected wall panels at the front doors, well-proportioned 12-paned sash and case windows surrounded by dressed stone margins and ornamental chimney heads all contribute to the attractiveness of the exteriors. The accommodation in the assistant keeper's house, the most southerly of the pair, originally consisted of a living/kitchen area incorporating a box bed, a tiny scullery, a bedroom, an 'artificer's barrack room', and a large storeroom. The box bed in the kitchen of each house must have been convenient for the keeper coming off watch, enabling him to warm himself before the coal fired range, have a cup of tea, and retire without disturbing the rest of the household. The house to the north was slightly larger than its neighbour, having two bedrooms, and was allocated to the principal keeper. This was done without regard to the size of the families of the respective keepers, but in recognition of the fact that the principal keeper would be asked at times to provide accommodation for visiting officials, official guests, or perhaps the attendant boatman when weather conditions forced him to remain on the island. An additional room and bedroom was provided for this purpose in the principal keeper's house, and his fuel allowance was correspondingly a little greater than that of his assistant. Each room in the houses had its own fireplace, the living/kitchens originally having cast iron ranges incorporating an oven and a boiler to provide hot water. The hallways and internal corridors have stone-flagged floors. A dry toilet, together with an ash pit, was originally sited externally at the north-west and south-west corner of each house. The design of the houses does nothing to exploit the spectacular views available to the occupants, and no windows on either house face north or south. The decision not to have a window facing southwards is perhaps understandable, as it would have been exposed to the most violent conditions brought by the prevailing southerly wind. On the north elevation though, a window would have been relatively protected from the elements and would have afforded the principal keeper a magnificent view of Kirkcudbright Bay and any approaching visitors. Oddly, a blank window is provided on that elevation, and is clearly shown as such on the original design drawings.

The second most dominant building on Little Ross is the north beacon, approximately 30 ft. in height and designed by the Stevensons to replace one of James Skelly's original two beacons. Square in plan and measuring 10 ft. by 10 ft. at its base, it is built of whinstone, battered on all four faces, and topped with a sandstone coping.

Two landing places were constructed by the Commissioners for Northern Lights, the first being a slipway on the north-west side of the island, approximately 230 ft. long and 8 ft. wide, extending towards low water mark in the sound between Little Ross and the mainland. This stone-built slipway, now partly surfaced with concrete, provides slippery access to small craft at all times and is generally sheltered from the prevailing wind. On extremely low spring tides however, a spit of shingle and stones, covered with seaweed prevents navigation through the northern part of the sound for all craft drawing more than a few inches. A hand winch at the head of the slipway enables small craft to be hauled clear of high water level. On the south side of the slipway, close to high water mark, a rectangular cutting has been made into the rocks of sufficient size to enable a cart or other vehicle to be parked there without obstructing access to the slipway. In the station's latter years an old Fordson van was kept there under a crude shelter. Severe gales and unusually high tides in the last few years have dislodged some of the very large stones at the lower and upper ends of the slipway, which will likely to lead to further damage. At the upper end, the land has been heavily scoured away by the same storms, exposing some of the strata of stones and shingle mentioned in Thomas Stevenson's geological report (see Chapter 1).

The second landing place was constructed at the north-east corner of the island in a rocky inlet, which may have been formed partially by the quarrying activities mentioned in Chapters 3 and 4. A small quay wall was hewn from the rock face at the south side of the inlet, and until recently it was faced with large baulks of vertical timber, between two of which an iron ladder was attached. This quay, although only 25 ft. long and 15 ft. high, enabled vessels of up to 30 or 40 ft. long to lie partially alongside, moored to both the baulks of timber and to iron rings, some of which still survive in the surrounding rocks. Although this inlet dries out well before low tide, it still enables vessels to readily discharge both passengers and goods for a few hours on each tide in settled weather. A small crane with a hand-cranked winch used to stand on a concrete slab atop the quay wall, and a smart little clinker-built dinghy bearing the name *Little Ross* was kept there in the latter years of the station's manned status. The dinghy and the crane were removed following automation, and the timber baulks and ladder have now rotted or rusted

The island's boat atop the east quay

away, to the regret of all who remember their convenience. A concrete and grass pathway connects with paths from the slipway, and from the white beach at the northern tip of the island the three paths meet beside the former cart-house/store at a rather incongruous looking domestic garden gate between concrete pillars.

The cart-house/store is a substantial stone building with a pitched slated roof and a chimneystack on each gable. The wall heads are neatly finished off with dressed skew stones, terminating in dressed stone skew putts over dressed quoins at each corner of the building. The building has double doors in its west elevation and one window in its north elevation. Inside, the floor is of close-fitting whinstone setts and there is a fireplace opening on each gable. It is surrounded by a stone wall nearly 7 ft. high, which wraps round the building and forms a narrow enclosure. The head of the wall is capped with whin coping stones, semi-circular in cross-section, and the surface of the enclosure is neatly cobbled. The enclosing wall has only two openings; the western one is 12 ft. wide and the northern one is 3 ft. and 9 in. wide. The door in the north elevation has beautifully made hinges, stamped with the letters 'N T N L' which are presumably an abbreviation for Northern Lighthouse. Whilst the building's name defines its purpose, the intended use of the chimneys is a matter for conjecture, as is the use of the enclosure referred to above. In recent years, the space between the cart-house and the surrounding wall has been protected by a lightweight lean-to roof structure. The tenants of the lighthouse cottages now use the resulting enlarged building as a workshop and store.

An unusual little building near the head of the west quay/slipway and a little to the south consists of a low stone wall with its coping stones taking the form of a parabola, roughly following the contours of the ground retained by the wall. The wall has a small opening in it, gated to protect what used to be a point at which water could be drawn by a hand pump from a cistern below. The cistern is believed to have been fed from a spring, supplemented by natural catchment from the grassy slope above and to the east. Following the departure of the keepers, the hand pump seized up and then disappeared. By that time, the water in the cistern had in any case become prone to pollution, as the protecting gate was no longer effective.

The track, uphill from the cart-house/store and landing stages towards the lighthouse, follows the roadway described by Thomas Stevenson (see Chapter 1). Strangers to the island who wander up this track may be surprised to find on their left-hand side, halfway up towards the lighthouse, a large 'L' shaped walled garden. There is also a row of what at first may appear to be single-storey cottages running east and west, separated from the north wall of the garden by a narrow alley. The siting of these building is such that they are concealed from many points within Kirkcudbright Bay from which the island is normally viewed. The walled garden is the better of two on the island, and was allocated to the principal keeper and his family. The purpose of the wall was partly to afford some degree of protection from the strong winds to which the island is exposed, and partly to deter rabbits from feasting on the fruits of the keeper's labours. In recent years, the tenants of the lighthouse cottages have built a small timber summerhouse in the garden.

Close to the garden at its north side is a small stone building and walled pen, generally believed to have been intended for use as a pigsty. The building is rectangular, 12 ft. 9 in. long and 6 ft. wide. It is built of coursed whinstone and the gables are topped with dressed skew stones. The wall head of the adjoining pen is finished with a neatly-rounded stone coping, matching that already mentioned at the cart-house/store. A full-height door in the west gable gives access to the building and a low door in its south elevation gives access to the adjoining pen, which is 12 ft. 9 in. by 9 ft. 9 in. The eastern gable has a small high opening, and a few cantilevered stones project from the wall below it. It seems possible therefore that the building may have accommodated either pigs or hens. The pen has its own external opening in its south face, which would at one time have been gated. Although the walls are generally in good order, the roofs have been removed and the materials used elsewhere. Pigs have not been kept on the island in living memory, but in both the 1950s and 1980s free-ranging goats were in residence for a short time.

The main building is constructed of coursed, roughly-squared whinstone, with beautifully dressed sills, lintels, inbands and outbands to doorways and other openings. The original slate roof was taken off after the departure of the resident keepers. The roof materials were subsequently removed and some were used for other purposes. Dressed skew stones are still in position at the wall heads of the end gables. The ridge line and the eaves lines both follow the same slope as the land on which the buildings are sited, demonstrating that construction was in accordance with a carefully prepared design rather than by a process of evolution over many years. The building, 71 ft. 6 in. long, is subdivided into six separate compartments, four of which have external doors on the south elevation, one on the north elevation, and one on the west elevation. The compartment furthest to the east is a blacksmith's forge, and has two small windows, one on the south elevation and one looking into a compartment to the north. The actual forge is on the east gable wall, and at the time the station was automated, it still had its large leather bellows in place. The bellows were later removed for their protection and are carefully taken care of by the tenants of the lighthouse cottages. What appear to be stone masons' marks are evident on the lintel of the forge and on some of the nearby masonry. The compartments adjacent to the forge and at the western end of the building are very similar in size and character. Neither has a window, but each has on its north elevation a neatly formed vertical slit in its masonry, such as one might expect to see in a byre. The purpose would seem to be purely for ventilation, as there is no indication that the openings were either glazed or shuttered. The floors of each of these two byre-like compartments are cobbled, but due to the sloping site, each has a step in its level. There is a drain in the corner of both of these compartments. Strangely, each compartment has a stone fireplace surround, fireplace opening, and a flue on its gable wall. The gables at the east and west ends of the building, and the gable which separates the forge from the other compartments, each have chimney heads, the design of the coping stones being identical to those at the cart-house/store. Between the two byre-like compartments are another two compartments, each 'L' shaped, and one with a door opening and ventilation slit on the south elevation, the other having a door and ventilation slit on the north elevation. An extension to the north of the main building houses the sixth compartment and has a wide door opening facing west, the purpose of which may have been to house a cart.

It is perhaps surprising to find that the construction of the forge at Little Ross was merited by the amount of metalwork necessary in the course of the station's construction and maintenance. The byre-like compartments may have been intended to accommodate a cow or cows, in accordance with Alan Stevenson's definition of the entitlements of a keeper (see page 100). It is also perhaps possible that one or more ponies may have been kept to pull the various carts that may have been used on the island. This does not however explain the presence of fireplaces in buildings not intended for human habitation. None of the fireplaces or flues show signs of extensive long-term use, other than that in the forge.

The Stevenson family were unusually skilful designers, who took pains to ensure that all their buildings, however humble, were technically sound, architecturally refined, and thoroughly practical. It is possible that they believed that a row of traditional-style buildings should have chimney heads in order to simply look right. It is even more likely that they realised that when building a gable end, it did not cost a great deal more to incorporate a fireplace opening, flue, and chimney, thereby providing considerable flexibility with regard to unforeseen future use.

No evidence has been found to suggest where the workmen, foremen, engineers, and any other site staff lived during the process of construction of all the quays, jetties, roads, garden walls, and buildings which comprise the station. A large workforce would certainly have been necessary for quarrying the stone and hauling it to wherever it was to be split, squared, and dressed prior to construction.

It would then have been hauled to wherever it was required, together with sand, lime, and water, before construction could even commence. Tidal conditions and weather combine to make it very difficult to envisage the work being completed on any reasonable timescale without the workforce living, eating, and sleeping on the island. One answer might be that firstly the main cart-house/store and secondly the two byre-like compartments that have fireplaces served as living accommodation during construction, doubling perhaps as workshops for stone masons and carpenters as the work progressed.

The shores of Little Ross do not attract driftwood to any great extent as both wind and tide tend to carry any flotsam to the mainland shores to the east of the island. Fuel must therefore have been brought from the mainland and its use carefully monitored.

On the south-facing slope of the island's seaward side is a second large walled garden. The potential benefit from its sunny aspect is however countered by the fact that it is extremely exposed to the salt-laden prevailing south-westerly wind, and it therefore presents an even greater horticultural challenge than the other garden. Perhaps for that very reason, it was allocated to the assistant keeper. A layout of paths and flower beds can still be discerned in the middle of the garden, evidence of considerable past efforts to create a garden that was attractive as well as productive. A small building and animal pen, similar to that described at the principal keeper's garden, is situated at its east side.

In 1845, a Parliamentary Select Committee was set up to look into the administration and management of lighthouse stations across the British Isles, reflecting the fact that there was still concern in some quarters about possible discrepancies between the standards maintained by Trinity House and the authorities that dealt with Scottish, Irish, and Manx lighthouses and buoyage. Alan Stevenson, having succeeded his father in the post of Engineer to the Commissioners for Northern Lights, appeared as a witness before that committee, and the following extract is taken from the official record of his interrogation, published in August 1845:

> We are informed that the Elder Brethren of Trinity House visit the lights occasionally; can you state how many visits they have paid since you have been engineer? – Since I have been engineer there has been only one visit.
>
> What year was that? – 1843.
>
> They paid a visit in 1836 – They did.
>
> Did you accompany them? – No.
>
> A Mr. Stevenson is mentioned? - That was my father.
>
> In 1843 did you join them on their visit? – I accompanied them in their inspection round the coast.
>
> How many lighthouses did they visit? – They visited all the lighthouses, but

I joined them at Greenock, after they had visited the Isle of Man, Little Ross, the Mull of Galloway, and Corsewall Point......

......Have you in the course of the last three or four years, had any serious complaints against the efficiency of your lights? – No, none whatever; the only case of complaint against the efficiency of the lights was by the corporation of the Trinity House with regard to the Little Ross light; but upon that subject I had previously reported to the Lighthouse Commissioners that I conceived the arrangement of small lenses, with a rapid revolution, was disadvantageous.

......Did they make any complaint on that visit? – Yes I mentioned before that they complained of the distinctive character of Little Ross light; they considered the flashes to be too short. I had previously reported to the board, as a defect of that apparatus, that the flash seemed to be somewhat too short for a marked appearance.

Has that been remedied since? – No, it could not be remedied without putting in an entirely new apparatus, and the defect was not considered of so pressing a description; the trade have never complained of it; they find the light very useful; and the Board came to a resolution upon my report, that upon the first opportunity, when that apparatus could be applied to another light with a different revolution, reflectors should be put in the place of the lenses at Little Ross.

Report of the Parliamentary Select Committee regarding administration and management of lighthouse stations in all parts of the British Isles (1845).

Trinity House, the general lighthouse authority for England, Wales, the Channel Islands, and Gibraltar is ruled by a court of 31 Elder Brethren, presided over by a Master. The Elder Brethren are appointed from the ranks of 300 Younger Brethren who advise and perform other duties as appropriate. The majority of Younger Brethren are former members of either the Royal or Merchant Navy, but others are people such as harbourmasters, pilots, and yachtsmen with extensive relevant experience. Three distinct and separate authorities exist to deal with all aspects of the provision of marine aids to navigation around the coast of the United Kingdom and the Republic of Ireland. They are: Trinity House, the Northern Lighthouse Board, and the Commissioners of Irish Lights. These three authorities liaise with each other to ensure their standards are compatible with each other and that there are no gaps between the services they provide.

Nowadays, most lighthouses round the coast of Scotland are painted white and their pristine appearance, rising from a grass-covered island, peninsula, or a seaweed-covered rock base is recognised by everyone on land and, more importantly, at sea. But the following extract from Alan Stevenson's interrogation makes clear that this was not always the case:

The Elder Brethren also report that with the exception of the Bell Rock and Skerryvore, the whole of the towers and dwellings being composed of dark stone, give the establishments a sombre appearance, and render them comparatively useless as beacons by day? – Yes, that is the case; that suggestion appears to me to be a good one, and steps have been taken in consequence to whitewash the outside of the towers, to roughcast them with lime; only one of them has yet been done, but two others are in progress this year. The operation would have gone on more rapidly, but we embraced at the same time the occasion offered by doing that operation to repair the joints of the masonry of the buildings, and it is entrusted to a workman who sees the whole thing done himself. I should add, that it had formerly been, many years ago, at Pladda, Corsewall and some others, but chiefly with a view to counteract damp.

Report of the Parliamentary Select Committee regarding administration and management of lighthouse stations in all parts of the British Isles (1845).

On 5 May 1845, Alan Stevenson was asked to explain to the Select Committee the nature of a dioptric fixed apparatus. He answered as follows:

The apparatus consists of several parts, of which the principal is a central or equatorial band of glass, like this shown on the model upon the table. The action of this instrument is not to collect the light from the sides, but simply from the top and bottom, or in a vertical direction. Its effect is to render the light parallel to the horizon, so that the rays are thrown out in the form of a flat ring, equally intense in every azimuth. The depth of this band is limited by its distance from the focus, because the highest and lowest ray proceeding from the lamp must not make at the inner surface more than a certain angle, otherwise, instead of proceeding through the refractor, it would be reflected backwards and lost. In order therefore to save the light which passes above and below this ring, the former practice was to use a set of curved mirrors of looking glass, each of which had its focus in the lamp. The loss of light from these mirrors being considerable, I proposed to replace them by means of *totally reflecting zones,* on the principle of the small apparatus invented by the French academician Augustin Fresnel. This is a model of these zones. The zones upper encompass the flame in the form of a bee-hive roof, and the lower ones are arranged in a cylinder; the effect is to intercept the light which would otherwise be lost: the light falls upon the inner surface of these zones, which are three-sided prisms. At this first or inner surface of each zone, the light is *refracted* so as to pass on to the second side of the prism, which it meets at a certain angle in such a manner as not to pass through that side, but to be *totally reflected* from it; after this *total reflection* at the second side of the prism. The light proceeds to the third or outer side, at which it suffers a second *refraction* and then emerges horizontally.

Report of the Parliamentary Select Committee regarding administration and management of lighthouse stations in all parts of the British Isles (1845).

Lighthouses, their accompanying dwellings and all their various ancillary buildings were designed and built to last and withstand some of the worst weather conditions in Scotland. Their design by the various members of the Stevenson family had evolved over a long period of time, allowing changes to be made as necessary when failures of either materials or building techniques occurred.

The buildings' maintenance was dealt with by the constant presence of the ever-resourceful keepers and their wives. Matters too complex or arduous for them to handle were identified during annual inspections by the Northern Lighthouse Board and dealt with either by their own staff or by contractors working under their supervision. The system may sometimes have seemed slow and labour-intensive to the residents, but it seemed to work. The lamps burned for over 50 years, and the daily routine continued with neither interruption nor significant incident. The following description of the lighthouse station at Little Ross, written 53 years after it went into service, could just as readily have been written on its first day in 1843:

> The station, consisting of a tower, two dwelling houses, and the necessary storehouses, is surrounded by a wall whitewashed, thus serving as a landmark by day. The tower rises to the height of sixty-five feet, and is crowned with a lantern, in which is fixed an early form of dioptric apparatus of lenses and mirrors, with a four-wick lamp in their common focus. This optical apparatus is made to revolve by a machine driven by a falling weight, and shows over the sea in the neighbourhood to the distance of eighteen nautical miles, with a flash every five-seconds — the power of each beam as it sweeps across the horizon being equal to upwards of 26,000 standard candles. The light is attended by two keepers, who mount a guard in the lighthouse as regularly as the watch on the deck of a warship. Each watch lasts four hours: and when the keeper on duty is to be relieved he summonses his comrade by the signal bells communicating between the light room and the dwelling houses. When a keeper is on watch in the lighthouse he dare not leave it, or the balcony, on any pretence. Nightly the keeper lights his lamp. And there darts forth a sheaf of rays of light to illuminate the darkness. The lamp must be kept burning bright and clear, free from smoke, and the flame must be equal to and never under the photograph of the standard flame hung in the light room. The weight of the machine, which causes the apparatus to revolve, must be regularly wound up. If the keeper omitted to do this and allowed the flashing light to become a stationary one, he would be instantly dismissed the service. Everything about the lighthouse is kept scrupulously clean and bright.

Rambles in Galloway, by Malcolm McL. Harper, (1896).

Far away from Little Ross Island though, knowledge of science and technology was advancing in ways that would revolutionise industrial power, transport, and communications. Early signs that the new technology might perhaps affect the inhabitants of Little Ross Island came on 20 May 1895, when Admiral Edward Field, Conservative MP for Eastbourne raised questions in Parliament regarding the provision of electrical communications for light stations. He asked that the President of the Board of Trade be required to advise whether or not the recommendations of the Commissioners on the subject had been approved and to reassure him that the work, when approved, would be carried out without unnecessary delay. Little Ross was one of the four lighthouses he specifically mentioned and the only one sited in Scotland. He also asked if arrangements would be made to display storm-warning signals at 25 listed lighthouses at the remarkably modest cost of one pound each. An underwater communications cable was eventually laid across Little Ross Sound, and a service was commenced to the island on 22 October 1897. The severed ends of parts of the cable can still be seen in places on the west shore of White Beach.

The lens that was in use at Little Ross lighthouse in 1960 was later generously gifted to the Stewartry Museum in Kirkcudbright by the Northern Lighthouse Board, and is now on permanent display there. That lens had replaced the original at an unknown date and had been made in Paris by Barbier, Benard & Turenne in 1896. Founded in 1862, this famous French company was responsible for the installation of Fresnel lenses, lighthouses, iron towers, and light-vessels in many different parts of the world. Fresnel lenses were named after their designer, Augustin-Jean Fresnel (1788–1827), an engineer who was at one time a commissioner of lighthouses in France.

Isaac Cookson and Company of Newcastle-on-Tyne had made the original dioptric lens that first went into use at Little Ross in 1843. This enterprising company, founded in 1728 as glass-makers, was also involved in coal and lead mining, salt and alum refining, and iron founding. They were manufacturers of lighthouse lenses between 1831 and 1845.

The magnificent clockwork mechanism which rotated the light and regulated the nocturnal lives of the keepers and their families for an unbroken period of 117 years was also gifted to the Stewartry Museum by the Northern Lighthouse Board and is displayed there beside the lens it caused to revolve for so many years.

Lantern and attendant keeper George Davidson DSM BEM,
courtesy of Keith Allardyce and the Museum of Scottish Lighthouses

CHAPTER 7

Dedication, Duty, and Domesticity

For hundreds of years, the lives of the men who have been employed as lighthouse keepers have inspired feelings in the minds of the general public ranging from curiosity, fascination, and suspicion, to respect, admiration, and gratitude. Few people however have had direct or indirect contact with the reality of lighthouse service, and in that situation, they were and still are more than ready to let their imaginations run riot. Perhaps the best and the most extreme example of this can be found in the words of the following earthy, but deservedly popular sea shanty:

> My father was the keeper of the Eddystone light
> And he slept with a mermaid one fine night
> From this union there came three
> A porpoise and a porgy and the other was me!
>
> Chorus-Yo ho ho, the wind blows free,
> Oh for the life on the rolling sea!
>
> One night, as I was a-trimming of the glim
> Singing a verse from the evening hymn
> A voice on the starboard shouted "Ahoy!"
> And there was my mother, a-sitting on a buoy.
>
> "Oh, where are the rest of my children three?"
> My mother then she asked of me.
> One was exhibited as a talking fish
> The other was served from a chafing dish.
>
> Then the phosphorous flashed in her seaweed hair.
> I looked again, and my mother wasn't there
> But her voice came echoing back from the night
> "To Hell with the keeper of the Eddystone Light!"

My Father was the Keeper of the Eddystone Light (Traditional).

Becoming a lighthouse keeper seemed for many people an escape from society, and could be likened either to running away to the circus or to joining the French Foreign Legion. Each of these activities required either talent and a high degree of physical fitness, or a sense of adventure and a minimum of concern about the consequences. However, the romantic image of the lighthouse keeper is that of a lonely and tortured soul, inadequate at dealing with his fellow men and women, possibly seeking seclusion to write poetry, a novel, or to compose a symphony, influenced only by the sea, the sky, and the wonders of nature.

Fortunately for mariners everywhere, the Northern Lighthouse Board took a different and more practical view of the qualities necessary in a lighthouse keeper. Candidates were often former Merchant Navy seamen or fishermen who sought employment closer to their families. Many of these men were tough, practical people from the Highlands and Islands of Scotland; they were self-reliant and versatile, not only familiar with the sea, but also capable of repairing equipment and improvising. The successful recruits were (almost unfailingly) well-suited to the tasks they were required to undertake and able to cope with the unusual lifestyle that their occupation and living conditions demanded. The Commissioners offered a reasonable salary, a pension, a low cost of living, free and decent housing of above average quality with all fuel provided, and perhaps most importantly, long-term employment with the prospect of promotion, albeit over a substantial period of time. Alan Stevenson, appearing as a witness before a Parliamentary Select Committee on lighthouses in 1845, was questioned about the remuneration and living conditions of keepers employed by the Northern Lighthouse Board:

> What is the number of persons at each lighthouse, and what is the salary of each? – At all our lighthouses there are two keepers, a principal and assistant; the principal receives £50 a year salary, and the assistant £40.
>
> Have they any other allowances? – They have a suit of uniform clothing, and grass for a cow, and a garden.
>
> What accommodation have they to live in? – They have a house attached to the lighthouse, not in the tower, but detached from it by about 50 or 60 feet.
>
> Do any of them live in the tower now? – Only when it cannot be avoided; only at the Bell Rock and Skerryvore.
>
> How long is it since they obtained detached houses? – I am not aware that any ever lived in the towers. I think not; my impression is they never did. I may mention, that when it can be avoided we consider it disadvantageous to have families living in the towers; the dust from the fires is injurious to the apparatus; and if it could be avoided at these two stations, it would.

There was some status attached to the job, lighthouse keepers being generally regarded by mariners and knowledgeable landsmen and women as trustworthy and respectable people engaged in important and useful work. In a typical career in the lighthouse service, a keeper and his family would be moved all around the coasts of Scotland and the Isle of Man, experiencing life in island stations such as Little

Ross, rock stations such as the Bell Rock, and mainland stations such as the Mull of Galloway. In mainland stations, keepers might have the opportunity to live with their families in either the lighthouse buildings or in keepers' cottages nearby. In these circumstances, it was usually relatively easy for their children to attend school and for them and their wives to play some part in local community life. In island stations such as Little Ross, although they could enjoy living with their families in a beautiful situation, their children might have to have lodgings in a mainland town or village to enable them to attend school, and their wives would be isolated from shops, friends, and mainland facilities. Provisioning depended entirely on a weekly visit from an attendant boatman, and would be subject to prevailing weather conditions. On a rock station, the situation would be more rigorous and extreme, in that there would be no opportunity for wives and families to be accommodated, and keepers would have to share their cramped and spartan living accommodation with their fellow keepers. In those situations, the wives and families of keepers were accommodated in lighthouse cottages at a nearby mainland or main island port. The keepers of course would also be able to enjoy living there when on leave. Supply of provisions to rock stations would inevitably be erratic, as landings could only be made during calm weather. On both rock and island stations, supply of fresh food was a problem. Obtaining fresh milk and vegetables was impossible on rock stations, but most island stations had gardens in which keepers with the necessary skills could grow some basic crops despite challenging horticultural conditions. The tensions potentially generated in rock stations by men, who were already missing their families and having to cope with cooking and preparing meals from a dwindling supply of ingredients, in close proximity to their superiors or inferiors in rank, can easily be imagined. Alan Stevenson described a surprising situation during his interrogation before the Parliamentary Select Committee:

> In the case the keeper himself should behave ill, or negligently, how do you obtain information? – We have no information excepting from one or other of the keepers, and generally find them very ready to give information against each other, for it is remarkable that they are generally on very bad terms. I know not how, but so it happens.

In assessing the capabilities and suitability of trainee or supernumerary keepers for full-time employment, the Northern Lighthouse Board was in the habit of stationing them for a few months in one of each of the three types of lighthouse station (rock, island and mainland). A candidate would only be offered full-time employment after completion of service in each of these types of station and the receipt of a favourable report from each respective principal keeper. In earlier times, the training related perhaps more to the different types of apparatus than to the living environment. Alan Stevenson gave an explanation for the choice of training stations in his answer to a question from a member of the Parliamentary Select Committee:

Now with regard to training; do you place the lighthouse keepers under any particular training? – They are required to reside six weeks at the Bell Rock, and six weeks at either Inchkeith or the Isle of May, so as to see both a dioptric light and a reflecting light.

Report of the Parliamentary Select Committee regarding administration and management of lighthouse stations in all parts of the British Isles (1845).

When the time came to be offered full-time employment and to be informed of the station in which their service was to commence, most married men hoped they would be offered a posting at which their wives could also reside, and married men with children generally hoped for a mainland posting with ready access to schooling. Some single men may have been happy to face the challenge and excitement of life on a rock station, but others would have hoped for a posting that offered at least some prospect of a social life. It is probable that at some time in his career, almost every keeper or his wife was unhappy with either the location of his posting, its duration, or the length of time he had to wait for promotion. Patience, stoicism, and an understanding family (where appropriate) were essential qualities which were not always easy to maintain. The romantic dream expressed so effectively in Erika Eigen's 1960s song *I want to marry a lighthouse keeper and keep him company* would not have been an easy one to realise, and the finding of 'treasure' during 'walks along the moonlit bay' of which she dreamed was an experience unlikely to be enjoyed by either lighthouse keepers or their long-suffering wives.

Lighthouse keepers at Little Ross, like their colleagues around the coasts of Scotland and the Isle of Man, had surprisingly little time to themselves. Forces of nature such as weather, tides, currents, sunrise, and sunset ruled their lives. Within nature's broad dictates, their daily routine was further subdivided by the ticking of the clock, the watch system, the turnings of the mechanism which controlled the revolving light, and a mass of chores, both professional and domestic.

Domestic chores and activities included tending to livestock (including any ponies), milking cows or goats, and feeding pigs and hens. Those keepers who did not have livestock had to make regular visits ashore to the dairy at Ross Farm for milk. Occasional Sunday visits were made to Borgue Parish Church (Borgue is the nearest mainland village to the island), and rare visits were made to Kirkcudbright, the nearest town, for any shopping other than the weekly food supply. Such visits were restricted to times when both the weather and tidal conditions were favourable. Particular care had to be taken to ensure that the dinghy would not be left high and dry by the tide, as the consequences of being late for the start of one's watch could be extremely serious. Coal, once delivered to the island, had to be taken up the hill to the houses by either a horse-drawn cart or a hand cart, though in the latter years of the station's manning, an old Fordson van that had been shipped to the island made this task much easier. Water had to be carried or pumped from the island's spring-fed wells to the houses. The flat roofs of the houses, which were used to collect rainwater for all purposes other than drinking, had to be kept clean and free from bird lime and from the remains of many dead birds that collided with the lantern during the night. The island's two gardens had to be cultivated and the endless battle with a huge and ever-growing rabbit population had to continue to be fought.

Professional chores, or perhaps more accurately, duties, centred on the care and maintenance of the lamp and the clockwork mechanism at the top of the lighthouse tower. Fuel had to be carried from the landing place to the lighthouse where it was stored in a tank in the basement. It was then carried up the narrow stone spiral staircase to the lantern room at the top of the tower as necessary. At dusk every evening the lamp had to be lit and the wick trimmed and adjusted so that it burned cleanly and brightly with a flame, the height of which was within the strict parameters stipulated by the Northern Lighthouse Board. A weight, suspended in a vertical shaft running through the core of the spiral staircase from top to bottom of the tower, had to be wound by hand to the top. This task could take up to half an hour to complete and had to be undertaken every two hours or so. The descending weight powered the clockwork mechanism which caused the lantern to revolve and thereby give the light its characteristic effect of a flash every five seconds. To forget the winding of the weight, to let the light go out, or to leave the lantern unattended for any purpose were offences punishable by dismissal from the service. One lighthouse keeper (not at Little Ross) is said to have slept on a pallet underneath the descending weight to ensure he could not possibly sleep through the final few inches of its descent. All night, every night, the two keepers at Little Ross took watch, in turns, every four hours. This was undoubtedly the most important and most arduous part of the work of a keeper, who was required to concentrate fully on observing the lantern's flame, and on winding the weight throughout this period. No reading, no listening to the radio, and no other leisure activity was permitted on watch, so four hours under the hypnotic effect of the lantern's flame and the regular ticking of the clockwork mechanism must have seemed an eternity. To be found asleep on duty would have triggered dismissal. At the welcome end of his watch, the keeper coming off duty could operate a mechanical bell pull in the tower which caused a bell to ring in the houses, waking the keeper about to come on duty (and presumably the rest of his slumbering family). The present tenants of the houses on Little Ross found an electromagnetically-operated flag system housed in a neat wooden box, which was operated by push buttons located in both the tower and the keepers' houses. It is presently located in the sitting room at Little Ross and has been wired into the house's low voltage DC power system to allow it to be demonstrated.

When daylight eventually came after a long night's duty, the balcony surrounding the lantern had to be cleared of the bodies of any dead birds which had collided with the lantern. This only seems to have been necessary when the original oil lamps were in use, as the light they emitted was considerably more intense than either of the later gas or solar powered lamps. The glazing to the lantern room had to be checked for chips and cracks caused by colliding birds, repaired if necessary, then cleaned and polished until all traces of salt or bird lime were removed. A particularly vital daily task was the careful cleaning and polishing of the lenses and mirrors that magnified and projected the tiny flame from the lamp into the beam of concentrated light which was the station's reason for existence. All visible and accessible brass work had also to be polished in the best nautical tradition, and all moving parts in the clockwork mechanism had to be regularly cleaned and occasionally lubricated.

The keepers were responsible for the day-to-day maintenance of the buildings at the station and had to coat all external walls of the tower and houses with lime wash annually to maintain their high visibility from the sea. Paths and tracks had to be scythed to keep weeds at bay, rain gauges had to be read, atmospheric pressure checked, weather records kept, and storm cones had to be raised or lowered from the station's flagpole as appropriate.

Somewhere between all these professional duties, time had to be found to cook, eat, sleep, and care for wives, children, and any other dependent relatives. Despite the obvious hardships of life in a lighthouse station, most keepers seemed to enjoy their work and took considerable pride in their position. In the course of a long career, most would eventually be rewarded by promotion to principal keeper, the status being gratifying and the increased pay being important to their eventual pensions. This resulted in many of the boys who were born in lighthouse stations going on to follow their fathers into the service and many of the girls eventually marrying lighthouse keepers, attendant boatmen, or crew members of the lighthouse supply vessels. After only a few generations, keepers might have parents, grandparents, aunts, uncles, cousins, sons, and daughters in the service of the Northern Lighthouse Board, who were rightly proud of this strong tradition of loyal family service.

The Northern Lighthouse Board kept a register 'Showing the distribution of the Principal and Assistant Keepers through the various Lighthouses, and the dates of their transferences from one to another.' Sixty-one principal and assistant lighthouse keepers served at Little Ross lighthouse for an unbroken period of 118 years. In addition to those 61 men, there would have been a large number of supernumeraries (trainees) and relief keepers whose names were not on the register. Periods of service ranged from an unusually short six weeks to the twelve years and ten months served by principal keeper W A McKay, between 1871 and 1884. The average period of service was however in the vicinity of four and a half years for principal keepers and three and a half years for assistant keepers. At Little Ross, there were always two keepers in residence so one of the was on duty at all time, night and day. During annual holidays, or in the event of serious illness, an experienced relief keeper would be brought in to ensure that the Lighthouse Board's standards were still being met.

Considerable efforts have been made to trace the details and family histories of the lighthouse keepers and their families who lived on Little Ross Island from 1842 until 1960. Information about the dates of their arrivals and departures has been taken from a variety of Northern Lighthouse Board records available in the Scottish Records Office. There are however occasional discrepancies in the dates of arrival and departure which are probably due to the fact that entry into the lighthouse service could have commenced on the day that a keeper boarded the supply ship, rather than the date on which the supply ship reached the appropriate lighthouse and was able to transfer passengers. For that reason, the records of an individual station occasionally differ from the records in the NLB archive.

In the entire history of Little Ross lighthouse, only three keepers were dismissed from the lighthouse service. A full account of the reasons for one dismissal are given in Chapter 12, but details of the reasons for the other dismissals have not been located. It is worth noting however that typical reasons for the similarly rare dismissals at other lighthouses were 'drunk and disorderly', 'asleep on watch', 'letting the light go out', 'letting the machinery stop', and perhaps most relevant to later events at Little Ross, 'showing symptoms of insanity'.

For a definition of the duties of light keepers from the 1847 Bye-laws and Rules and Regulations of the Commissioners of Northern Lighthouses, see Appendix I, and for a list of all the keepers who served at Little Ross, see Appendices II and III.

CHAPTER 8

The Keepers and their Families,
1842–1881

The first principal keeper appointed to Little Ross lighthouse station was Thomas Ritson, whose service commenced there on 22 June 1842. Thomas Ritson, who had entered the service of the Commissioners of Northern Lights on 4 July 1831 when he was 29 years old, had been an assistant keeper at the Mull of Galloway, so did not have to travel far to his new posting. To be promoted to principal keeper and to simultaneously be put in charge of a brand new lighthouse station must have been an exciting and challenging experience. Assistant keeper Alexander Law was appointed on 2 November of the same year. The lighthouse was not scheduled to go into service until 1 January 1843, so the two keepers must have spent their early months and weeks at Little Ross working together with the builders and commissioning engineers and learning how to understand and look after what was at that time regarded as one of the three most advanced lighthouses in existence. They would also of course have had the great pleasure of moving into their brand new houses, the arduous work of attempting to break new ground in their sizeable gardens, and the exhausting task of moving lighthouse stores, personal stores, furniture, livestock (if any), and fuel to appropriate locations, uphill and downhill in their new domain. Their appointments would have been a source of pride and satisfaction to both men and their families. The Northern Lighthouse Board members must have had particular confidence that the knowledge, experience, character, and judgement of the newly appointed keepers would ensure that the lighthouse's commissioning would be efficiently accomplished and that a high standard of care and maintenance would be set for subsequent keepers to emulate.

No records have been found of who was the first attendant boatman to Little Ross Island, but it is likely that several local part-time fisherman would have vied with each other to secure what was a humble position, but one which nevertheless provided a steady income, long-term security, and some satisfaction. It also perhaps provided the opportunity to be equipped with a new boat, built to the high standards required by the Commissioners of Northern Lights. On 7 June 1843, the Commissioners considered the matter of providing an attending boat for Little Ross, and after appraising two tenders, one from Messrs Thomas Wishart & Co., and the other from Mr. James Hutton, they authorised acceptance of the offer from Thomas Wishart & Co., amounting to fifteen pounds and sixteen shillings, which was three pounds, four shillings, and sixpence lower than that of James Hutton. There was a boat-builder in Kirkcudbright at that date called Thomas Wishart whose premises were at the Fish House on the west side of the River Dee and it is probable that he was the successful tenderer.

A distinguished early visitor to the lighthouse station provided the following tribute to the manner in which the station was maintained, and to the capability and pride displayed by the keepers during what must have been a fascinating and rather arduous day:

> Yesterday was given to an expedition to the lighthouse on the island of Little Ross, about six or seven miles below Kirkcudbright. Some rode and some drove, and George Maitland walked till we all came to the ale house on the peninsula of Great Ross, where we took boat, and after a mile's sailing were landed on the island. It is one of the lesser lights. All its machinery was explained to us by a sensible keeper. I never understood the thing before. The prospect from the top, and indeed from every part of the island is beautiful. I was more interested in the substantial security and comfort of the whole buildings, both for scientific and domestic purposes. No Dutchman's summer-house could be tidier. Everything from the brass and the lenses of the light to the kitchen, and even to the coal-house of each of the two keepers was as bright as a jeweller's shop. Eleven people lunched at the ale-house on our return upon oatcakes, cheese, butter and ale of the house and in a frenzy of generosity I resolved to pay the bill and was rewarded by finding that it amounted to only one sixpence. There is a hotel for you! George Maitland and I walked home — a rough tramp. But it lay all the way upon the shore.

Circuit Journeys, by Lord Cockburn, (1889), referring to a visit made in 1844.

Thomas Ritson and Alexander Law had obviously impressed their visitor. They would probably never read the foregoing account, as 45 years were to elapse before its publication, but hopefully word would have filtered back to the Commissioners in Edinburgh of the success of the visit.

Thomas Ritson was 40 when he was appointed, and his wife Anne was 35. Both were born in England, possibly in Cumberland, where the name Ritson is common among seafarers and shipbuilders. The 1841 census records that while Thomas was a keeper at the Mull of Galloway lighthouse, he was accompanied by his wife Anne and son James, who was 12 at the time. It is not known if James accompanied his parents to Little Ross.

Alexander Law married Agnes Robertson on 17 November 1844 at Borgue Parish Church, and on 28 August 1845, Borgue parish records show that a son named Alexander was born to Alexander Law and Agnes Robertson of Little Ross. It has not been possible to determine where young Alexander was actually born, but if it was not on the island, he would certainly have been brought there from the mainland shortly after his birth, making him the first infant known to have lived on the island.

A very severe storm struck much of Galloway on 10 October 1846, and principal keeper Thomas Ritson reported that the weather was particularly awful at Little Ross, resulting in several panes of glass being broken after hail had covered the ground to a depth of 12 in. He also reported having sighted six waterspouts from the top of the lighthouse tower.

On 17 November 1846, Alexander Law and his family were moved to Cairnryan lighthouse in Wigtownshire. Richard Cumming was appointed as his replacement on the same day but he resigned in 1847 and was replaced by Robert Burnett in June 1847. Robert Burnett had been born at Stoneykirk in Wigtownshire in 1827, and was the son of a lighthouse keeper who was later stationed at the Point of Ayre on the Isle of Man. Robert's wife Elizabeth Crowe had been born at Lezayre on the Isle of Man in 1823, and they married there on 22 June 1847. Robert and Elizabeth Burnett remained at Little Ross for just over ten years, and though little or nothing is known about their life there, they certainly must have been both productive and busy as they brought up six children on the island. Robert Alexander Burnett was born on 4 May 1848, Janet Anne Burnett on 4 December 1849, Elizabeth Burnett on 26 September 1851, Catherine Emma Burnett on 23 August 1853, Margaret Burnett on 25 April 1855, and Edward Burnett on 22 March 1857. All of the births were registered in the Parish of Borgue, and four of the children were also recorded as having been christened at Borgue.

Their eldest son, Robert Alexander Burnett, became a prominent businessman in Chicago, having gone to Illinois to farm there in 1867. From farming, he progressed to being a produce merchant, and in 1876 he formed the firm of Connor, Burnett and Co. He bought out all other interests in the firm in 1880 then traded under his own name until 1892, when the firm became R. A. Burnett and Co. and he became president of the Wholesale Fruit and Produce Association. Perhaps his interest in agriculture had been inspired by his early childhood experience of helping his father tend the rather bleak and exposed garden allocated to the assistant keeper at Little Ross.

The 1851 census records the following eight people being residents of Little Ross Island on the day the census was taken:

Thomas Ritson, age 49, Married. Occupation: Lighthouse Keeper (principal). Born: England. Anne Ritson, aged 44, wife of Thomas Ritson. Born: England. Jane Forsyth, aged 18, Household of Thomas Ritson. Occupation: servant (house). Born: Kirkcudbright. John Lachie [sic. probably intended to be Leckie], aged 44, visitor in household of Thomas Ritson, married. Occupation: attending boatman. Born: Kirkcudbright. Robert Burnett, aged 24, Married. Occupation: lighthouse keeper (assistant). Born: Galloway, Wigtownshire. Elizabeth Burnett, aged 27, wife of Robert Burnett. Born: Isle of Man. Janet Anne Burnett, daughter of Robert Burnett, aged 1. Born: Borgue. Robert Burnett, son of Robert Burnett, aged 2. Born: Borgue.

The mention of the last two children being born at Borgue refers to the parish rather than the village. It is therefore possible that the births took place at Little Ross.

The contrast between the households of the two adjacent and similar cottages at Little Ross was marked. In normal circumstances, Thomas and Anne Ritson would have been the sole occupants of their slightly larger principal keeper's house. The census however must have coincided with either bad weather, inconvenient tides, or both, forcing the attendant boatman to spend the night on the island. Thomas Ritson's slightly higher salary apparently enabled him to employ a house servant, which must have made the Burnett family very conscious of their lower rank and status as they struggled unaided to bring up their children. A handwritten note on the first page of the Register of Keepers for Little Ross records the Principal Keeper's salary as £50 and that of his assistant, £40. Later but undated pages show an increase of £5 to each salary, and also the payment of £10 to each keeper 'in lieu of ground'. Jane Forsyth, at the age of 18, probably had a hard and lonely life on Little Ross, with no company of her own age and little opportunity to get to the mainland. The 1841 census had recorded Jane Forsyth, aged 7, living with her parents Thomas and Sarah, at Tongue of Bombie, near Kirkcudbright. Jane was the fourth of five children, and her father Thomas was an agricultural labourer.

Principal keeper Thomas Ritson retired from lighthouse service and was replaced by Hugh Fitzsimons on 18 February 1852. Hugh Fitzsimons, born in Ireland in 1818, had entered the lighthouse service on 15 May 1844 after marrying Jessie Watt in 1837 at Kirk, Rushen, Isle of Man. Jessie Watt had been born in Arbroath to John Watt and Ann Hepburn. John Watt was a lighthouse keeper who had served, among other places, at the Calf of Man in the 1830s. Hugh Fitzsimons served for seven years at Little Ross and was then transferred to the remote and beautiful island of Sanda, close to the Mull of Kintyre, on 23 February 1859. The couple were together at Davaar lighthouse near Campbeltown in 1871 when Hugh was principal keeper there, so it seems likely that he was accompanied by his wife Jessie when he was stationed at Little Ross. Hugh retired from the lighthouse service in 1879 and Jessie died at Campbeltown in 1882. Hugh married again to Catherine McKechnie in 1884.

By 1857, when Robert Burnett's ten years of service at Little Ross came to an end, his family had increased to six children. One of them, Catherine Emma Burnett later gained a minor place in history when she married Henry Bird in April 1880 in Edinburgh. Henry Bird was the driver of the first train to cross the Forth Bridge. Robert and Elizabeth Burnett went on to have four more children after leaving the island on 15 July 1857 on their transfer to Covesea Skerries. Robert and Elizabeth eventually followed their eldest son to Chicago and Robert died there in 1899.

Thomas Saunderson commenced service as Robert Burnett's replacement on the same day that Robert and his family departed; he was accompanied by his wife, Jessie J. Saunderson. Jessie Saunderson gave birth to John C. Saunderson in 1858 and to Margaret J. L. Saunderson in 1860. Both births were registered in the Parish of Borgue, so it is probable that both children were born on Little Ross. Thomas and his family were transferred to Skerries lighthouse in 1861 after three years and three months on the island. At that time, Thomas Saunderson was aged 30, his wife Jessie J. Saunderson was 36, John C. Saunderson was 3, and Margaret J. L. Saunderson was one year old.

Alexander Craib entered the lighthouse service on 15 January 1843 when he was 23 years old, and commenced duty as principal keeper at Little Ross on 23 February 1859, having arrived there from Kirkmaiden in Wigtownshire with his wife Catherine and their seven children. He had previously been stationed at the Mull of Galloway, where he was the principal keeper. In early 1861, another child was born and the whole family is recorded in the 1861 census as living together on the island:

Alexander Craib, aged 37: principal lightkeeper. Catherine, his wife, aged 39. James, their son, aged 18: scholar. Ann, their daughter, aged 16: scholar. Catherine, their daughter, aged 13: scholar. Alexandrina, their daughter, aged 9. Georgina, their daughter, aged 7. Flora, their daughter, aged 5. Margaret, their daughter, aged 3. Mary Gordon, their daughter, one month old.

The foregoing statistics show that the population of Little Ross Island in the early part of 1861 consisted of four adults and ten children – surely the highest it has ever been. How could all of these people have been accommodated in two small cottages? How did Little Ross's modest water supply cope with the demand, and how did the off-duty keepers manage to make up their lost sleep when surrounded by the chaos that ten children could create? Perhaps the row of buildings adjacent to the forge and to the principal keeper's garden was used, officially or unofficially, as sleeping accommodation for some of the family. It is probable that the three elder Craib children had lodgings ashore to enable them to attend Borgue Academy for at least part of the year, but in the summer months they might have been able to commute from the island to Borgue. Their journey would have begun by walking from the lighthouse to the west quay then launching a rowing boat, which would not have been an easy task at low tide. On landing at the mouth of Ross Bay (the nearest accessible part of the mainland shore), they would then have been faced with a walk of four and a quarter miles in each direction. In bad weather, this journey could have been either dangerous or impossible. Even in good weather, the long walk would frequently have had to be undertaken in wet clothing. But perhaps it was worth that to be able to enjoy a childhood that few would not envy, with every opportunity to swim, fish, catch rabbits, and to explore every crack and crevice in the romantic rocky landscape that surrounded their home.

Alexander Craib was transferred to Barra Head on 11 March 1863, and James Pithie took his place as principal keeper at Little Ross on the same date. James

Pithie was 25 years of age when he entered the lighthouse service on 18 October 1848. A lighthouse keeper by the name of Pithie was stationed at the Bell Rock Lighthouse in 1818 and was very likely to have been related to James Pithie. James was born in Forfar/Arbroath in 1822/23 and married Elizabeth Brown on 20 November 1850 while he served at Pentland Skerries lighthouse. Elizabeth was the daughter of the principal keeper at Pentland Skerries, so the marriage was another example of the close nature of relationships between the families who depended on the Northern Lighthouse Board for both their homes and their livelihoods. Elizabeth and James Pithie had a son, also named James, who was born on 6 August 1853 at South Ronaldsay in Orkney. It is presumed that all three were resident at Little Ross. On 20 March 1861, Robert Watson took over from Thomas Saunderson as assistant keeper at Little Ross. Robert had been born in New Lanark in 1829 and had married Margaret Bertram from Biggar on 24 June 1852. The Watsons arrived with their four children, Margaret aged 7, Jane aged 3, James aged 2, and Johanna who was aged only three months. Another child, William Riddell Watson, was born at Little Ross on 14 August 1862, but died there on 11th June 1863, of hydrocephalus/dentition, aged only ten months. A sixth child, Jannet (sic), was born on 10 February 1864 at Little Ross and her birth was registered at Chapelton, Borgue on 22 February.

Robert Watson was an experienced keeper, having joined the lighthouse service on 4 October 1854, aged 24. He had then served for four years at the shore station of Ardnamurchan and three years at the rock station of Skerryvore, during which time his family would have lived in the station cottages at Hynish on Tiree. Sadly, his years of varied experience and training did not save him from a cruel fate. Articles in the *Galloway News* of 8 April and 13 May 1864 tell the story:

MELANCHOLY ACCIDENT – TWO MEN AND A BOY DROWNED.

On Tuesday afternoon, about four o'clock, Robert Watson, one of the lighthouse keepers on the Little Ross Island, near Kirkcudbright, having been in town purchasing provisions, left the quay on his way home in a small boat, accompanied by John Leckie, a fisherman, residing in Kirkcudbright, and his grandson, David Leckie, a boy of 14 years. Nothing was heard of these parties until between eight and nine o'clock the next morning, when a sack containing 10 stones of oatmeal was washed ashore at the Gibhill, which was identified as having been taken in the boat with them. Shortly after this the sails and mast of the boat were found along the shore. The finding of these articles aroused a suspicion that all was not right, and three men were sent down to the lighthouse to make enquiries if they had reached there, but they returned in the afternoon with the melancholy intelligence that the boat had been cast ashore near Senwick Wood, fairly split in two halves, and that no doubt existed that the whole three had met with a watery grave. Later in the evening the body of the boy was found washed ashore near Senwick churchyard. Yesterday (Thursday) several parties went in search of the other two bodies, but up to last night no word has reached the town whether they had been successful or not. It is thought in attempting to get over the bar the boat struck the ground and filled with water. Both Watson and Leckie leave large families, and great sympathy is felt for them.

THE LATE MELANCHOLY ACCIDENT AT KIRKCUDBRIGHT

The body of Mr. Watson, the lighthouse keeper, who was drowned at the Little Ross a few weeks ago, was found last Monday in the Ross Bay.

Kirkcudbright Bay is a relatively benign place compared with either Ardnamurchan or Skerryvore, but its shallow waters can be dangerous when winds and tides act against each other to generate waves. John Leckie, an experienced boatman (almost certainly the same John Leckie who stayed in the Ritson household during the 1861 census) would probably have sought to take the flood tide for the five mile passage up the estuary to Kirkcudbright. The foregoing account of the incident shows that the shopping mission had been accomplished and that the party was returning down river with the ebb tide towards Little Ross when disaster overtook them. They may have been taking a shortcut across Milton Sands on the west side of the bay and been caught by a strengthening south-easterly wind which would have slowed their progress, resulting in them perhaps being overwhelmed by breaking waves in the increasingly shallow water. That however implies that they made a misjudgement, which may not have been the case. If they had followed the channel which crosses to the east side of the bay, the same freshening wind could have easily caused them to capsize and founder while crossing the bar at the mouth of the river channel. In either case, the outcome would have been the probable swamping and destruction of their boat as it eventually grounded in the heavy seas, and broke up.

Robert Watson was buried beside his son William in the beautiful little churchyard of Senwick, on the west side of Kirkcudbright Bay, overlooking the scene of the tragedy. Many other unfortunate seafarers share the same calm and peaceful resting place, but most of their graves are unmarked. A handsome sandstone headstone over the grave of Robert and William bears the following inscription:

ERECTED
BY
MARGARET WATSON
IN MEMORY OF
her Husband Robert Watson
Lightkeeper at Little Ross who
was drowned 5th April 1864,
aged 35 years.
And their Son William R Watson
Who died 11th June 1863
aged 10 months.

On 18 May 1864, the members of the Northern Lighthouse Board met in Edinburgh, and after studying a will that Robert Watson had made in favour of his wife, authorised their secretary to make payment of the unstated amount of his insurance, to her. This would have been at least some comfort to Margaret Watson and her children, in an age when the poorhouse was an ever-present threat to most people in her unfortunate situation.

Following the tragedy, the Procurator Fiscal in Kirkcudbright sent the following letter to the secretary of the Northern Lighthouse Board:

> Procurator Fiscal's Office,
> Kirkcudbright, 19th April 1864.
>
> Sir, I have been directed by Crown counsel to whom I reported a precognition touching the death of Robert Watson Lightkeeper at Little Ross and two others by drowning, to bring under your consideration, that with a view of preventing a similar occurrence, it might be well that your Commrs. should provide a safe boat for the use of the Keepers at Little Ross, in order that their lives may not be endangered when they require to visit the mainland. The Coast betwixt Kirkcudbright and the Little Ross is often a dangerous one.
>
> I am etc. (signed) Will. Milroy Pro. Fiscal

The reply from the Board was brief and firm, but probably fair in all the circumstances:

> Northern Lighthouse Office
> Edinburgh 26th April 1864.
>
> Sir, On my return from an official absence, I have to acknowledge receipt of your letter of the 19th Curt. which I shall lay before the Commissioners of Northern Lighthouses at their first meeting. The present arrangement for Attending Boats is not one which has arisen from inadvertence. The Commissioners did supply Boats, but they found the parties so careless of what was not their own property and so reckless of damage where they did not repair, that some years ago they were induced in every instance, to make the Boat the property of the Boatman.
>
> I am etc. (Signed) Alex. Cuningham (sic) Secy.

At a subsequent meeting, the Board endorsed the opinion expressed above by their secretary, and agreed to inform the Procurator Fiscal that they saw no reason to change the practice regarding a boatman's vessel. They further stated that according to their information, the accident in question was not caused by any insufficiency of the boat, and that they did not infer from the Crown Counsel's direction that they considered that it was so.

There was clearly a high degree of public concern and grief about what had happened. The Chief Constable had also written to the Board, drawing attention to the destitution of the boatman's wife and his remaining grandson. The Board again had to inform all concerned that they had no power to apply any portion of their funds to the relief of such cases.

Archibald Turner was appointed as assistant keeper on 18 May 1864 in place of the ill-fated Robert Watson. This was Archibald's first appointment as an assistant keeper, aged 27, and he served at Little Ross until 26 April 1867, when he was transferred to the Isle of May. On the same day, Murdoch Morrison commenced duty as his replacement, but departed on leave of absence only three months later on 10 July 1867. Little information has been found about either Murdoch Morrison or the reason for his early departure from Little Ross. The 1891 census however records that a Murdo Morrison, crofter and retired lighthouse keeper, aged 60, was living at Scalpay in Harris with his wife and five children. Some of the five children were from a previous marriage, but if he was ever a keeper at Little Ross, it would have been as a single man.

Joseph Dick was then appointed as assistant keeper, arriving to take up his duties on the day that Murdoch Morrison departed. James Pithie was still principal keeper, but was transferred to Inchkeith on 5 February 1868. Joseph Dick's stay at Little Ross was relatively short, but his subsequent career was sufficiently interesting and unusual to merit extended mention. Joseph was born in Edinburgh on 12 June 1842 and the 1851 census records him living at Dildawn near Castle Douglas, where his father was a land agent. At the age of 12, Joseph was apprenticed to the Earl of Selkirk in Kirkcudbright as a gardener. The 1851 census shows that the Earl's gardener at that time was David Dick, aged 48, whose household included his elder son John, also a gardener, and two assistant gardeners, who were lodgers. It seems probable that the young Joseph was related to the Dicks and may have lived with them during the early part of an apprenticeship, which they may have helped him to secure. In 1861, the head gardener was Walter Ford, aged 27, who was in charge of four gardeners and two apprentice gardeners, and who employed one domestic servant. Joseph Dick was one of the two apprentices, and shared a bothy in the estate grounds with the other five gardening staff. St Mary's Isle Estate gardens were close to the southern end of St Mary's Isle peninsula and the lighthouse on Little Ross was prominent in the view southwards, as the lighthouse tower was on the axis of the main path and flanking borders. It is said that the young Joseph developed an ambition to be a lighthouse keeper in the early years of his apprenticeship.

He succeeded in fulfilling his ambition, and after training with the Northern Lighthouse Board at various other stations, was appointed as assistant keeper at Little Ross on 10 July 1867. On the 15 July, he was married in Penicuik, to Jessie Wilson Milne; presumably he had obtained special leave to marry before he commenced his duties. Little Ross lighthouse station was therefore his and Jessie's first home, and on 22 October 1868, it became the birthplace of their daughter, Alison. Earlier that year, the peaceful scene at Little Ross was disturbed by a minor marine calamity which must have been witnessed by the lighthouse keepers and was duly reported in the local newspaper:

Joseph Dick, courtesy of the Dick family

The smack *Nancy and Jenny* of Belfast, McIlroy Master, from Kirkcudbright to Belfast in ballast, on the 1st June drove on the rocks, off Little Ross, and has become a total wreck. The vessel is not insured.

Kirkcudbrightshire Advertiser, Friday, 12 June 1868.

At that time, the principal keeper was John Fullarton, who had been appointed on 5 February 1868. John Fullarton was a Campbeltown man who had married Margaret Conn of Kilwinning in Ayrshire in August 1845 and entered the lighthouse service on 7 January 1846. He was 52 when he came to Little Ross, and had previously been principal keeper at Noss Head, Wick.

Joseph Dick served at Little Ross for two years and three months, leaving officially on 13 October 1869. At the end of service at a particular lighthouse station, it was usual for the register of keepers to record a keeper's posting to a station in Scotland or the Isle of Man. Joseph's posting however is described as 'Japan – out of Commissioners' service'. His transfer to another country is unique in the records of Little Ross lighthouse. Periods of service not ending in transfer normally ended in either retirement or, in very rare cases, dismissal. It seems possible that Joseph Dick was either seconded or amicably transferred to Japan in a special arrangement made by the Northern Lighthouse Board.

The Government of Japan was making efforts to facilitate foreign maritime trade through, among other things, the provision of a modern system of buoys and lighthouses in their coastal waters. The British Ambassador to Japan, Sir Harry Parkes, is believed to have recommended the Stevenson family firm as suitable engineers and advisors to assist in this task, and they were instrumental in their associate, Richard Henry Brunton from Aberdeenshire, being appointed to lead the project. Joseph Dick is believed to have been part of the team selected by Richard Brunton, in consultation with the Stevensons, to travel to Japan with him and to carry out the necessary work.

In the next few years, Joseph settled very well into a new way of life and work in Japan. He became involved in the training of lighthouse keepers and he assisted Richard Henry Brunton in the construction and maintenance of some 25 lighthouses, including Tunoshima, which is now a museum to Japan's lighthouse service. In Tunoshima Lighthouse Museum there is a desk and Japanese chessboard that were used by Joseph, and a sculpture of him sitting at his desk.

Joseph Dick prospered in Japan, and after his lighthouse service ended, he engaged first in taking charge of signalling for the new Japanese railway system on Richard Henry Brunton's recommendation, and then in trading, importing, and exporting. Joseph's business prospered partly because of the Sino-Japanese and Russo-Japanese wars and Japan's consequent need for the charter of ships from overseas. These wars of course caused great hardship in all the countries involved; many Japanese families suffered losses, temporary absence of breadwinners, and there were ever-increasing numbers of orphans. Joseph Dick is said to have been concerned about this state of affairs and to have used some of his wealth to personally distribute rice and other basic foodstuffs to the needy.

Joseph's wife Jessie appears to have been less happy in Japan however, and eventually returned permanently to Scotland in 1875 with her children, Alison, Joseph (born on 8 March 1870 in Penicuik), John (born on 12 January 1872 in Yokohama), and Catherine Sharpe (born on 10 December 1873 in Yokohama). Joseph Junior's birth in Penicuik implies that Jessie must have made a previous return visit to Scotland. After Jessie Dick's final departure with her family, Joseph Dick took a Japanese 'wife', Fuji, daughter of Samurai Oida, by whom he had three children (a boy and two girls). After an early upbringing in accordance with Japanese tradition, they were educated to Western standards and were made familiar generally with a Western way of life. Joseph never returned to Scotland to visit his legitimate wife and family, but according to family sources, kept in contact with Jessie by occasional letter, always addressing her as 'my dear wife'. The census of 1891 records his 'dear' wife Jessie living with her mother and sister in Penicuik, while employed as a lady's nurse. His daughter Alison had married James Borrowman and was living in Penicuik. Joseph Junior was a plumber living in lodgings in Falkirk, John Dick was a 'van-man' in Penicuik, and Catherine Sharpe Dick was a paper mill worker at Calendar's mill in Penicuik. It is understood from family members that Joseph did send at least some money home to his wife and family, but it does not appear that they shared to any great extent in his prosperity and status.

The following obituary for Joseph Dick was taken from an unidentified cutting in a Japanese magazine, probably the *Japan Chronicle,* which was published in Kobe, in English, between 1902 and 1940:

By the death of Mr. J. Dick at his residence in Kobe on Friday, after a long illness, another link between Old and New Japan is broken. Mr. Dick arrived in Japan in 1869, and never left the country he settled in as a young man of twenty-seven. For about 35 years, Mr. Dick resided in Kobe, and until a couple of years ago was hale and hearty. After one or two brief spells of illness, which his strong physique was able to resist, Mr. Dick was taken seriously ill on January 4th last while on his way home from his store. He was carried home and put to bed, and he never left the house again, though he was able to get up and read and talk to his friends. In spite of his convalescence, however, it was realised that the end was not far off. The cause of death, we believe was a complication of brain and stomach trouble.

Mr. Dick was born at Corstorphine in Scotland, on June 12th 1842, and was thus in his 73rd year when he died. As a lad of 12 he left home to serve his apprenticeship as a gardener on the estate of the Earl of Selkirk on St Mary's Isle, and it was one Sunday afternoon, on seeing a lighthouse nearby, that he made up his mind to become a lighthouse keeper. He learned the duties at the Little Ross and the Mull of Galloway lighthouses, and went back to gardening until he was old enough to qualify for the post. He was eventually called up for service as assistant at the Bell Rock light, but soon after the assistant at Little Ross light was drowned, and Mr. Dick was appointed in his place. In 1859 Sir Harry Parkes sent from Tokyo to the British Government asking for men to volunteer to come out to Japan for five years as lighthouse keepers, and Mr. Dick was one of the men who volunteered and whose application was accepted. Accordingly Mr. Dick, accompanied by his wife, came out to Japan, where his first duty was to assist in superintending the erection of the lighthouse at Shigame, in Tokyo Bay. One of Mr. Dick's reminiscences — and the one he was proudest to recall — was in connection with the visits of his late Majesty to the lighthouse. The Emperor showed the greatest interest in the building and apparatus, and thoroughly inspected every room. From Shigame Mr. Dick proceeded to Rock Island in Tokyo bay, and after being there a year was sent to Oshima. There were no steamers running in those days, and the voyage by junk took him a fortnight. After various other appointments, Mr. Dick went to Noshima in 1877. In a severe typhoon that year three barques were wrecked nearby, one of them a German ship, the 'Madagascar.' From this ship four men were saved, one of them - Bruhn - later on became Mr. Dick's partner in business. A German warship came along shortly after, having heard of the wrecks, and picked up all the survivors and took them to Yokohama. In recognition of the services rendered by Mr. Dick to the crew of the German barque, the German Government presented him with a pair of binoculars and a complimentary address.

In April 1870 Mr. Dick came to Kobe. There being no more work to do just then in instructing Japanese lightkeepers, he was sent south to assist in the work of laying the telegraph lines from Kobe to Osaka. This work was in charge of Mr. George Gilbert, but on Mr. Dick's arrival Mr. Gilbert went north and finished the Yokohama-Tokyo lines. After a few more years in the service of the Japanese Government as a lighthouse keeper Mr. Dick retired, and in 1880 joined the firm of G. Dormany and Co., compradores of Yokohama. Later he came to Kobe and joined Langfeldt's and in 1885 started in business on his own account as a ship's chandler. Soon afterwards he was joined by the man whom ten years earlier he had picked up shipwrecked, with 'nothing more on him than he was born with,' as Mr. Dick used to say – Mr. Bruhn. The partnership was quite successful, but came to a tragic termination. Mr. Bruhn married and went home for a holiday, but dropped down dead from heart disease, the very night he set foot in Heligoland, which was his birthplace. The firm of Dick, Bruhn and Co., however was continued, and the senior partner took an active part in the business up to a couple of years ago.

Mr. Dick was a man of genial disposition, and was greatly respected by all who knew him. He had a vast store of reminiscences of early days in Japan, especially in regard to matters connected with ships and sailors, and he was probably one of the best known men longshore in this part of the world. Mr. Dick was a sturdy old Scotsman of a type such as is rarely met with so far away from the Highlands, and the humble but useful part he played in educating Old Japan was his proudest recollection.

In 1875 Mrs. Dick left Oshima with the children for home, and has since resided in Scotland.

The funeral took place on Saturday afternoon, Pere Fage officiating. Mr. Olsen, deceased's partner in business was the chief mourner.

In the mid-1860s, Japan was a developing country, having for example, no paved roads, no iron ships, and no lighthouses. The Europeans who were brought in to help introduce new technology included many Scots who occupied important positions. Joseph Dick had no education beyond basic elementary school and was certainly not an engineer, but in Japan he came to be regarded as a Western expert and was rewarded accordingly. Despite his lack of formal training, he must have stood out among his colleagues and shown great personality and promise to be selected by the Stevensons and Richard Henry Brunton for such an important and high profile mission. One can quite see why, following the practical end of his marriage, he did not return to Scotland, where he would have been most unlikely to have risen beyond the status of a principal lighthouse keeper.

Donald McKerrell was appointed as Joseph Dick's replacement on 12 August 1869. Little Ross was his first posting as an assistant keeper, aged 23. Since the date of Joseph Dick's transfer to Japan is recorded as being 13 October 1869, it seems likely that Joseph had actually left Little Ross on or about the 12 August. This would also make reports of his arrival in Japan in 1869 more credible. Principal keeper John Fullarton was transferred to Cromarty on 15 March 1871. His successor at Little Ross was William A. McKay, who took up his duties on the same day, having been promoted from the post of assistant keeper at the Mull of Galloway. The 1871 census recorded the following people being resident on Little Ross at the date of the census:

> William A. Mackay, aged 36, unmarried, principal lighthouse keeper, born: Reay in Caithness. Elizabeth Mackay, aged 30, housekeeper, sister of William A. Mackay, born: Reay in Caithness. Donald McKerrell, aged 25, married, assistant lighthouse keeper, born: Islay, Argyllshire. Elizabeth McKerrell, aged 23, wife of Donald McKerrell, born: Stoneykirk in Wigtownshire.

Donald McKerrell and his wife were transferred from Little Ross to the Point of Ayre, Isle of Man, on 19 July 1872 and went on to serve at Canonry and Tarbetness until Donald retired on 6 December 1901. John Martin commenced duty as his replacement on 18 July 1872. He had previously served at the Isle of May and Auskerry, but was only at Little Ross for a year and three months before resigning from the lighthouse service on 16 October 1873 due to ill-health, aged only 27. George Craig took over as assistant keeper six days later and remained in that position until his transfer to Buchan Ness on 8 August 1879. Little is known about George Craig, but his name and that of principal keeper William McKay each appear in registers recently discovered in the head office of the Northern Lighthouse Board, which record the names of the occupants of each lighthouse station, the distance they had to travel to attend church, and the number of times they attended church in the years 1873 and 1875. William McKay attended Borgue Parish Church six times in 1873 and seven times in 1875. George Craig attended twice in 1873, and nine times in 1875.

William Gilmour then stepped into the role of assistant keeper on the same day that George Craig departed. The explanation for so many transfers and replacements occurring successfully on the same day is that keepers, their families, and their possessions would normally arrive and depart on board the same lighthouse supply vessel. By that means, if there was bad weather, the transfer might occur later than the keepers had hoped for, but the light would never be without two guardians, other than in the direst of circumstances.

The 1881 census records the inhabitants of the two households on Little Ross as being:

> William McKay, unmarried, aged 46 principal lighthouse Keeper, born: Reay, Caithness. Elizabeth McKay, sister of William McKay, unmarried, aged 42, Housekeeper, born: Reay in Caithness (Elizabeth had seemingly gained an additional two years in age over the previous decade). William Gilmour, unmarried aged 24, lightkeeper and seaman, born: Kirkmaiden, Wigtownshire. Jane Gilmour, sister of William Gilmour, aged 28, unmarried, born: Kirkmaiden, Wigtownshire.

An eyebrow or two might be raised at the fact that two unmarried brothers were living with their two unmarried sisters on a remote island. Probably however, like many other lighthouse family members, Jane and Elizabeth were merely waiting patiently for the right unmarried assistant or, better still, principal keeper to come into their lives. Their only other prospects of romance would seem to have arisen from the weekly visit of the attendant boatman, or the annual visit of the Northern Lighthouse Board supply ship and her crew.

CHAPTER 9

The Keepers and their Families, 1882–1919

In 1882 William McKay's stay at Little Ross exceeded the ten years served by Robert Burnett, making William the longest serving keeper at Little Ross. Assistant keeper William Gilmour was transferred to the Butt of Lewis in the Outer Hebrides on 16 January 1883 and was replaced by Robert McIntosh on 2 February 1883. Robert had entered the lighthouse service on 9 February 1880, aged 25, and had previously served at the Butt of Lewis. William McKay finally left Little Ross on 21 January 1884, bound for Lismore lighthouse, off Lismore Island in the Firth of Lorne, after twelve years and ten months on the island. In that time he must have become familiar with every corner, every rock, and every nook and cranny of his tiny domain. His cumulative knowledge and experience of the tides, currents, horticulture, and the wildlife of Little Ross Island would be second to none and yet nothing is known about him, his thoughts or his aspirations. Like the great majority of lighthouse keepers, he apparently quietly got on with his job, always ready for, but never knowing, when his next transfer would occur. His replacement, James Ferrier, had arrived on 18 January 1884. James had been born in Arbroath in 1842 and was one of ten children. The birthplaces of the ten children in Kirkmaiden, Arbroath, and Bute provide clues to the fact that their father, Lawrence Ferrier was also a lighthouse keeper. James had entered the lighthouse service on 16 March 1864. He married Elizabeth Boa in 1868, at Kilmory on Arran, and their first two children were born at Pladda lighthouse. At the time of James and Elizabeth's arrival at Little Ross, they had four children, Walter, Lawrence, John, and Christina, and it is assumed that they were all also residents at Little Ross.

The periods of service of James Ferrier and William McKay overlapped by a few days, so James had an opportunity to be briefed by a man who was more familiar than anyone else with the island and its lighthouse. After a little over two years at Little Ross, James Ferrier was transferred to Noss Head, near Wick, on 5 March 1886 and Neil McDonald took over as principal keeper on the same day.

According to *Bartholomew's Gazetteer*, the population of Little Ross in 1887 was six people. Neil McDonald was married but had no children at that time, so it seems likely that Robert McIntosh must have had both a wife and family.

Early in January 1891, in an attempt to reduce the time taken in sending aid to vessels in danger in the vicinity of Little Ross, the lighthouse keepers there, Neil McDonald and Robert McIntosh were supplied with rockets for use as distress signals.

Robert McIntosh was transferred to Chicken Rock, Isle of Man, on 11 March 1891, later serving at another rock station, Skervuile lighthouse, to the east of Jura. On 12 March, Simon Fraser, who had previously been based at Port St Mary, Isle of Man, was appointed as assistant keeper and the national census for 1891 recorded that the eight inhabitants of Little Ross were:

Neil McDonald, principal lighthouse keeper, aged xx, born: Tiree, Argyllshire. Elizabeth McDonald, wife, aged 39, born: Isle of Man. Maggie Ann Caley, niece, aged 20, unmarried, born: 18/1/1871, Bride, Isle of Man. Neil McDonald and Elizabeth Joughin had been married at Bride, Isle of Man on 21st June 1871 (Bride is close to the Point of Ayre Lighthouse). Simon Fraser, assistant lighthouse keeper, aged 34, born Tarbat, Ross shire. Jessie Fraser, m.s. Robertson, wife, aged 34, born Tarbat Ross shire. Margaret Fraser, daughter, aged 7, scholar, born: Isle of Noss, Bressay, Shetland. James Fraser, son, aged 5? Scholar, born: Tain, Ross shire. Isobel Fraser, daughter, aged 6 months, born: 13/9/1890 Port St. Mary, Isle of Man.

Principal keeper Neil McDonald must have been contacted by the Rev. William Andson regarding assistance with research work. The Rev. William Andson was joint librarian of Dumfries and Galloway Natural History and Antiquarian Society and had a keen interest in meteorology. The following entry in the society's journal illustrates yet another example of the careful and patient work occasionally carried out by lighthouse keepers in addition to their official duties:

Transactions of Journal of Proceedings
Dumfriesshire and Galloway
Natural History and Antiquarian Society
1890–1891
Observations on the temperature of the River Dee and its estuary
during the past year, by the Rev. William Andson

Rev. Mr. Andson read a paper embodying the results of observations on the temperature of the River Dee at Tongland, taken by the Rev. W. I. Gordon, and of its estuary taken by Mr. Macdonald, lighthouse keeper on the island of Little Ross….. the observations in this case (Little Ross) were taken daily, for a whole year, from 1st August 1889 to 31st July 1880.

The number of inhabitants of Little Ross increased temporarily in early October 1891, when a small trading vessel came to grief on the island. Her captain and his crew were reluctant visitors there and were lucky to have escaped with their lives:

WRECK OF A SMACK

On Sunday last the smack *Lady Buckley* went ashore on the Little Ross near Kirkcudbright, where she remains a total wreck. The *Lady Buckley,* a smack of 37 tons register, under the command of William Thomas was bound from Bangor to Silloth with a cargo of slates. She left Bangor on the 23rd September but was forced into Ramsey Bay by stress of weather. Leaving there on 31st September, she encountered a hurricane, and a heavy sea washing over her carried her boat against the pump which was rendered useless. On Sunday morning the Master observed that the smack had sprung a leak, and being in the vicinity of Little Ross, he beached her there. Both vessel and cargo are fully insured.

Kirkcudbrightshire Advertiser, Friday, 9 October 1891.

Simon Fraser was transferred to Covesea, Lossiemouth, on 18 May 1893. His replacement as assistant keeper was James Gair, who took up his duties at Little Ross on the same day. Neil McDonald was transferred to Cape Wrath on 6 July 1893 and Peter Nicholson was appointed principal keeper at Little Ross on the following day. Peter Nicholson was transferred to Rona lighthouse, to the north of Raasay, on 19 Dec 1895 and Donald Georgeson was appointed as principal keeper at Little Ross on the same day.

Donald Georgeson was born in Caithness on 6 May 1842, and he and his elder brother Alexander were both destined to become lighthouse keepers. Donald married Isabella Watt on 17 July 1867, establishing yet another link in the complex relationships of the Northern Lighthouse Board's employees, as Isabella Watt's father, William, was first officer of the Leith-based supply ship *Pharos.* Most, or perhaps all, of their seven children had been born in lighthouses at North Ronaldsay in Orkney, Chanonry, near Rosemarkie on the Black Isle, Unst (Muckle Flugga) in Shetland, Monach, to the west of North Uist, and Mull, and there are indications that Annie S. Georgeson, Isabella Wilson Georgeson, and Fred Georgeson lived with their parents at Little Ross. Their second son, Hugh Fitzsimons Georgeson, was probably named after Hugh Fitzsimons who had been principal keeper at Little Ross from 1852 to 1859. Hugh Fitzsimons had been married to Jessie Watt who may have been related to Isabella Watt. A fourth son, Alexander, died in a tragic accident at Rona Lighthouse near Raasay just two months before Donald Georgeson was transferred to Little Ross. Alexander, aged only ten years, had fallen from a steep staircase in the ruins of Raasay Castle and died almost instantly on 21 October 1895. The exchange of Donald Georgeson and Peter Nicholson as principal keepers at Rona and Little Ross was perhaps made in recognition of the distress the Georgeson family must have felt at seeing the castle on Raasay as a constant reminder of the tragedy that had occurred there.

It is during the period of service by Donald Georgeson that the first indication is given of a hobby or leisure activity engaged in by a keeper at Little Ross. There was little time for the following of such pursuits, and few of them that could be undertaken during the long hours of watch-keeping without detriment to duty. One such activity however was ornithology. The process of removing dead birds from the lantern balcony and from the roofs of the houses below would have been hard to carry out without making some observation of the astonishing diversity of wild birds found among the casualties. In the following extract from an 1885 magazine article, the writer pays tribute to the quality of the information submitted by Donald Georgeson while he was stationed at the Monach Isles, earlier in his career:

> Monach Isles.-Donald Georgeson—Three quarterly schedules. Mr. Georgeson's schedules are able and masterly; and if we could have all our schedules returned in a similar epitomised condition, no doubt much time might be saved; but in the meantime, schedules coming from a few stations out of so many stations, so epitomised, whilst the rest adhere rigidly to the columnar arrangement, makes it more troublesome to arrange details. Uniform attention to the columnar arrangement is simplest for the ledger work.

> *Report on the Migration of Birds in the Spring and Autumn of 1885*, by J. A. Harvie-Brown, Mr. J. Cordeaux, Mr. R. Barrington, Mr. A.G. More and Mr. W. Eagle Clarke. Seventh Report, (Vol II, No 2, 1885)

> Edinburgh: Printed by McFarlane & Erskine, 14 and 19 St. James Square (1886). Price Two Shillings.

James Gair was transferred to the slender and beautiful lighthouse at Auskerry, off Stronsay in the Orkney Islands on 8 August 1898 and Robert Murray Anderson was appointed as assistant keeper on the same day. This was Robert's first posting with the lighthouse service; he had previously been employed as a fisherman. On the 3 October 1899, Robert married Ann Sutherland at Whalsey Manse in their native Shetland. Principal keeper Donald Georgeson retired on 14 June 1900 and George Irvine was appointed principal keeper, again on the same day. George had entered the lighthouse service in 1884.

Little Ross's population in 1901 consisted of six people:

George Irvine, married, aged 44, principal lighthouse keeper, born: Isle of Man. Jessie Irvine, wife, aged 42, born: Govan, Lanarkshire. Mary Irvine, daughter, aged 8, scholar, born: Govan, Lanarkshire. Georgina Irvine, daughter, aged 2, born: Islay, Argyllshire. Robert Anderson, married, aged 25, lighthouse keeper, born: Skerries, Shetland. Annie Anderson, wife, aged 23, born Skerries, Shetland.

Assistant keeper Robert Murray Anderson was transferred to the Flannan Isles on 19 May 1904, and on the same day, Mr. R. Watt was appointed in his place but was dismissed on 26 October 1904, after which, John Hugh McLeod was appointed as assistant keeper on 2 December 1904. John Hugh McLeod had entered the lighthouse service on 25 June 1901 and brought with him to Little Ross the useful skill of having been a blacksmith to trade. If he retained any affection for his previous trade, he would have been delighted to find that his new station was equipped with a complete and functional forge. Hugh had married Mary-Ann Bisset on 17 June 1904 at Crimond in Aberdeenshire and their first son, also named John Hugh McLeod, arrived while John was serving at Little Ross, the baby being born at Crimond on 8 September 1906.

Principal keeper George Irvine was transferred to Hoy High lighthouse, Isle of Graemsay, Orkney, on 11 December 1906 and Robert Brown took over as principal keeper on the same day.

On 31 March 1908, the Kirkcudbright lifeboat *Hugh and Ann* was launched to take Kirkcudbright's Dr. John MacMyn to Little Ross to attend a lighthouse keeper's wife in labour in a strong west-south-westerly breeze:

> One of the last services rendered by the *Hugh and Ann* is so unique that it deserves chronicle: For the wife of one of the lighthouse keepers, the hour of travail was fast approaching, but the sea was rough and hazardous for the doctor to cross from mainland to the island in an open boat. It was stern necessity however and human life was at stake. The distress flag was run up for the Kirkcudbright lifeboat, for the Ross Lighthouse is a signalling station as well, and the doctor was taken across the stormy waters in this most unusual way. All ended happily. The child was a boy, and rejoices in the name of Hugh, as some recognition of the *Hugh and Ann,* and the part she played in his entry into the world.
>
> From *The Galloway Lifeboat Service,* by Dr. J. Maxwell Wood in the Gallovidian, about 1908.

The last sentence in this report sadly seems to be either fanciful or based on inaccurate reporting. A baby boy was indeed born at Little Ross lighthouse on 31 March 1908 at 10.30am. His parents were John Hugh MacLeod and Mary Ann Macleod, née Bissett. The birth was registered at Borgue on 18 April, but the baby's name was Joseph B. MacLeod rather than Hugh. The reporter may have been confused by the coincidental presence of the names Hugh and Ann in the parents' full names. The lifeboat *Hugh and Ann*, a sailing and pulling vessel, was in service from 1887 until 1910, when she was replaced by the last sailing and pulling lifeboat at Kirkcudbright, the *George Gordon Moir.*

Assistant keeper John Hugh McLeod was transferred to Chicken Rock, Isle of Man, on 26 May 1910; on the same day, George Mackie succeeded him at Little Ross. Robert Brown was principal keeper at that time, but he was transferred to the Isle of Ornsay, near Skye, on 23 October 1910, and his duties at Little Ross were taken over by James Mercer McCulloch on 2 November 1910. James M. McCulloch, a cabinet maker to trade, was born in Coldingham in Berwickshire, and was the son of a lighthouse keeper, David McCulloch. James was 44 years old

The RNLB 'Hugh and Ann', courtesy of the Stewartry Museum

and a single man when he came to Little Ross. In 1912, a local lady, Agnes Gillone was employed there as his housekeeper.

It is not known whether George Mackie followed an initiative by his superior officer James M. McCulloch, or whether he was the instigator, but both men cooperated in the study of ornithology and submitted their observations to *The Scottish Naturalist*, the editors of which included observations from Little Ross in their annual 'Report on Scottish Ornithology' for several subsequent years.

Principal keeper James M. McCulloch and assistant keeper George Mackie reported to *The Scottish Naturalist* the following extensive range of birds sighted at Little Ross during 1914:

Starling, Yellow Hammer, skylark, tree-pipit, pied wagtail, goldcrest, spotted flycatcher, willow warbler, blackcap, whitethroat, fieldfare, missel thrush, thrush, redwing, blackbird, wheatear, whinchat, redbreast, wigeon, oystercatcher, golden plover, lapwing, curlew, snipe, jack snipe, water rail.

Information taken from 'Report on Scottish Ornithology in 1914' published in *The Scottish Naturalist* No. 43, July 1915.

George Mackie, courtesy of Catherine Quirk

125

James Mercer McCulloch was transferred to Inchkeith Island in the Firth of Forth in December 1914, and William Begg or Beggs (he used both spellings at different times in his life) was appointed as principal keeper at Little Ross on 22 December 1914, following his transfer from Inchkeith.

Earlier in his career, William Begg had been selected to replace James Ducat as principal keeper at the Flannan Islands after the mysterious disappearance of all the keepers at that station in December 1900. One imagines that the Northern Lighthouse Board would have had a difficult task in deciding what to do in the aftermath of a disaster that still provokes great speculation and a never-ending stream of outrageously contrived suggested explanations. The new principal keeper would have had to be someone in whom the Board had complete confidence, not only in his technical ability, but also in his courage and management skills in holding together the spirits of his assistant keepers.

William Begg was evidently a highly experienced man when he arrived at Little Ross. Born in Portpatrick in 1857, he had served at lighthouse stations on Mull, the Isle of Man, Inchkeith, and probably other places in addition to the Flannan Islands. While stationed at the Isle of Man, he took part in the particularly daring rescue of three of the crew of the schooner *Lyra*:

SCHOONER WRECKED AT PORT ST MARY. THE CAPTAIN DROWNED: THREE MEN RESCUED BY THE PORT ERIN LIFEBOAT.

Castletown Lifeboat – Wreck of the Schooner "Lyra" 1888

Driven before the fierce wind and no less violent sea, the schooner went with a fearful crash on to the Carrick, and with the aid of glasses there could be seen from the shore several men clinging to the rigging, and repeatedly covered by the waves which swept clean over the vessel. The enforced inactivity and helplessness of those on shore, whilst waiting for the lifeboat, grew unendurable, and, with a courage that cannot be too highly praised, a number of men put off from inside the pier in a harbour boat, rowing double manned oars. The names of these brave fellows are–Wm. Kelly, coxswain (owner of the boat), who resides in Port St Mary; Wm. Watterson of Cregneish; Joseph Kinvig of Cregneish; Wm. Watterson of Howe; J. J. Sansbury, banker, Port St Mary, H. Creggen, John Shimmin of Glenchass; and W. Begg, one of the Chicken Rock lighthouse keepers who happened to be ashore on leave.

Manx Sun, 7 January 1888.

By 1914, William Begg was a married man with ten children and was accompanied to Little Ross by his wife Julianna. It is not known if any of their children were full-time residents at Little Ross, but many of them stayed there for holidays and more prolonged visits, particularly their daughter, Catherine Sheila Eversfield Begg (always known as Eva), who had been born at the Sound of Mull lighthouse in 1891. William Begg was already known as an enthusiastic and extremely knowledgeable ornithologist and was a frequent contributor to the *Galloway Gazette* on the subject. His grandson also reports that William contributed many articles to what was then the *Manchester Guardian*.

William Begg, courtesy of Ian Begg and Catherine Quirk

William Begg and George Mackie reported to *The Scottish Naturalist* birds sighted at Little Ross during 1915. The list consisted of:

Black redstart, Snowy owl, Kittiwake, Raven, Peregrine falcon, Rook, Jackdaw, Starling, Green finch, Linnet, Chaffinch, Skylark, Rock pipit, Grey wagtail, White wagtail, Blue titmouse, Goldcrest, Chiff chaff, Willow warbler, Sedge warbler, Garden warbler, Whitethroat, Fieldfare, Missel thrush, Thrush, Redwing, Blackbird, Wheatear, Greater wheatear, Redstart, Redbreast, Hedge Sparrow, Wren, Swift, Kestrel, Greylag goose, Brent goose, Oystercatcher, Ringed plover, Golden plover, Lapwing, Knot, Curlew, Whimbrel, Snipe, Woodcock, Common tern, Corncrake.

Information taken from 'Report on Scottish Ornithology in 1915', published in the *The Scottish Naturalist* No. 54, June 1916.

William Begg's interest in natural history was not restricted to ornithology, and he also contributed valuable information to *The Scottish Naturalist* concerning the insect life on Little Ross:

In September, Mr. W. Begg, formerly stationed at Inchkeith, kindly sent about forty moths (representing twelve species) and a beetle from Little Ross lighthouse, on the coast of Kirkcudbrightshire. These were especially welcome, seeing they came from a station not previously on the contributing list.

Taken during the summer, prior to 15th September: Moths : Leucania pallens; Xylophasia polyodon; Charaeas graminis; Agrotis strigula; Noctua xanthographa; Triphaena pronuba; Amphipyra tragopogonis; Xanthia flavago (silago); Cirrhoedia xerampelina; Calymnia trapezina; Plusia gamma. Dung Beetle: Aphodins rufipes.

From 'Lepidoptera etc at Scottish Lighthouses in 1915', by William Evans FRSE, *The Scottish Naturalist,* No. 54, June 1916.

On 28 January 1916, the daily routine of the inhabitants of Little Ross was dramatically interrupted when the 60 ton schooner *Charles* of Gatehouse of Fleet, bound from Whitehaven to her home port with a cargo of coal, was stranded on the east side of the island in 'half a gale' from the south. Kirkcudbright lifeboat crew were on their way to the boathouse when they were told that the schooner's crew of two had got ashore safely on the island and were in the care of the lighthouse keepers. It was therefore decided that the lifeboat's services were no longer required. The sight of the *Charles* nearing the Ross would be a familiar one to William Begg and George Mackie, and they must have been very shocked if they witnessed her being driven on to the rocky eastern shore of the island. The *Galloway News* of Friday 4 February 1916 provided the following account of the incident:

> The members of Kirkcudbright Lifeboat crew did some quick work on Friday morning. At ten minutes past nine, Superintendent Robertson had telephone intimation from the Ross lighthouse of the wreck of the *Charles* schooner. He at once warned Coxswain Parkhill, and within a very short time the bursting of two rockets summoned the crew, and they were hurried off to the boat in a conveyance from the Royal Hotel. Fortunately their services were not required, as the two men on the schooner were lucky enough to effect their own landing on the Ross Island, but the lifeboat crew had at any rate done enough to show that they were 'ready, aye ready'.

The Northern Lighthouse Board's rules were very precise in covering situations such as this. If on duty at the time, keepers were not allowed to leave their posts to offer assistance and were expected merely to observe and report accordingly. To the credit of the Board, it seems those rules were interpreted with a degree of unofficial flexibility, as there are records of keepers receiving awards for bravery in their attempts to rescue potential victims of similar incidents.

The arrival of 23-year-old Catherine (Eva) Begg at Little Ross just before Christmas 1914 must have made an impression on assistant keeper George Mackie, as despite an age difference of 19 years, they were married on 25 February 1916 at Borgue Manse, by the Rev. W. J. Pennell. Their courtship on the island, living in adjacent houses and constantly under the watchful eyes of superior officer William and his wife Georgianna, must have required discretion, restraint, and perhaps even a degree of daring.

On 5 September 1916, Catherine (Eva) Mackie gave birth to a daughter, Mary. The timing of Mary's birth in relation to the date of George and Catherine's wedding was probably the source of some tension between George and his father-in-law, who may not always have made George's life easy. Family members report that a copy of George and Catherine's wedding certificate in their possession has had the date altered in George's hand to 1915, which is evidence of his discomfiture at the situation.

At the time of Mary's birth, George commenced a personal diary, which he continued to write in regularly for the next 20 years. The diary is concerned almost entirely with family matters of relatively minor consequence, mingled with occasional remarks on the awful progress of the First World War as interpreted from the peaceful isolation of Little Ross. No mention is made of matters ornithological, or of ships and boats which passed the island, and only rare reference is made to people who visited. Nevertheless, George's observations, his religious faith, and his deep concern for the welfare of his children provide a rare insight to a lighthouse keeper's hopes and fears. Shocking revelations about his childhood help to explain the intensity of his focus on the care of his own children, and hence the degree of his loneliness during their occasional absences. Although nothing specific is said, it seems evident that his relationship with principal keeper James McCulloch was much better than that with his father-in-law William Begg, which was perhaps inevitable in the circumstances. They nevertheless managed not only to live and work together, but also to cooperate in their spare time to prepare the most meticulously detailed information before or since about the island's birdlife and some of its insects. George's relationship with all the other Begg family members seems to have been an excellent one, and he makes many references in his diary to their kindness and assistance.

In 1916, principal keeper William Begg and assistant keeper George Mackie reported to *The Scottish Naturalist* the following birds sighted at Little Ross:

> Siberian chiff chaff, Raven, Jackdaw, Starling, Chaffinch, Skylark, Meadow pipit, Yellow wagtail, Grey wagtail, Blue titmouse, Goldcrest, Pied flycatcher, Chiff chaff, Sedge warbler, Garden warbler, Whitethroat, Lesser whitethroat, Fieldfare, Missel thrush, Thrush, Redwing, Blackbird, Redbreast, Wren, Nightjar, Wryneck, Shelldrake, Tufted duck, Storm petrel, Oystercatcher, Ringed plover, Golden plover, Lapwing, Turnstone, Sanderling, Knot, Dunlin, Redshank, Curlew, Whimbrel, Snipe, Common tern, Water rail.

> Information taken from 'Report on Scottish Ornithology in 1916', *The Scottish Naturalist* No. 66, June 1917.

One of William Begg's sightings in 1917 was particularly enthusiastically received by the editors of *The Scottish Naturalist*, who added their comments on the importance of his observation:

Siberian Chiff Chaff (Phylloscapus collybita tristis) at Little Ross Lighthouse, Kirkcudbrightshire:

On the morning of 3rd December 1916 with a light breeze from the north-east and a drizzle of rain, and haze, there were numerous birds at the lantern at Little Ross. Curlews, Lapwings, Redwings, Fieldfares, Thrushes, Larks, Knots, Golden Plover and Snipe were plentiful, also various other waders. I was out capturing a curlew when I saw a tiny warbler fluttering against the lantern. On examination, I saw it was something uncommon, as the lateness of the season led me to expect, I therefore sent it to Miss Rintoul and Miss Baxter, who inform me that it is a Siberian Chiff Chaff.

William Begg, Little Ross Lighthouse.

[This is a very interesting and important record, being the first time this little visitor from the East has been recorded from South West Scotland. It has been known to occur on the Orkney and Shetland Islands and the Isle of May, but with the exception of Sule Skerry, there is no record from the West, nor has it hitherto been noted as far south in Scotland as Kirkcudbrightshire – Eds.]

From *The Scottish Naturalist* Vol. 61, January, edited by William Eagle Clarke, Williams Evans, Percy H. Grimshaw (1917).

This article by William Begg demonstrates both his extensive knowledge and his ability to write about a subject he clearly loved:

AUTUMN MIGRATION AT LITTLE ROSS LIGHTHOUSE, KIRKCUDBRIGHTSHIRE.

Summer with its genial glow has fled, so also have the summer birds; the woods are vacant, the hedgerows deserted; the orchard where once were life and song is now all quietness, not a chirrup nor a twitter is now heard. The time has arrived, the instinct gifted by Nature tells the birds, that they must leave this northern clime and seek their southern winter quarters. The geographical position of the island of Little Ross renders it among the most favoured stations in Scotland for observing the departure in autumn of our own breeding birds; with these, migration begins very early as soon as the middle of August. Amongst the commonest migrants at this time are Willow-warblers, Whitethroats, Spotted Flycatchers, Garden-warblers, Sedge-warblers, Robins, and Corncrakes. I sent the Robins that were killed at the lantern for inspection, and they proved to be of the British race, so were evidently our own birds going south. One might raise the question, why do they migrate so early? It can't be for want of food: insect life is abundant for insect-eaters, and seeds of all kinds plentiful for seed-eaters. Their migration flight takes place when the weather is still warm and genial, therefore it cannot be cold nor want of food which prompts this early departure. Another of our earliest migrants is the Swallow: it is a traveller by day. In all my service in the lighthouses, which is now thirty-two years, I have never seen a Swallow amongst other birds at the lanterns, but during the day they rest here in thousands; they care not whether the winds are strong or light, weather conditions don't seem to matter; they go on their long flight, feeding as they fly, towards their southern clime.

After these early movements migration goes on steadily throughout September and October and into November; in the first-named month all the above-mentioned species, as well as Chiffchaffs, Redstarts, Thrushes, and many others, are common at the lantern on suitable nights. All the Thrushes got early in the season belonged to the British race, though one that I got in November 1916 (and doubtless many others in the big rushes late in the season) was of Continental origin. This species is always very numerous on suitable nights: sometimes they darken the rays, and the death-roll is often enormous.

From the end of September onwards, Redwings are nightly visitors, and when weather conditions are suitable, they, like the Thrush, are very numerous, and the death-rate is always large: the court below, the tops of the flat roofs, and all round about, are literally strewn with the dead. Then come the scavengers : Kestrels and Gulls appear and make a clean sweep, the Gulls picking them up as a hen picks corn. Fieldfares and Blackbirds too are very numerous on migration, and many are killed at the light. This season has been a record here for Ring-ouzels ; as many as fourteen have been counted sitting round the lantern at a time, whereas for previous seasons just an occasional visitor would be recorded. Missel-thrushes I find erratic in their movements one night very numerous, then on the following night only a few; again, several nights pass and only an occasional one will be seen, then a big rush may occur and many will be killed.

Finches and Linnets gather here for a day or two in great flocks, then proceed in undulating flights to the South: they are daylight travellers, and prefer a light easterly wind and clear atmosphere. The Grey, Pied, and White Wagtails travel principally by day; their movements and those of the Wheatear were stronger this autumn than I have ever seen. The Wheatear seems to me to travel both by day and night, I have seen them passing in great numbers over the island on a southern course during the day, and at night in numbers round the lantern. Robins and Wrens have been unusually plentiful on migration this autumn, being regular visitors to the lantern, and up to the time of writing (mid-November) a great many Wrens are still on the island. An interesting visitor came during the third week of November this year, namely, a Wryneck, which struck the lantern and was killed; it seems a late date for this species to occur so far north. Golden Plover and Lapwings are at times very numerous; being large birds, they show up prominently in the rays, also they are heavy, and when they strike are instantly killed. One night I was standing out on the balcony right among them, when one struck me on the side of the face and left me fairly dizzy for some time. After a big migration night I have picked up in the court below and round about the tower as many as thirty-six Golden Plover, the wounded, too, are thickly scattered over the island. The mortality among the Lapwings is even greater, we collect them, and have stews and pies, but even so, many have to be buried or given to the Gulls. Skylarks and Starlings also pay heavy toll at the lantern. The former appear as soon as the end of August, and strong rushes take place in September and October, a larger percentage of Larks is killed than of any other bird. Starlings we have at all times; every hazy night brings some to the lantern, but during October the great migration rushes of this species are a feature of the nights. Besides these migrant Starlings, we have many residents, the caves and fissures amongst the rocks are full of them roosting at night. They are very reliable weather prophets, leaving these roosting quarters when a change is going to take place. It is wonderful what an attraction the light has to most land-birds, yet there are others which it never affects. The Rock-pipit, for instance, though locally very numerous, rarely appears at the light, and the same may be said of Owls and Hawks (Peregrine, Kestrel, and Sparrow-hawk): these, though resident in the district, rarely visit the lantern, and then only in search of food. Curlew I have caught in the light-room, having on some nights to leave the door from the light-room out to the balcony open, owing to condensation: these birds walk straight in, and make no attempt to fly.

It is a wonderful sight, standing on the balcony on a big migration night, with the revolving rays above one's head and these myriads of birds flying and screaming about the lantern. As I stand there I conjecture the distance these feathered mites have travelled before they reached here, and the yet greater distance many of them will have to journey before they reach their destination.

By William Begg.

From *The Scottish Naturalist,* No. 61, January 1917.

William Begg's reference to consumption of large numbers of lapwings in stews and pies may be distressing to ornithologists, vegetarians, and conservationists in general, but is an interesting illustration of how a lighthouse keeper could

John 'Hubby' Poland,
courtesy of Robert Mitchell

sometimes compensate for lack of fresh provisions and at the same time prevent the unforeseen victims of the beam of light he tended from going entirely to waste. Older mariners in Kirkcudbright have told tales of how attendant boatmen such as John 'Hubby' Poland used to return from the weekly supply delivery to the lighthouse with sacks full of dead birds. The sacks were allegedly delivered to the poorhouse, where their contents went into the stockpot 'heid feet tail an'a".

William Begg and George Mackie told *The Scottish Naturalist* in 1917 that these birds had been sighted at Little Ross:

Starling, Skylark, Yellow wagtail, White wagtail, Chiff chaff, Willow warbler, Grasshopper warbler, Sedge warbler, Garden warbler, Whitethroat, Thrush, Redwing, Ring ouzel, Blackbird, Wheatear, Redstart, Swallow, Sand martin, Cuckoo, Oystercatcher, Ringed plover, Knot, Common sandpiper, Redshank, Woodcock, Black headed gull, Herring gull.

Information taken from 'Report on Scottish Ornithology in 1917', *The Scottish Naturalist* No. 78, June 1918.

In 1918, William Begg and George Mackie informed *The Scottish Naturalist* that the birds sighted at Little Ross were:

Skylark, Rock pipit, Grey wagtail, Goldcrest, Chiff chaff, Willow warbler, Fieldfare, Song thrush, Redwing, Ring ouzel, Blackbird, Wheatear, Swallow, Swift, Whooper swan, Scaup, Oystercatcher, Golden plover, Lapwing, Sanderling, Knot, Dunlin, Redshank, Curlew, Water rail.

Information taken from 'Report on Scottish Ornithology in 1918', *The Scottish Naturalist* No. 91/92, July/August 1919.

The following birds sighted at Little Ross were reported to *The Scottish Naturalist* by William Begg and George Mackie in 1919:

Starling, Greenfinch, Skylark, Tree pipit, Meadow pipit, Grey wagtail, Goldcrest, Pied flycatcher, Sedge warbler, Whitethroat, Lesser Whitethroat, Song thrush, Blackbird, Wheatear, Redstart, British Redbreast, Swift, Ringed plover, Golden plover, Lapwing, Knot, Curlew, Common snipe, Water rail.

Information taken from 'Report on Scottish Ornithology in 1919', *The Scottish Naturalist* No. 103 and 104, July/August 1920.

George Mackie's service at Little Ross ended on 16 October 1919 when he was transferred to the Isle of May in the Firth of Forth. Although he was disappointed not to have been sent to a mainland station, the Isle of May was at least closer to the family's many relatives in Leith. George and Catherine's family continued to expand over the next few years with the birth of a son, John, at Leith in 1919, a daughter, Julia, at Leith in 1920, a daughter, Catherine, at Dunnet Head lighthouse in 1923, and a son, William, at Stroma lighthouse in 1925.

In 1933, George bought a Monington and Weston piano for 99 guineas. Astonishingly, that piano then travelled with the Mackie family to George's various postings, and his eldest daughter Mary recollected that the crew of the NLB Tender *Hesperus* had great difficulty in carrying the piano over rocks at the landing place near Douglas Head lighthouse on the Isle of Man! Two of George's great-great-grandchildren still play on that same piano, and in 2016, they won the pianoforte duet class at the Manx Music Festival in Douglas. George would have been very proud of them.

CHAPTER 10

A Keeper's Journal

From the diaries of
Assistant Lighthouse Keeper

GEORGE MACKIE

The following extract from George Mackie's diary covers the period of his service at Little Ross after the birth of his first daughter Mary, and is reproduced exactly from a transcription generously made available by George's granddaughter, and William Begg's great-granddaughter, Catherine Mackie Quirk.

N.B. Some words or phrases have been placed in round brackets by either George Mackie or Catherine Mackie Quirk. Comments in square brackets have been added by the author to provide further clarification. Throughout the transcript, spelling, grammar and punctuation have been left as in the original diary:

> I am writing this in the hope that some day, the records of these little events may be of some interest to my daughter, Mary, when I have passed beyond the bourn of time and my hands can no longer care or work for her — but I trust that some others will be kind and watch over her. Still my greatest wish is that she may be spared to grow up to be a most useful, kind-hearted Christian woman, always to trust her God for everything and, in whatsoever position in life she may be placed, to fulfil that to the very best of her ability. And whenever the hour of death shall come, may she be found ready.

1916

5th September Mary born, 11lb in weight. First outing when 10 days old with Mother and Nurse. Got her photo taken along with nurse. Trust one may be kept for her to see in after years if spared.

25th September Mother, Aunt Dot [Colina Begg] and Baby arrive home to Little Ross. Baby nothing the worse of her long journey, slept most of the time and proud was I to kiss her and see the likeness of her father. But after 6 weeks all alone, the stirs and cry of a baby seems strange to me. Still pleased to see them safely home as I felt very lonely. For the following month or so, got a good many small presents for Baby and think (her) more fortunate than her father ever was.

George and Catherine (Eva) Mackie, courtesy of Catherine Quirk and Ian Begg

18th October Rev W. J. Pennell arrived, (same that married father and mother, and christened baby). Not a long job, dinner the longest part of it. Still I enjoyed a piece of good fowl. At 3 months old, took Baby over to dairy to have her weighed. She turns the scale at 15lbs. Getting on fine and a good wee soul.

14th December Got her vaccinated, had a sore arm for the following 10 days but soon got over it as she is strong and healthy.

1917

February 26th First two teeth cut (bottom ones), mouth bothering her but still sleeps well at night and likes plenty of nursing during the day. Fortunate to have her grandmother and Aunt Dot near at hand. Very kind they are and no less is wee Freddy [Frederick William Begg was the youngest member of the Begg family, and was also a frequent visitor to the various homes of the Mackie family].

5th March Mary 6 months old today. I wish it was as many years to see her go to school. No food given yet but she sips a little soup or milk pudding at dinner.

13th March Took Baby over to Dairy. It was a lovely day and she enjoyed the outing. Freddy kept very near her in case we would leave her behind for he will have none of that. Baby got 2/6 in a present and Freddy 6d. Mary is getting heavy to carry about much, still very fat.

Saturday 14th March Baby had her first food. Corn flour made ready for her today and ate the full of a saucer but must get some kind of good food for her soon as she seems quite able and willing to take it.

Sunday 18th March Took baby to bed with me this afternoon but a very little of this is enough. A look or two round about to take her bearings, then the twisting and serpentine movements are brought into play. Of course the crying soon follows and Mother has to come and lift her, then (Mary) casts a smile back at me as much as to say 'It's all right now'. Yes, Mary is getting a bit wise. Took her out for a walk late in the afternoon. The evening was cold but how she enjoyed the outing, she is all smiles then. Keep her, O Lord, under the shadow of thy wing this night. Protect her from every disease and every danger, to which we are continually exposed.

21st March Mary down at the garden this forenoon with her Mother, seeing her Father plant the first of his potatoes. This is also my birthday, 45 years of age. I seem to be getting old.

Sunday 1st April Baby gets some 'Allenburys Food', and can take it fine. This is the first food that I have bought for her. If spared, I wonder tonight when she will take her last?

Advertisement for Allenbury's Milk Foods, courtesy of the Wellcome Library, London

2nd April Hard frost and snow.

Sunday April 22nd Had Baby over at Dairy today, enjoys the sail and outing, a beautiful day but she is afraid of strangers. I suppose seeing so few causes this. Her Aunt Dot, Nettie [Janet Begg] Gordon [Gordon Begg] and Freddie were all along with us. The want of fresh milk every day for her food is a drawback here. Still if she could manage to get plenty of soup or potatoes, they are much more to her liking but these things are hardly suitable for her yet. I am very fond of these things, nothing I enjoy better. May the good God bless and keep her.

Sunday May 6th Mary and Mother returned home today. They left here on Tuesday to see her Aunt Nettie away from Kirkcudbright who was here spending a fortnight holidays. Mr. and Mrs. McKenzie have been very kind to them and enjoyed the short holiday. But Baby is a bit restless tonight, her mouth seems to be bothering her again, must be her teeth. However, the weather is fine and will have a chance of getting out more, may help her …. And we have house cleaning all done. I missed them when away but Dot was very kind and done most of my housework and cooking so that I was not so badly off. I suppose if my wee girl is spared, she will read of this terrible war and the destruction is has caused. No potatoes to be got, sugar also very scarce and 6p per lb and bread not too plentiful. I paid £1.15/-for 10 stone of flour the other day and lucky to get it. In fact, everything about double in price. Truly this is an awful time and probably things may get worse yet. But I trust the like will never be seen in our country again. Surely this is a warning to the rising generations.

Sunday 20th April Boat trip. My day to attend church but the morning was threatening rain so that I remained at home. Wee Peggie and Mary McKenzie came down with their father and spent the day which turned out fine. We had all a sail over in the motorboat to the Ross Bay and Baby enjoyed it. There was no sign of sleep near her, being too much taken up with the wee girls. Company is a change for her.

Sunday 2nd May Baby has got another tooth, a top one this time, this is the third one and she can give my fingers a good nip now besides pulling my moustache. She can do this furiously, more especially with her left hand (which) is most used. In fact all along she has used this hand more than the right. I trust she will get out of this and I am beginning to wonder if any hair is going to grow on her head at all for up to date, it is seriously scarce. I daresay one might see as much on a gooseberry but probably time will cure all this. For I can remember well when mine was fair and curly and my Grannie would hardly allow it to be cut. Through time it got dark and now alas it is getting white again. But I trust that I may be spared to see my wee girl grow up and fit to do for herself and, Lord, when our days of trial and endurance are ended, may we all meet together in thy heavenly kingdom, where true joys are to be found.

June 5th Baby 9 months old today and still getting along fine but I think hardly so fat as she was. Probably the teething may be the cause of it. But she can pull at things and lift herself up a good bit. Sometimes when the day is warm, she is put outside in her bath as was done this forenoon, there being a terrible rush on, our steamer coming with the Superintendent and stores. Mary of course had to be got out of the way. Her mother lifted bath and her out on the grass but soon after, she was heard crying. Her mother went out, only to find poor baby and her bath upset, lying with her face on the ground. I, of course, had to become nurse then but soon after she was dressed up and looking her best for the occasion. But I trust these sorts of visits will never bother my wee girl, if spared to grow up. There was some mention of a shift for us today. I hope that when it comes, it will be to some place where we can get a little fresh milk every day for Baby. The want of this is a drawback here as she can take a good drink out of a cup now. It seems as we would have been away from here, had it not been for the wars, as I am 7 years here now, my longest time at a station so far. Yes, Baby is a consideration now.

June 11th Mother and Baby left here this forenoon for Kirkcudbright to meet her Uncle John [John Begg]. I boated them across and carried her over the rocks and through a field but she is getting heavy now. I was all sweating, it being very warm. Mother and Dot will have her to carry 2 miles. I don't envy them their job on such a day. But Baby could be always out, nothing pleases her better. Her little red cheeks and dressed all in white, she looked a picture. But I miss her here tonight, the cradle empty, no one to steal a kiss from. Yes, my wee girl will never have another earthly father who will think more of her. Still, I trust she will always keep herself humble, never seek the praise of others, nor entertain their praise with delight, never try to rub herself against her 'betters'. May the good God keep her from such.

June 12th Mother and Baby returned home. Boating takes no effect on Baby, in fact she seems to enjoy it. She is getting more teeth, two bottom and two top and can fairly bite my finger now. Eats almost most of what we do, sups porridge, a piece of an egg and very fond of soup and potatoes. She would rather have these than anything made for her, in fact will not eat Allenbury's food but usually gets bread and milk before going to bed. When I look on her sweet wee face and takes her hand in mine, I wonder what the future holds in store for her. Surely her life will be an improvement on her father's, at least I trust so. May the Lord bless her and keep her throughout her life.

June 19th Had Mother, Baby and Dot over at the bay today for the afternoon. Baby enjoys the outing. Has got 6 teeth, 4 top, 2 bottom. She has had a slight cold these last few days but I think about all right again. But Baby is getting on in many ways. When she does not get what she wants, there is a noise and when at our meat, pulls the table cover, makes grab at knives, forks, plates and everything. Yes, she likes to be moving. But sometimes I see her getting a bit hit on the hands for it, only to forget a moment later. And strange, everything goes to her mouth, probably the teething has something to do with this. She can say 'Dot', and 'ta ta' and tries Daddy so my wee girl is getting on all right so far.

Sunday June 24th Took Baby for a walk, it being a fine day. We sat down on a little grassy slope to enjoy the sunshine and what a beautiful view. Away to my right was the great stretch of blue sea with the sun sparkling on the water and the Cumberland Hills faintly seen in the distance and the smoke rising high out of the vast furnaces. To my left lies Kirkcudbright nestling in the hollow, surrounded by the budding trees, a place of beauty. In front of me, just across the narrow stretch of water, is the Countess of Selkirk's house [Balmae House, now demolished] standing among a clump of trees, with the green fields all around and the high cliffs stretching away in the distance to Abbey Head. Around me the butterflies are sporting themselves and I hear the cry of the sea birds. All appear to enjoy the sunshine. I trust that if spared, some day my wee girl will come back here and view the scene of her early childhood. It may be when the hand that is writing this is stilled forever but may the Lord keep her.

26th June Took Baby over to the dairy to have her weighed. She is now 21lbs and can eat almost anything. An egg she can eat quite easily but also very fond of chewing the blankets. Bits she pulls out of the hearth rug, all goes to her mouth. She must have a grand appetite .

Saturday June 30th Had Mother and Baby out at the fishing and caught a few small flounders - it being a lovely night, stayed to near 10 o'clock. Baby had a sleep but soon wakened up as bright as ever. Boating seems to take no ill effect on her, in fact she seems to enjoy it but anything to get out in the open air.

21st July Mother and Baby at Kirkcudbright and enjoyed the outing, it being a lovely day. How well Baby likes these. I went over to the bay and met them. Mrs. McKenzie, her sister (Belle), also Alick McDowell (their brother) is all down staying for their holiday and as I looked on their faces and heard what was once familiar voices, my thought carried me away back to city life. Oh what changes the years bring. This family that I went out and in among for so many years in Glasgow now alas has practically passed out of my life. How well it is that we cannot read the future because God has meant it to be held from us and we must trust him day by day and believe in his loving wisdom. Hoping that my wee girl will do this throughout her life.

July 26th (Thursday) Had Mother and Baby over at the Bay House, invited by Mrs. McKenzie to the wedding feast as Maggie McKenzie was married this afternoon. We had a fine afternoon and had plenty to eat. Fowl and salmon and a few songs after, an enjoyable afternoon, a very rare thing here and my wee girl was as good as could be. Seemed to enjoy the fun also but we had to keep her awake coming home in the boat as she was tired out and also it was her bedtime. She has 7 teeth now and I have seen her eat a bit biscuit and can crawl a little on the floor. She can also lift herself up in her crib and tumbled out one day — give us a fright but fortunately no harm done but we have got to watch her now as she is getting a bit lively. And can open her mouth to give us a kiss now, when in the notion. Yes, it gives me joy to look on this sweet little face. Love's chain links this heart of mine to thee. Often I wonder if this life will end all this or will me meet our loved ones beyond. Someone says 'On that happy Easter morning, all the graves their dead restore. Father, sister child and mother meet once more'. If such be the case, it will be grand.

August 4th (Saturday) Mother, Baby, Dot and Freddie away on a drive to Kirkcudbright seeing their Aunt Maggie away, also to meet Gracie [Grace Begg]. Went over for them in the afternoon but what a job getting them aboard the boat. Had to take off my boots and wade out to carry them on my back. A nasty swell rolling in on the shore and a very low tide. This makes a very bad landing here at all times. But they all enjoyed the day and Baby always good on such occasions, more especially when her Aunt Dot is there. They are fond of each other but of course she has nursed Baby a good deal from the first and has been very kind to her all along. They will miss each other when parted.

August 12th (Sunday) Baby got a present last Thursday of a bangle from her Aunt Dot, also a small brooch from John Munro, her mother's cousin. They are all very kind to her.

August 26th (Sunday) Baby is weaned now with no bother and getting on fine. She can stand up at a chair by herself quite easily. She takes more watching now than ever, creeps into all corners and scatters everything about, pulls and hauls at whatever she gets her hands on, makes for the fireplace every chance there is. In fact, I nurse her more now than ever and someone has always got to watch her. But sleeps well at night and eats well during the day. Two strong points in Mary.

September 17th I have just returned from holidays, from 1st till 15th and spent them at Portpatrick. I love to visit the old home and the scenes that was once so familiar although many changes since those days. Many, very many of the old faces gone and all my relations but one, Sarah [George's great aunt], who is now a frail old woman. But ah, how I miss my grandmother. Her smile and her welcome, no one shall ever fill her place to me on this earth, a dear friend from first to last. Her memory can never fade and as I visit her grave each year, it but reminds me how soon we must all follow. My wee girl has passed her first birthday on the 5th September. She was sick for a few days during my absence but all right again. Her teeth seem to be bothering her very much. Mother and her met me at Kirkcudbright and we stayed all night there but she was very restless and got little sleep. The following day was good and we all arrived home safe. I took the money out of Baby's bank before leaving on holidays. She had £1.5/-. My intention was to have it put into the bank but afterwards thought otherwise with the result I spent it but I will soon have it all refunded with good interest as I would like to always encourage her to be careful. I bought her a pair of brown boots when away. This is her second pair and also a frock but it is too small, a doll and a rattle and Sarah sent her a nice shawl. Yes, Baby has done very well for her first year and what a difference it has made to me nursing and the cry of a Baby after long years spent as a bachelor. Indeed sometimes I think it all seems strange but I don't mind for this, so long as she is spared to grow up to be a good and faithful woman. This is my one desire. Oh Mary, fix your dependence on Him who sayeth, 'Lo I am with you always, even unto the end of the world'.

Sunday 30th September We were all over at the Bay today I got baby weighed, turned the scale at 23lb. She is getting big now and I think hardly so fat as she used to be and of course, her teeth may be the main cause of it. But still strong and healthy and can creep along like a hare, can walk by holding on.

Saturday October 13th Baby just beginning to walk alone now but oh the mischief she gets into and the knocks she gets. The whole day long, tumbling about the floor and nothing can be left down within her reach or it soon goes to the floor, more especially at feeding time. Her mother was busy baking today and Mary was hovering around. Caught her cans of buttermilk and spilled the whole affair but it seems as she got smacked for it and she has burned her fingers several times at the fire so poor Mary has a rough passage sometimes. She sleeps in the room at night along with us and very often there is bother getting her to sleep but once she does, there is little bother with her to morning. Mother usually gets up before us to make the breakfast but it is not long after till Freddie makes his morning call, usually only his nightdress on. Then the fun starts and certainly it (keeps) me busy watching that she does not tumble out of bed. I am much better up then.

Saturday November 2nd Baby getting on fine and busy running about the house all day and into every kind of mischief. Poking at the fire gets her fingers burned. Pulls and hauls at everything and must get it or cries. She is not so easy put off and her poor wee head gets many a sore bump. What a grand appetite she has, can take a fill up of anything, more especially soups, broth and potatoes she is very fond of, also milk puddings. We have little bother with her food and takes porridge for breakfast when we can spare the milk, as sometimes it is very scarce here.

Sunday December 2nd Mother and Mary accompanied by Neil [Neil Begg] left here yesterday for Leith. Neil has been here spending a week after coming out of hospital having been gassed in France. But I feel the house dull and quiet today. I miss wee Mary with her clogs running about the house for she seldom rests and into all kinds of mischief. But wee Freddie is missing her also. I rose out of bed last night about 7pm and he was sitting at the kitchen fire crying. I asked him what he was crying for, was it for Neil? No. Was it for Eva? No. Was it for wee Mary? A nod of the head. 'Yes, if she would but come back, he would not hit her again.' Poor wee Freddie is very fond of her. He trails her around all day and carries her in and out but I told him that his playmate would soon be back again. However, I am not so badly off so long as Dot is here as she helps me a lot. Still I do not like being left alone as I weary very much.

Saturday 15th December Dot left here yesterday for Leith on holiday and I feel more lonely now than ever as she did all my housework and cooking and was very kind to me. Mother and Mary are away a fortnight today and the time seems to me long. I had a letter today from her and they are both well so far. Mary now has 10 teeth, had only 7 when she left but the rest was almost cut through before leaving. But how I am longing to see her. The cradle in the corner, her toys lying about, all these continually keeps her in my mind. Her wee prattling tongue is missed. For all the bother and worry there is in bringing up children, how fondly we cling to them. Still Mary has been a good baby and very little bother so far. May her life be made up of meekness and modesty, always ready to sympathise with others in their trouble and sorrows.

Sunday 30th December This year is fast drawing to a close and what a year of sorrow it has been but I believe history will bring out the true facts of the losses in this terrible war. And food scarce here at home and very dear — everything almost controlled prices. Still I have no reason to complain as I have always got sufficient to do my home so far, wanted for nothing so that I am thankful. Although I must say that this has been a very dull Christmas to me. I feel lonely being all alone. But sometimes there are inconveniences in life one has got to put up with and this is one of them so there is no use complaining. Only I hope that we may all be spared to enjoy many Christmases together yet. My wee girl is getting on all right in Leith but I wish she was home as I am longing to see her. I got a present of a frock for her the other day from John Mackie and I bought a few tickets for a prize drawing in Borgue last Friday night, raising money for the soldiers and I won 1½ lbs of butter and a rabbit so I was lucky. I will send the butter to mother as it is very scarce in Leith.

1918

New Year's night (Tuesday) Received a wire last night (Hogmanay) from Leith that I had got a son and heir. May the Lord bless and keep him, sanctify him in body and soul.

23rd January (Wednesday) Mother, Dot, Mary and baby returned back home today and all seemingly doing well and glad was I to see them as I was tired of being all alone. Baby was 12lbs when born, one (pound) heavier than his sister and what a fine wee fellow To be called for myself and very like me but trust if spared that he will be a much better man in every way and I hope and trust that throughout life, you will always be kind and considerate to your sister, no matter what her failings may be, under all conditions to love her and help her if it is within your power. For as long as I live, I will try my best and do for both of you what I can and I expect you to take my place some day and that you will watch over and not neglect her. This is a charge that I leave with you to fulfil and I trust that throughout life you will remember it when your father's task will be finished and hope that you may be spared to grow up to be a good, honest, upright, Christian man. For it isn't where you start — it's where you leave off that counts. Whatsoever a man soweth, that also shall he reap.

How well I would like to see my family grow up and into honourable positions to do well for themselves. Surely there would be some recompense, some joy in a father's heart to see this after all the care and trouble in bringing them up. May the good God direct all your steps during the eventful pilgrimage of this mortal life and when our days of trial and endurance are completed, may we all meet together in thy heavenly kingdom.

2nd February Baby doing well, sleeps on, it seems a bother for him to wake up. I used to think that Mary slept a lot the first three months and so she did but George is beating her so far. However, at the end of three months, Mary soon found out that there was more to life than sleeping. Her brother may also find out the same before long as he is a fine strong wee chap, at least he appears that to me and Mary is very fond of him, kisses and cuddles away at him. May this love always continue.

March 2nd Baby continues doing well and what a good wee soul. I used to think Mary was very good but so far George is a far more contented child and gets far less nursing than his sister got. I got his sugar card the other day, or rather I should say his ration card but he gets all his rations from his mother. Want of sugar or anything else has no concern for him. Yes indeed, happy childhood. I often look at him at night, how he cuddles into his mother, sound asleep and quite content. He seems to like this. Mary at his age very seldom slept with us, always in her cradle but George seems different, prefers company and I never hear him disturb us. He is very fat, the war and scarcity of food seems all to be agreeing with him. We were out this day a little but it was very cold. Mary is doing well and can eat anything and plenty of it also but she never rests from morning to night. She is continually in some mischief. She is also beginning to say some words now quite distinctly. Yes, sometimes it is a very cheery house but I hope and trust that they may be spared to grow up a loving brother and sister and may God bless and keep them.

Tuesday 12th March This was our bread day so we crossed over early as we also had to take over a bale of wool that we found some time ago. When I returned about 1pm, word had been sent down by the minister that we were to be over at the dairy at 2.30 to meet him there to christen baby. There was a rush to get dinner, shaved and etc but as all the rest were about ready, Mother Mary and baby, Dot, Gracie and Freddie, I was not long completing my toilet. I took Mary ,Freddie and a basket with a few refreshments down the hill and reached the slip. This as a general rule is slippery so I got Mary in one arm, my basket in the other to carry them both down. But unfortunately among other things I had changed was my boots for finer ones, consequently I had no sooner started than away my feet flew from me. All went flop. I tried to save Mary but her leg got a little under me. She started crying and her grandfather declared it broke but fortunately Finlay, the farmer, had come over with us so he examined and declared it only slightly hurt and marked a little so we all proceeded although I had hurt my elbow and no doubt Mary (had) a fright. We pulled over against a strong tide but reached the bay all right. I had to moor the boat far out in case of ebbing as the tide was going out fast and we would require to hurry back. Away we went and reached the dairy. Very soon the minister came, the Rev W. J. Pennell who married us and christened Mary and, as I held (George) up for the water to drop on him, he looked into the minister's face and smiled. Ah the things that rushed through my mind when I looked at that wee innocent smiling face and so far as good a baby as ever was. As the service proceeded, I thought how frail a being I was to fulfil those vows that were being laid on my head. But I hope and trust that my little namesake, this young life that has just been consecrated to God, if spared, will be a big improvement on his father. Yes, I desire of him to live a good life and I will try and do my best for my children and when gone, may our heavenly father watch over them. We had a little refreshments, they had luckily escaped the downfall and I hurried away back to the boat with the rest following only to find I was too late. Before I could get her launched, the tide left her high and dry on the sand. Here I was in a fix, not yet 5pm and me on duty to light but of course this did not matter. They all arrived wanting home but alas, hopeless. We waited on, darkness came, all cold and the children cross. However, we got safely back at 7.45pm, all tired out and hungry — an eventful afternoon. Of course it was the children I was anxious about, although the day was fine but it got a bit cold at night, especially with us hanging around, we felt it more. We will all remember George's christening.

Thursday March 14th Mother and baby left here by the boat for Kirkcudbright to get baby vaccinated. This done, they were to return the same day but owing to the big tides, they could not get back to the following morning when they returned safely. Mary remained at home with Dot, she is a little lame since we fell, hurt her knee but I think not much worse. She is beginning to speak a good lot now but oh, what mischief she gets into, never halts but otherwise getting on fine. Can eat any amount and anything we like to give her. She gets an egg every day. We are fortunate to have a few fowls, otherwise we could hardly buy them. I got 4/-per dozen not long ago but 3/6 now. I sell very few, uses most of them.

Thursday 21st March – My birthday Yes I am getting up in years and surely with my wife and growing children around me now, I have more to live for than ever, if it should be God's will. We had roast mutton for dinner and duff for tea. Ham and eggs for breakfast, rather high living as things go nowadays, all in honour of the event. Meat of all kinds is very scarce here. I do not think, if spared, that ever my family will live to see the like. After returning from getting the milk, went down and put in the first of my potatoes. The day was good so mother, Mary and baby was down also but I had to keep shouting at Mary, trampling all over the place. What a restless wee girl she is. Baby has a very sore arm but it should be about at worst now. I wish it was better for he is such a good wee soul, makes one feel more sorry for him. Still I think it best to have it done before teething starts. That is the reason of me having him vaccinated so soon. In fact, he is a little sooner done than Mary was.

31st March (Sunday) Baby 3 months old and getting on fine. His arm is nearly better but the scab is still on it yet. Did not affect him much as fat as ever, not that either of us is living very high just now. Butcher meat especially very scarce here, therefore we do not get broth or soup as often as we would like and often I feel sorry for Mary when I know quite well she ought to be getting something better. But fortunate that she can take a good fill up of anything, nothing comes amiss with her. This is a terrible war and probably things may get worse yet, still we are not the only ones suffering. Everyone is feeling the effects of it, at least mostly the poor as everything is scarce and very dear. I have all my potatoes in so it will be house cleaning next. Not a very nice job for me.

Sunday 7th April I was at church today for the first this summer. It has been a fine day but it is a bother getting my bike over when the tide is low, carrying it over the rocks. We have got through most of our house cleaning and I can hardly think that we will ever had to do it again at this station as I am looking for a shift at any time. Baby has been 'shortened' today and he looks much bigger with his wee blue frock that I bought for Mary when on holiday last year. But of course, I have little idea of sizes so it was far too wee for her but has come in handy for George. His arm is nearly better now and simply rolling with fat. I believe that he has a larger face than Mary and looks much older than his age, one of the best of children. Mary is also doing well, a restless wee girl, never out of mischief and can speak a good lot now, some words quite plainly.

Tuesday 23rd April We were all over at the dairy today. Baby got 2/-in a present and Mary 6d, so much for their bank. It has been a fine day and they enjoyed the outing but baby is heavy to carry. In fact, if he gets much fatter, we will require to roll him about, at least I don't see much else for it. However I daresay once teething starts, it will pull him down a bit for Mary seems to have lost all her fatness but she is growing fast and perhaps the amount of exercise she goes through every day may count also. But they both fell asleep coming home in the boat. Baby does not get near so much outing and nursing as Mary got. I think he will be a different nature, at least he seems to me at present to be far more contented than her. Of course time may alter all this. For Mary was also a good baby but has altered very much, ever on the trot and very fond of sweets or toffee that her mother makes. Likes to get down with me to carry the hens corn, feed them and carry home the eggs. She cannot slip down out of the door yet but she does the next best. Goes down on her hands and knees in the lobby and backs out of it. She calls me 'George' sometimes and her mother 'Eva'. Of course this is hearing the rest. When I am going any place, she runs after me calling 'hand, hand' wanting me to take her hand. Sometimes it is a job getting clear of her. I wish wee George was fit to run around but it is strange how soon they come on and I trust may be spared to grow up and lead useful lives.

April 28th Sunday It has been a fine day. We had baby and Mary out for a walk and had our tea on the shore. Mother and Dot came home and made it and brought it down so we all enjoyed ourselves, with Mary and Freddie as usual doing the big share. Baby got restless and fell asleep so he was laid on the grass and I think enjoyed his nap for he was all right when he wakened up but after a couple of hours, we all got home again and both children were ready for bed. Being out in the sunshine and fresh air makes them sleep better.

May 9th (Thursday) This has been washing day and a fine one, sunshine all day. Baby was laid outside in a bath covered up while his mother was busy and me over for the milk. In the afternoon baby, Mary and myself lay down for a little but neither slept very long so I had to do the nursing after. I took him out and he was good but terrible heavy to move around. Washed and sleeping now, he sleeps in the crib at night and Mary in bed. I hear her just now wanting someone to bring her up the stairs to Daddy. She was up the last night I lighted but I am afraid to learn her this habit as she might easily fall about the stairs and get hurt. Gracie [Grace Begg] left here a week ago so she is missing her chum as she trailed her about all day and was very kind to her. Moving around suits Mary.

Sunday 2nd June This has been a lovely day. We were all out for a walk in the evening and I had baby out in the forenoon. He is getting on fine and likes to be out but heavy to carry about. Sometimes he lies in the bath outside and sleeps, no doubt but he is good. Mary is never out of mischief and follows me about. When I do get away without her, she usually soon misses me and kicks up a terrible row. Her face is all skinned just now with the sun but seemingly does not make her hair grow much as she has still very little. We had the *Hesperus* here on Friday 31st May and sorry was I to ask a shift from here. Such a fine wee easy station, I will probably never have the like again. But these last two years, my life has been none too happy. Therefore my home has suffered also. But at some future date, if spared, I will hand down the reasons to my children in the hope that they will remember them. Probably my first 5 years here was about as happy as ever I had in the service but ah, what a change. I am a nothing now. May be some day I will have my turn, at least I hope so. But wherever I may go, I trust to be able to do justice to my children and I hope that they may be spared to grow up to be good and mete out justice and consideration to those they come in contact with and not a case of self every time for it is terrible, the outcome of a selfish life.

Saturday June 8th What a splendid day. Doctor came and extracted a tooth for me. It has been bothering me for some time. I have very few left now, in fact I should have them all out. Baby is still doing well, sleeps in the crib at night and very little bother. Mary sleeps in bed with us but oh what a mischief.

June 10th Mary got in among the preserved eggs today and broke about half a dozen. She got a sound whacking from her mother but she soon forgets these things.

Monday June 24th Baby still getting on nicely but I think that his mouth is getting bad. Still I see no sign of teeth yet. He has been getting a little thin porridge at night this last week but still very fat. I am sorry I cannot get him weighed. He takes some long rests lying on the kitchen hearth rug before the fire with a pillow below his head, lies and kicks and sucks a spoon if dipped into the sugar and Mary cuddles and kisses him but not in a very polite way sometimes but very fond of him all the same. He got a present of a nice wee frock and pinafore yesterday from Aunt Maggie in Glasgow, very kind of her. I also got Mary her first strong wearing boots and paid 6/6 for them. Everything is a terrible price and even although plenty things cannot be got at any money, our meat is difficult to get, more especially ham and butcher meat. I kill a rabbit sometimes, helps us along but many a day we have only potatoes a piece of butter and a little milk for dinner, certainly we don't live too high these troubled times. But if we are suffering a little, it is nothing to be compared with our poor soldiers and sailors. What a terrible war this is. I hope that the rising generation will never see the like. But I know if spared, my children will have their trials and troubles. They come to all and sometimes seems as if we must sink beneath the sorrows and hardships that beat upon us like great angry waves. But no matter how fierce the storms may rage, we shall come to no harm if we are following Jesus who is ready and willing at all times to help us if we only trust him.

July 4th (Thursday) I have been looking after baby all forenoon. Mother busy washing and I soon tire of nursing and he is heavy to lug about much. Mother had him over at Dairy last Sunday. They weighed him and he is about 25 lb so he is much heavier than Mary was at the same age. He is fond of being taken out, likes the fresh air and getting more lively but I think that his teeth is bothering him. Still for all he is a good wee soul, sleeps in his crib and little bother. Mary is very fond of him, likes when I put him on her knees to hold, kisses and cuddles him, sometimes most severely, at least not to his liking. Often she leans over the bed and gets at him in his crib and of course wakens him up then. Of course, the row starts for sometimes it is a struggle to get her asleep at night. The night that I don't light up, I take her to bed with me and I know many a pounding I get before she is asleep, jumping all over me and kicking and seldom goes to sleep but what she is pulling and working with my hair. She has a sleep mostly after dinner for an hour or two but apart from that she should be tired when it comes to bedtime, considering the amount of running she does in a day. She has a slight touch of the cold this last two days but I hope will be better soon.

July 14th (Sunday) Had Baby and Mary out a little this forenoon but too heavy for me to carry very far. He is bothered with his mouth, a bit restless but likes to get out into the fresh air. Mary is not taking her meal very well this some time back and has got thin. At least, she is not very heavy and I trust may soon get all right again. I don't know what is wrong with her and she would follow me all day. Kicks up a terrible row when I don't take her. I often think how wondrous strange are the chequered scenes of this fleeting life.

August 17th (Saturday) Baby still getting along nicely and has got two teeth just cut through. This is the first of them. He is longer in getting them than Mary was. Perhaps he may be a little more restless got but not very much. Sometimes lies in his crib awake long spells but also sits in the bath and cloth basket for long, only sometimes upsets out of the latter, getting over strong for it. Gets a little pudding at dinner time and some thin porridge at night. This is all the meal that he has got yet. Mary also doing well but still full of mischief and can speak very well now, in fact say too much sometimes — and still very fond of baby. We are all looking forward to our holiday and a visit to my dear old home and again to see Sarah.

August Saturday 31st I am on watch 4, will be extinguishing the light in another hour and we are all packed up for to leave early with the boat on our holiday. I trust that the day may keep fine for the sake of Mary and Baby, it is a very early start for them but we must be in Kirkcudbright before noon to catch the train. Mary is quite uplifted at going away. She says she is going in the Puff-Puff to see Aunt Sarah in the Port. Well, if we reach there safely, it will be my children's first visit but I trust that if they are spared, they will also love it like their father. Daisy [Margaret Begg] and Nettie are here on holidays but going away today and Freddie is leaving along with them to go to school so Mary will lose her chum and she will miss him very much but he is school age and must go.

September 15th (Sunday) Returned today from holidays and we all enjoyed our change and old Aunt Sarah thought there was never children like mine, so pleased to see them. Baby was extra good all the time and many admired him. He is such a big and fat boy and has cut through another tooth since we left. He has three now, two under and one top so he has a sore mouth just now. We got the loan of a coach when in the Port for him as he is so heavy to carry, therefore got out plenty. We also got his photo taken in Stranraer and would have gotten Mary taken along with him but unfortunately Mary had fallen on the street a few days before and skinned her nose. With her rubbing it, made things worse so she had to be left out. She was very sick all night after we arrived and the following day. In fact the whole time did not seem in her usual health. I think the change upset her and followed me everywhere, would not leave me and I had to put her asleep at night or she would have been crying for George Mackie. She slept along with me all the time. But what a change it has been, my first holiday spent with my children but I trust, if we are all spared, to spend many a one in my beloved little native place yet — and when my work is finished in this service that I may be able to retire there and finish all and that some kind hand may lay me to rest in the place that I have loved so well. I first left it when about 10 years of age and ever since, there has been very few years that I have missed paying it a visit, in fact when in Glasgow, twice a year. Very true my friends are few there now. Still the place remains dear to me.

October Friday 18th I am afraid that this little diary of mine is falling behind a bit, not so much through neglect on my part as in fact it was through our boatman always forgetting to bring me this new book. However, baby is still doing well. He has got six teeth, four top, two bottom and for all, still as contented as ever. Sits most of this time in the big zinc bath but beginning to raise himself up now on to his knees and reach over to the floor for whatever he sees or wants and how he enjoys his bath at night. Likes to get splashing in the water and then goes to bed and little bother with him till morning. We got his photos the other day and they are very like him. I hope one may be kept for after years. I also bought him a war certificate, 15/6 - in five years it will be worth a pound, his first investment. Mary got two with the money out of her bank. George had only 8 shillings. Mary's nose is better now but I am afraid also getting a bad wee girl, perhaps a bit spoiled. At any rate she soon says 'No' to anything she does not want. But I trust, if they are both spared, that this life, this school of hard experience which they will pass through will make them good and honourable. Yes, I would like to be spared to see them able to do for themselves — otherwise to leave them young and helpless without a father would be terrible. But I know these things are ruled by a higher power, by One who sees all and He sees best. Therefore we must trust Him for everything. When we begin to count our many blessings one by one, truly we have much to be thankful for.

November Saturday 2nd Baby is still getting on fine, eats anything and can eat plenty. Gets an occasional tumble out of his bath where he sits but soon gets over it. He gets no nursing such as Mary got but for all seems quite contented. I have now got him other four War Certificates making five for him, which in five years will be five pounds. I have also got the same for Mary. This is their first investment but I trust that some day they will have something worth mentioning, for to be careful and saving is a good point in life. I don't mean to be hard and stingy. There is medium in everything – and as for pride, never think of such a thing, leave the fancy dress and glitter to others, for in our position in life (to be proud) is nothing else but pure ignorance. Rather to exercise a thankful heart to God for all his kindness. Do not ask for riches, for honours, for the good things of this world. These things cannot calm the troubled mind nor ease the conscience. Rather would I have you to commit yourself to God's protection and guidance which is far better.

November Sunday 10th Baby still doing well. He is beginning now to stand on his feet and can raise himself up in his bath where he sits, quite easily. But he is time enough yet being so heavy and bad with this mouth just now. Mary is also doing well and as restless as ever.

November Monday 11th We have just received word this afternoon that this terrible war has finished. Peace proclaimed. Germany beat. What rejoicings there will be in the country but if we have won, it has been at a terrible cost. I don't mean money although it was costing this country something like seven millions per day but it is the young lives it has cost, that has been the sad part of it. Thousands upon thousands lie in France never to return but let us hope that their lives have been laid down for what we believe to have been a good and just cause. We at home may have suffered also but cannot complain much, very true all food was scarce and very dear. Still we always managed to get enough to do us. Surely the like can never happen again. In fact I can hardly think that the rising generation will ever fully realise that this has been. They will read about it in their school books but still it will give them but a faint idea of the terrible anxiety it caused in this country. Yes, undoubtedly for a long time, things looked very black for us but I think one of Germany's great blunders was not trying to keep America out of it because once she entered, it very soon gave the balance of power in our favour. But Germany thought her power greater than all, alas, her warlords have been sadly mistaken.

December 14 Sunday Baby still getting on fine, can stand up and creep about the floor. It is getting dangerous putting him in his bath now where he has spent so many, I hope, happy hours playing for he gets up and tumbles out and hurts himself for he is very heavy. I think he has seven teeth and can eat like a ploughman, anything you like to give him. Can eat an egg, a very simple matter with him. Mary is also doing well, growing fast and bad at the same time.

December 19th Baby still creeping around and standing on his feet but making no attempt at walking yet but I daresay he has quite time enough as he is very heavy. When he wakens up through the night, he pulls himself up in his crib and tries to get into the bed beside his mother but he is always kept to his crib as Mary sleeps with us and there is no room for him. Besides I think it is best but he is a good wee soul. I found him not long ago sitting up fast asleep with his head bent down on the clothes. When Mary was like him, the minute she wakened, she was soon heard but George is different. Without a doubt he has been a good baby. I daresay perhaps there was more life in Mary at this age but then she got plenty of nursing and maybe demanded attention. Perhaps this may account for some of her brightness. George laid inside the zinc bath on the floor — that has been his chief nurse and there for hours remained, quite content. But he is about past this now as he comes tumbling out of it. He would rather be creeping about and into all the corners to see about him. I often take him up on my knee and wonders, if spared, what his like will be. Surely better than his father's and I trust much better equipped for the battle of life to begin with because as a matter of fact, I had a terrible poor start, without education, ah without anything. I started to work when about 10 years of age and got very little learning after that. At fifteen I went to my trade ….A year later, thrown out on the streets of Glasgow not knowing where to lay my head. Between me and death not as much as a halfpenny. Had to go and seek shelter from a stranger. Yes, this was what a mother did and what a step-father thought perhaps a good thing. But I will give you a brief outline of what led up to this. Born in Portpatrick I was brought up with my great-grandmother Jane until about 7 or 8 years of age. I am not quite sure the date of her death but she was fond and kind to me. Even yet I can well remember her loving kindness for me but her death left our home broken up. My grandmother, Mary, was out at service working for her living. Sarah was also out working, these two always were at home with my great-grandmother. Therefore I went with Sarah to live, for how long I am not very sure, but she was not in a very good position to look after me. However, I daresay when about nine years of age, my mother came home and got married. Shortly after I had to go and stay with them and let me add, it was against my will because I had practically no desire for her. It was very seldom I had ever seen her unless when home on holiday. Still, she was very anxious to have me, yes, I can well remember this. Well, when about ten years of age, we all migrated to Glasgow but by this time, there was other three of a family. John the eldest and twins (two boys), the latter died some time after when about fifteen months old. They were two fine wee boys. Well I remember them. Many a time I had to carry them about in a shawl and I used to have a box with wheels on it, both of them laid inside and me running and pulling them up and down on the pavement like a hare. Ah but these were sad years for me, little to eat and not a bed to lie on. We were but a short time there when she got me into a factory to work. I would be about ten years of age then or eleven, not very sure. Worked one day all day, the next went out as usual between 5 and 6am but had to walk a few miles to start at 6am, worked till 9 then walked straight away to school a few miles further away and returned to work after school closed and worked, I think, till 6pm. Had 3/6 per week with school fees paid, no free education in those days.

I can well remember it was always four scones I got with me for to do me all day. No tea or anything else. It was very seldom I got loaf bread but I sometimes used to change with the girls and some of them were very kind to me, occasionally giving me a little extra and very often a drink of tea. Of course, some of them had plenty and they were fond of scones. No doubt good enough for she was a splendid baker but I was well fed up with them, more especially when I had nothing to wash them down. However, all this was hard enough on a young boy but when I look back over it all, the worst was the education. I was learning nothing, they would not allow me to pass the standards, not having the attendance. I never got beyond the 4th. Of course I did not mind and cared less.

When I returned home at night after this long day, the sad thing about it was the treatment I got, harsh to come from a mother to her own child. One can well look over many things in a poor home. I can well forgive her for the scarcity of food. I can easily look over and understand why my bed was thrown on the floor or an empty room and me lying down all huddled up with little in me and about the same on me. But however poor a home may be, parents have it still in their power to exercise a kindness to their children. However, things did not vary very much until I was about fifteen years of age. Still I have very little doubt in saying that a more abler pen could easily write and hand down some interesting events in my life between ten and fifteen and all connected with hardships, even to begging a piece of bread. But at fifteen, as I have said already, I started to serve my time as a ship joiner in Stephens of Linthouse with perhaps as little prospects of ever finishing it as ever anyone had. But such was to be and I became a joiner after serving five years. About a year after, when about sixteen, they turned me out. My flitting was no great show, assistance was conspicuous by its absence, a little bundle under my arm and so far as I remember, an old jacket was all my worldly possessions. I had made my entry into this world with nothing and I had help good. But however hard this was on me, at the time it was the turning point in my life for the better. Yes, I was parted now from my step-father and my mother for ever, cast out in a great city, a mere boy among strangers not knowing where to lay my head or where my breakfast was to come from. Surely the outlook was dark enough but however, dark the night, morning breaks and youth must have its day. But it is not in any spirit of envy or ill will towards any that I recall these things, far from that for my step-father I believe is long since dead and this I write about is somewhere about thirty years back. But I can quite well recall his memory for he was a hard-working industrious man and an exceptionally clever one. For years, he held the position of Foreman Rigger in Stephens. He was never idle in his youth, he followed the sea and when at home in the Port was at the fishing. He was fishing when my mother married him. I never remember him lift his hand to me although perhaps he might have been a little more kind but I never harboured any grudge against him for I have long since forgave and forgot all.

My mother is still living somewhere in Govan, it is about twenty years since I saw her last. Perhaps my children will think that it is very cold and indifferent in me never going to see or to ask after her but you must remember that she has been a mother to me only practically by name and the few years that I lived along with her only served to drive my feelings farther and farther away from her. Even after the lapse of all these years, I can quite well recall her cruelty to me. When one would fain forget and forgive all, they flash across my memory and cause me sad thoughts. At no time was there any reasonable excuse for such treatment as was meted out to me, especially by a mother, for however poor she may have been, it was well within her power to have been kind to me. It would have cost nothing more and there can be little doubt but what it would have altered the whole course of my life. Perhaps my children when reading this, may think that their father must have been a really bad boy. Well, I must honestly say that at no time in my long life have I been able to hold myself up as being a great example, I am only too conscious of my many failings. But never have I seen the boy who would or could work in the house as I did. When about twelve year of age, she got me entirely clear of the school. I could do almost anything in the way of house cleaning, run all messages, even sewing the patches on my clothes. No getting out at night to play as other boys, one hour per week was about my allotted span. If I forgot myself, a thrashing. Well I believe most boys require this at times but hardly in the form it was administered to me. Ordered to strip and perhaps left black and blue with whatever came most ready to her hand. Once after a thrashing, I went to my work the following morning, not able to lift my arms, they were all bruised. But somehow two men in our shop found it out, I do not remember how. There was another apprentice worked also with me who lived up the same stair, probably he may have told as he knew all about me. At any rate, they asked me what had done it. I told them it was playing at football. However, after examining me, they soon saw what was wrong and I had to admit what had done it. They bathed my arms all in hot water and after that I felt them much better. But the cat was out of the sack. I was more afraid now than ever as they threatened to go to my step-father who as I have said already worked in the same yard and was well known. Now I knew quite well that this would only make things worse for me so they promised not to do so in the meantime. But they determined if the like would happen again, they would assuredly see about it and me just as determined that they would never know about the like again, I was so afraid. But little did I think at the time that this little affair was to serve such a good purpose for ever after, one of these men was to be one of my best friends. He was the wood turner of our shop and an old soldier but a first class tradesman. He had a stern commanding voice and you may be sure liked obedience. His name was John McKenzie but John had a good heart for all that and became very fond of me. He used to tell me if ever anything would happen to me at home, I was to be sure and tell him. Of course I paid very little attention to this at the time but later I was fortunate to have such a friend. However, time went on and I got about the first year in but had no tools whatever. I was working all this time among the machines.

Just about this time, I went home one night, what had gone wrong, I do not remember but got orders I was to clear out the following night. Of course, such things were quite common in my life so gave little attention to them but I think I got a lashing this night for something — that was also common enough. However, the following night did come. I came home from work as usual, got my tea, washed up the dishes, did my regular routine of work then got the order to evacuate. I hesitated a bit but she would brook no delay. Nothing for it but to clear out and try to get out as quietly as possible as I was terrible afraid of her and for very good reasons. I remember clutching at what was supposed to be my Sunday jacket hanging aback of the door. It came out of Paddy's market but it was my all. Forth I went out into the street. White Street they called it but God knows it was dark enough looking to me, out into the cold world, out among strangers. Where was I to go, I had nowhere to lay my head, no money to pay for lodgings, I was destitute. But youth is not so easily daunted. It is hard to crush the young life and yes, I would make a hard fight for it. I would go to my old friend, John McKenzie and tell him all. He lived not very far off but if I went straight from here, someone may follow me and kick up a row. This would be a serious matter. But if I cut a semicircle and run for it, no one can follow me. Well, this is what I did and arrived at the house, knocked at the door and was told to come in. I told my story to him, it was all true — so after hearing it, he told me to go back and get my stepfather to write a line for me to the effect that they wanted nothing more to do with me. This was a crusher on me without a doubt as I was afraid to look near them again but it must be done so I soon arrived, knocked at the door several times and at last it was opened by him. I think they were in bed as they usually went very early. However I told him my message but the answer was 'to clear out from here immediately' and a lot more I don't remember but it was the last time he ever spoke to me in life. I came away very sad but glad to get out of their reach. I soon arrived back and again told what he had said. Well, it was all right, I was just to stay where I was in the meantime and go to my work as usual in the morning. But let me say I never was in their house again, Only sixteen years of age and never again to have a father or mother's guiding hand. I never spoke to him again although I saw him every day in the yard. I spoke to her some twice after this.

A few years after, she met me coming from my work and wanted money from me as he had been badly for some time and she was hard up. I had only some 9/- or 10/-per week, my time was not out yet. I told her I could not help her when this was all my pay. But she began to cry and told me that I could get it for her if I would write to my grandmother but this I would not do for the simple reason my grandmother would not send her money. But when my children are reading over this, surely there is a stern lesson for them here. Just think the very one who had despised and rejected me and threatened what she would do if ever I would enter her house again, now humbly begging money off me. What a change. But I will take a jump over a good many years and tell you about her next call on me. Somewhere about a year before I entered the service, probably I would be about twenty-nine years of age, I was lodging with an old lady in Govan . I was the only lodger in the close, I mean on the whole stair, and was attending the night school at the time. This particular night, I had just got down onto the second flat when who should I meet but my mother. I knew her fine. She asked me if I knew anyone who kept lodgers here. I told her there was one woman on the top flat who kept one. She did not know me and of course, I passed on and said no more but it was my custom to call in at the paper shop just at the close mouth and I did so as usual, still wondering how she had got on. Well, I had not long to wonder because my landlady told her where she would probably find me — or otherwise if she could not find me, then who would she say had called. 'Oh' was the reply 'only his mother.' and walked away. My poor old landlady was thunderstruck as she never knew I had a mother, always kept these things to myself. However, the first thing I heard was her calling me from the door. I knew that once familiar voice but George was not afraid now. We stood in the close out of the heavy rain. I asked her what she wanted. She replied 'Nothing'. I suppose only wanted to see me. We had a long conversation and something to the effect why I would never think in coming down to see them, nothing was her fault, blamed it all on him. Of course I told her it did not matter now for I would never bother them again. But what a difference now, she was very nice to her boy but alas, it was too late. There were two children along with her. I spoke to them kindly and gave them something each, bade them goodbye and hurried away to the night school. This was our last meeting and I left her with a sad heart for I knew quite well that she could have nothing but remorse in hers. It was for her I was sorry, surely this was a lesson for me to remember throughout life and for all that have children under their care, to do their duty to the best of their ability. Then and only then may they hope for the same in return. However, I will have to leave my story in the meantime but will resume it later on and tell you a little more of my life.

The foregoing entry makes for sad and difficult reading. The thought of George, in middle age, putting such a history and such sentiments in writing in the solitude of Little Ross is hard to bear. It seems highly likely that he stretched the rules and put all these personal and private thoughts on paper while on his lonely duty at the top of the lighthouse tower as his family slept peacefully in the cottages below. What contrasts had taken place in his life, and how pleased he must have been to have provided a relatively spacious comfortable and attractive home for his wife and children! It is also remarkable that despite his self-confessed lack of education, and his consequent lack of concern about matters grammatical, he was able to express his conflicting emotions so clearly and fairly:

> **December 25th Wednesday, Christmas night** I was on watch this morning from 4am until extinguishing time 8.20. Had Mary's stocking and Baby's hung up for them when they got up. Father Christmas brought Mary a nice fancy stocking full and a box of fancy tin dishes to play with, also a ball. George got something, I think like a dog or between that and a teddy bear, hard to say which, in fact I think neither but very nice, also a ball so they did not so bad. Mary was in high spirits with her box and tin dishes. We had a good breakfast of ham and eggs, also a nice dinner as I had bought a fowl and we all enjoyed it so much that little of a tea satisfied all of us. But Mary is not taking her meal very well just now, nor for some time back. As for Baby, he can eat like a wee pony, no wonder he is so fat and a terrible bother just now. You could not watch him creeping around into all kinds of dirt and throwing everything about on the floor. But Mary was much the same when creeping, in fact maybe she was worse. He makes no attempt at walking yet. Well, this is his first Christmas on earth. I wonder where he will spend his last. If spared, it will hardly be at a lighthouse for I trust he will have some better position in life where there will be some little enjoyment for there is not much variation in this one, year in, year out. It is much the same routine and never a proper night's rest unless at holiday time, the only break. Still I do not say that there is a very great advantage in a tradesman's life for I have had experience of both, worked about ten years or near that after my time was served. Certainly there is more money in a trade but it is equally true that you have got to work for it and the outlay is much greater. But I have had little reason to complain because I have always had sufficient to do me so far. I have much need to be grateful for the many blessings.

> **December 31st Tuesday** This has been a beautiful day and it is Baby's first birthday. I hope and trust that he will have many, very many beautiful and happy ones before him yet, that he may be spared to grow up and be a credit to those who reared him. That is my one great desire that my children may do well for themselves and I will try and do my duty to each of them so long as I am spared to be with them. Perhaps I may never be able to give them all I would wish but I will do my best and I trust that they will do the same. Each got a frock in a present from their grandmother today which was very kind of her. Their Uncle John [John Begg] also arrived home on a holiday from France. He is not clear of the army yet but thank God the war is finished. And this year with all its changes, its troubles and its trials is also fast drawing to a close, dear knows where we may be this time next year. The future all unknown. However, I must say that George has been one of the very best of babies. Yes, he has been good, he can look back on this with some little pride and now I will finish up the year thanking God for his remembrances, the mercies we have all enjoyed, the dangers we have escaped and the consolations and support we have experienced.

1919

> **January 1st Wednesday evening** New Year's Day is fast closing again but how little difference it makes to me now. Rose as usual and had a good breakfast, ham and eggs. Dinner roast pork and etc so we did fairly well considering as far as eating goes. But it has been a gale with heavy rain all day which kept me indoors but working a little as usual as there was no friendly visiting to wile away the time

*Robert Stevenson,
oil painting by John Syme,
courtesy of the Scottish
National Portrait Gallery*

Oil painting of the ketch Windward, *courtesy of the Stewartry Museum*

*Thomas Stevenson,
oil painting by Sir George
Reid, courtesy of the Scottish
National Portrait Gallery*

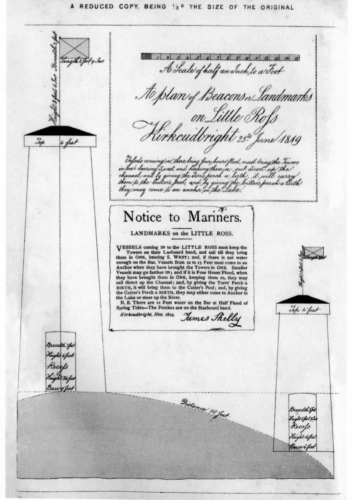

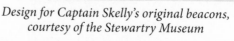

*Design for Captain Skelly's original beacons,
courtesy of the Stewartry Museum*

*Robert Cutlar Fergusson, oil
painting by Sir George Haytor,
courtesy of Daniel Shackleton*

Little Ross Lighthouse tower from the south east

The principal keeper's garden and the byres and forge, from the south

The principal keeper's pig sty and its relationship to the lighthouse tower

The control panel for the solar powered lantern, courtesy of Graeme Macdonald and the Northern Lighthouse Board

Douglas Molyneux at the west quay, courtesy of Keith Allardyce and the Museum of Scottish Lighthouses

Detail of the forge in the smithy at Little Ross Island

A stonemason's mark at the forge

Roger and Rosie Wild

The lighthouse station from the south east

The entrance to the lighthouse tower

The lighthouse station from the west

The clockwork mechanism that caused the lighthouse beam to rotate

The north beacon and Kirkcudbright Bay

Shore House and the slipway, Kirkcudbright - for many years the home of the Stitt family, and the departure point for the Little Ross supply boat.

The author's boat Speedwell, *and Little Ross Island from the north east, courtesy of Alistair C. Gillone*

Sunset over Little Ross Island, courtesy of Philip Dunn

otherwise. Surely if I am spared, I will see a more happy New Year's Day spent at a lighthouse yet. At least I hope so. In the meantime it is all right, no fault to find. But I would thank God for all the goodness we have experiences at thy hands. What have we which we have not received and now it is on thy power and wisdom and goodness that we depend for the future guidance and protection for we know not what is in reserve for us in the course of the year on which we have entered. But to thee we entrust all our interests, now and for evermore.

February 2nd Sunday This has been a beautiful day but cold with easterly winds. We had baby out round the island this afternoon and how pleased he is to get out but what a weight to carry. I think the sooner he walks the better, otherwise it will come to a case of having to roll him. He has been weaned this last week but as he can eat and drink any amount, it did not bother him very much. He stands up in the armchair at the end of the table and plays with anything he can get for he makes a sore mess of things when he gets on the floor. Mary is also doing well growing big and, sorry to say, bad. Still I am glad to say that they are both strong and healthy.

February 23rd Sunday I had baby and Mary out for a little today but it was cold for him and as both of them have got a touch of the cold, I did not stay long. He went into his crib after dinner and I lay down in bed beside him and we had a good sleep. He is getting more teeth, I think he has about nine now. He is also beginning to walk, in fact he has been doing a little of it this last week back but being so heavy, he moves along very slowly.

February 25th I am three years married today by the date and oh what changes. Yes, there is nothing but changes. At the same time I am thankful that through them all we have always managed to get what would do us. My two wee children are not very well tonight and I feel a bit sad. Mary has eaten nothing today and anything she did take only made her the more sick. But they both have got a dose of castor oil and off to bed. Baby is not just so bad but I think that it is a touch of the cold as they have not been over well this last few days back. I hope that they may be all right by tomorrow.

March 2nd Sunday Baby and Mary is about all right again, they have still a slight touch of cold but much better. Mary is still eating very little and I would like to see her with a better appetite.

March 9th Sunday Baby and Mary are both well again. I had both out playing around about the house most of the forenoon. Baby is getting a little smarter on his feet but still heavy on his legs. In fact they seem bent out a little but I trust may come all right through time. He can say 'Thank you' but that is all we can make out as yet. I must say it seems a very mannerly start. He gets into all corners, turns out everything in fact getting just as bad as Mary used to be at his age. I was just saying today to his mother that I often wonder what he will turn out to be. If such a thing could be that a father could watch over his children when gone, how gladly I would do so to help them where I have failed. But I hope they may put their trust in God.

Sunday 23rd March My birthday has passed the 21st without an entry as I had not time. Yes, I am one year older, one year nearer the grave. But oh how I hope to see my young children grow up into mature years, to be able to look after themselves for it would be awful to part with them so young and helpless, left without a father to look after them yet a while for no one can ever fill a father's place. Although I am coming up in years and perhaps not the amount of energy I had twenty years ago to work after them much, still I love them dearly and would not part with them for the world. And I trust that they may be spared to grow up and lead a good, useful life. I have just lately finished a small workbox and small chest of drawers for Mary and also a box to George. It may be useful to them some day, perhaps when I am gone, they will look on them as something their father made them. It was only a bit of wood I got on the shore, nothing great but still it done all right. I have all or most of my joiner's tools yet. Still it is hard to make a very good job of anything as they get out of order and no proper grindstone to sort them properly.

April 2nd Wednesday We had the doctor down yesterday seeing baby as he is walking very bow-legged and seemingly getting no better. The doctor examined him and said that the body is too heavy for him to stand much yet. Also that there was a touch of rickets attached to it and for to give him plenty of milk and cream, porridge and rather fatty substances. Well, I can quite well understand about his body being too heavy for his legs and keeping him off his feet as much as possible but as for rickets, it seems something strange to me. If he was in any way delicate I could understand but he can eat anything and eats like a wee pony. However we will try and fulfil the orders the doctor has left and I trust they will come all right. I am sure that we are both anxious and willing to do all we can for their good. For my own part I have no other desire in the world that to see my children right. They are my all now. Gracie was here for a fortnight and away again. During her stay, she looked after baby and we got well through with house cleaning. I also got in the first of my potatoes last Monday. I am about half through with them now and if weather permits, would not be long getting them all in.

April 14th Baby and Mary both well but keeping baby off his legs as much as possible. I am getting him a little cream now and food they call 'Virol' to harden up his joints or rather trying it but it is difficult getting fresh milk here, a great drawback of this place. However it is causing him to be more confined to the house, a thing he does not like. Sometimes I take him down with me to feed the hens, carries him on my back and how he likes this. He cries on them for their food or rather tries to but can say very little yet. I should certainly say that Mary at his age was more clever but his weight is sore against him in walking but I trust that he may soon come all right as he does not care about being tied into a chair.

Jar for Virol, 'the ideal food'

Mary is not taking her food very well yet but she is never at rest, running about the whole day with her curly hair flying — but she has no great quantity of it yet. Strange. George has very little hair also. He lies in his crib at night but in the early morning usually wakens up, then he has to get into bed. He has slept in his crib all along and always in the room. We used to keep Mary in the kitchen, in fact, I believe, till she was near walking. We used to sleep there ourselves but I think that the room is more healthy. Mary is getting very tall, growing fast and we can make out most of what she says. In fact, sometimes she says too much. When a baby she was fat and plump, now she has lost it all and got quite thin. It is wonderful how soon children grow up but ah what a bother and trouble is with them, no use denying it.

April Sunday 27th This has been a splendid day. I was ashore and attended Church, 'Easter Sunday', came home and went to bed in the afternoon with baby in his crib beside me. He had a short sleep as Mary wakened him up, a usual occurrence. Had tea and then all of us went down to the hens and lay down on the grass for a while. He likes to get out. I do not know if his legs are improving much. Still awkward at the walking but full enough of mischief in the house. Tosses everything around with the greatest of pleasure but of course, only to himself. We are through with all our housework and not a very easy job when there are children running around. I trust the steamer may come soon and get it passed as these visits are a terrible bother. I trust that my children will be clear of these things and try something better in life. It is my desire that they should do so.

May 4th Sunday Mother and Mary left here for Leith last Thursday 1st and George is left with the Grannie and Dot and I am once again left all alone. However, I am not so badly off as Sonnie (NB This is the first time George is called Sonnie in the diaries, the 'family' name that lasted all his life.) Comes running around and keeps things more lively, otherwise I have no doubt that we would feel the quietness more. Dot does most of my housework and cooking. She is very good, I must say. Still I do not like now to be alone in the house as I have lost all notions of housework. When I entered the service first, I thought nothing of this, now all is changed. The years have brought their changes in my life. Still I have not much reason to complain as yet we have all got what has done us so far. Very true we can use up our pay very easily now as children take something to keep them but I do not grudge it as long as they are right. I don't care so much for myself but I was a bit careful before I got married and saved a few hundred pounds and I hope to add a little to it as time goes on for the sake of my family for it anything were happening to me, I would be anxious to leave them as much as possible. They are so young and helpless. Today I sent away the titles of my house in Portpatrick as I agreed to sell it to James Wither for £200. My idea for doing it is to try and make a little more out of this money as there is not much (to be made) in house property by the time taxes and repairs comes out of a rent of £12 per annum and one has not a great amount of interest left. I have done it for the best and I will try and be careful and get it invested as best I can. I have also £100 in war loans drawing 5 per cent interest which is much better than the house and no bother. But even with all I have it would be little divided up with a woman left with a young family. But I trust we may all be spared to enjoy each other's company for many a long year to come and may we always trust the good God for everything.

May 7th Had a letter from Mother today and a parcel. She sent George a pair of new boots for lacing tight over his ankles to try and strengthen them, for his legs are still bad and one cannot keep him tied up in a chair. In fact he will not do it, he must be out if possible and when in the house, you could not watch him for he is continually in mischief.

May 14th Wednesday Wee George is still getting on fine, never seems to miss his mother or Mary, quite content. I carry him down to feed the hens every night, carries him on my back. He is such a weight but he has got a burned foot just now and cannot get on his boots and he is never content unless someone takes him out. He is always ready for that. When he is in the house what a mischief, you could not possibly watch him, coals in the kettle, coals in the water pails, in fact coals scattered all over. The hens potatoes that I boil for them is a favourite place. He can make them fly, he knows where to find everything. But I miss my wee lassie, yes I do but I hope that the change will do her good as she was not taking her meal over well before she left nor for some time previous. I do not know any difference on George, his legs are just the same. He gets what the doctor ordered but under the present circumstances it is impossible for me to keep him off his legs, Perhaps if things had been different, he might have had a better chance in this respect but I trust they will get right as he grows up because he is strong and healthy and can take his food well.

May 16th Friday Had a wire today from Leith telling me that I had another son, one more to the family circle, one more given into my care.

May 18th Sunday trip but I did not go to church as the boat was too late of coming down. There was also a lot of visitors here. It was a splendid day. Had no further word from mother. I had George out all forenoon among the visitors, he was afraid among so many but he got a few sweets which pleased him. There is no doubt but what he can work away with them. He has got a burned foot still and cannot get on his boots, but he can run around all right. There is no doubt he could have done to be the baby yet for a while. However, there is no use complaining, we must just do the best we can. I have just received payment for my house sold. If spared, I must try and put the £200 to good use for the sake of my wife and family because if anything happened to me, I am quite sure they would require it all and far more.

June 1st Sunday This has been a splendid day and I ought to have been at church but the boat was too late of coming down. I took George out for a walk and this pleases him, he likes to get out. He gets on fine and never seems to miss his mother or Mary. He is growing fast now but his legs are still bad. Mother and baby are both well and will be back home on the 14th if all goes well. No doubt my house, once they all return, will be a bit lively. Still if baby is anything like George, he will be little bother for he was a good wee soul sure enough although I cannot say that for him now for he is a perfect mischief got. I also hope that the change will do Mary good. I am thinking long for to see her but of course one feels lonely left alone. The time is rather long, they are away a month now and I have a lot of work with my garden and busy preparing for the steamer coming. No doubt but what it is a rather awkward time, however I must manage some way.

June 15th Sunday Mother Mary and baby all arrived back home last evening Saturday night and all seemed nothing the worse of the journey for it was a splendid day which was in their favour not perhaps so much in regard to the railway journey as in getting down here. Well, the baby is called for his Uncle John who is staying here at present and he is a fine wee chap. His mother did not get him weighed so I cannot say what it will be but I have little doubt in saying that he is not so heavy as George. I often think how well I would be repaid if I but knew for a certainty that they would or will turn out anything like I wish them to be, an improvement on their father, yes and I trust a big one. May they always remember to ask help and guidance from the One who is always able and willing to give it and throughout life may they remember this when the hand that is writing this shall assuredly be forever stilled. But with all my faults and failings, may God ever help me to do my duty to them while here, it is all I can do.

I do not think that the change has made any improvement on Mary as she is very white and thin and has a touch of the cold. We have just been putting her and George into the kitchen bed tonight to try if they will sleep together as there is no room for us all in the one bed. Freddie came back along with them, he got clear of school a fortnight before holiday time so he is fine company, the three of them together.

July 7th Monday Mr. Pennell, our minister, came here today and christened baby. He has named my three children and I must say that he is very nice and most obliging. Fortunately it has been a lovely day. He arrived here about 3pm. I went over for him in the boat and as I heard and answered to the vows, those cares which a father promises to fulfil, I trust that God will help me to do so and that my wee boy may be spared to grow up worthy of the blessings that has been asked for him today. Well, we had a little wine after the ceremony, then a good tea, fowl and roast mutton. There are two lady visitors here just now so we all enjoyed ourselves. Baby is called after his Uncle John who is staying here just now. Mary and George are both well. Mary is growing up fast. George also is coming on but very slow at speaking, he cannot say much yet and his legs are still bad. I doubt if they will ever be right but smart enough at mischief especially among water.

July 11th Friday We had the *Hesperus* here yesterday and landed our oil. Superintendent was telling me he was going to see about shifting me as I am so long here. Well, no doubt it must come soon now. I am nine years past here, a long spell at the one station but what a difference it will make with me shifting now. I had only a housekeeper to consider before but now a wife with three children. Yes, it is a big change but life is really full of them, nothing but change. However, I hope that we may get a more convenient place for children.

July 17th Thursday Last Tuesday mother took baby to Kirkcudbright and got him vaccinated, returned the following day but it is not bothering him so far. He is a good wee soul and sleeps well at night. I think he is going to be more like Mary than George and seems to be getting on fine so far, with little nursing compared to what Mary got. Mary is sleeping alone in the kitchen bed now. We tried George in also but it was a failure as he rolls about like a ball so he is in along with us in the room and baby in the crib. Of course when I go down now at midnight, I go in with Mary but she seldom wakens before dawn but she likes me to go in beside her. Of course she is just young enough to be left alone.

July 19th Saturday night This has been a general holiday for most but makes little difference to us This is the Celebration of Peace and when I look out, I see plenty of bonfires and fireworks for it is a lovely night for their enjoyment We sent up a few of our rockets, they give a very loud report but for all that, they did not waken any of the children who are in bed fast asleep. How fortunate that these things have no concern for them yet.

August 2nd Saturday Baby's arm is not better yet, it must be a sore thing this vaccination. I feel it to see the little one suffering but it is done all for the best and I hope he will soon be all right again. All the family were here from Leith for the fortnight's holidays but the last of them left today. We miss them as it is cheery when all here and Gracie and Nettie were very good at the nursing. Gracie is very fond of children. We had two parties during their stay and we all enjoyed ourselves as it is very seldom that we have anything of the kind here.

12th August Tuesday Baby's arm is better now and he was shortened yesterday or rather I should say on Sunday and getting on fine. He had a sore arm but it did not seem to affect him very much. He is a nice wee baby, not near so heavy as George was or even Mary. I think he is the lightest of them but quite healthy and not by any means a bad wee soul. I think gets less nursing that any of them got, however he may be nothing the worse for that. Mary is also getting on fine, growing tall and very thin and fond of her Daddy but don't know but what George is quite as much as he follows me about everywhere, that is if he gets the chance and he is by no means easily done. His legs are still bad but I trust will come all right as he grows up but still very fat and heavy and a big boy for his age, chocked full of mischief. Strange how most people take to him and although I say it myself, he is a fine wee chap with his ruddy cheeks and white hair but I do not think he is going to be so curly as Mary. She has nice hair but rather short. I suppose she takes this from her father as I used to have the same. Yes, and mine is getting fair again but we cannot stay the onward march of time, it leaves is mark on each and this is one of them. Oh that I had been a younger man, I think it would have been better for my little ones but things must be as they are and I only hope I may be able to do my duty to them and that they might remember me when gone as having been a good friend to them. And I trust that if my wee boys are spared, they will be kind to their mother and think on all the bother she has had with them in trying to do her duty and never to forget Mary but to remember and be kind to her at all times. These little wishes of mine, I hope that my boys shall fulfil. Well, I am purposing leaving here on Friday 15th on holiday. I hope that the weather keeps good for a fortnight.

Catherine (Eva) Mackie, née Begg and her children.
Back row, Mary, Catherine (Eva), and George (Sonnie).
Front row, Ian, Catherine (Rena), Billy, and Julie.

September 2nd Tuesday Returned from holiday after a very enjoyable fortnight. Visited my little native place once again, had also a few days in Glasgow and even had a run through to Leith and spent the night there. Of course my business through there was to visit our office in Edinburgh to ask permission, in the event of anything happening to Aunt Sarah, to be allowed to go through to bury her to rest. This was granted to me on condition that I pay the Occasional's expenses.

September Saturday 6th Received wire today to join *Pharos* on 22nd inst. for Isle of May. Long looked for come at last. Well, I am only sorry that it is another island station. I would have liked on to the mainland for the sake of my children but must go where sent. Well, I am sorry in a way for to leave this grand little station but there are other considerations I shall never forget. At the same time I can never hope to have a better station, nor more kind neighbours to my children, in fact too much so. I shall never forget Mrs. Begg's and Dot's kindness, in fact I shall give them all full credit on this point. At the same time, Dot has been our main help, she has always been ready and willing where anything was wanted with the children and Mary is very fond of her. I am not the least ignorant of the fact but what we will miss her help very much. However, these changes happen to all in this service, we must go where sent. But so long as I live, I can never forget the changes in my life since coming here. They have been varied and many. I came here a bachelor and leave a married man with a wife and three of a family. It is altogether for their benefit that I would have liked a better station.

September Monday 8th We have been busy packing up all day and Mary is in high spirits going in the Puff Puff to Leith. George of course does not realise it yet but he has been busy all day in mischief, he is an awful wee boy. One might easily be thrashing him all day and now that the house is being turned up a bit, he is simply in his glory. Poor wee souls, if they but understood.

November 9th Sunday (written from the Isle of May) It seems a long time since I have made my last entry in this little book but much has happened and we have all been kept busy, trying to get settled in our new home. Mother and children left the Ross on the 15th October and I left the following day with attending boat, after our shift being put back twice. The first I don't know the reason but the second was owing to the railway strike. Then again, we ought to have all left together on the 15th but the occasional did not turn up and us sitting all ready waiting when he spoke down and told us that owing to a sore eye he could not come. We immediately wired to the office and an assistant from the Mull of Galloway arrived the following day but as I have already said, we were all ready for the 15th so we wired up for a motor. Mother, Dot and the children left and travelled to Glasgow and spent the night there. I travelled the following day direct to Edinburgh and arrived near midnight. Took a cab to Henderson Gardens and joined all the rest as they had travelled the same evening from Glasgow. But let me say that as I took a farewell of my old home, that little lovely island that had seen so many changes in my life, I could not help but feel sad after spending about nine and a half years there, a long spell at one station. You may be sure that many of its memories will ever remain with me.

We spent about a week in Leith and stayed with Daisy, fortunate to have a place so handy. She was very kind to us and we all spent a most enjoyable holiday. We joined the *Pharos* at Granton at 10am on the 22nd October and about an hour later, we started. Fortunately it was a good day and we enjoyed the sail, arrived on the May about 2pm but we were hardly right aboard till Mary fell on the deck and cut her lip. The music of course started right away but Daisy and Dot came down with us so with Dot near, she was soon all right again but the parting soon came. Yes, the best of friends must part.

We were soon under way and it was a quiet day so we had a pleasant journey and landed about 2pm. They were all very kind to us on the steamer *Pharos* and when we landed, women and men were all down to meet us. We had a nice tea in the Principal's house, they were very kind. There are two sets of men here, three for the engine room and three for the tower, one occasional or what we call one and the Principal, eight all told. Well, I was for the Tower so we soon arrived there and found the accommodation less than we had at the Ross, no pantry nor store room but a large kitchen and it is a very cold house but one very handy thing, the electric light, but it is all that here, all electric plant. I got a week to learn, went on watch with another then started on my own. I found out that the work would be much heavier here and everything different to what I had ever seen in the service. The tower from outside is a beautiful building, not like a lighthouse at all, more like some big gentleman's house inside. The stair is also very nice, carpet up the whole way but the light room is a poor place, hardly any room to move about and what a noise this lamp makes, like a saw mill, sometimes more like bagpipes. We have a foghorn and gun. This latter we lightroom men look after, it is a long way off and a terrible job getting down on a dark night. However, we are beginning to get settled down again and I hope that our stay will be short here. I am about 6 or 7 on the list for promotion so if all goes well, a couple of years will about do me.

Mary, for whom George Mackie's diary was intended, fulfilled her father's hopes for her future. She moved from Scotland to the Isle of Man in 1933 and died there on the 31 October 2010, aged 94 years, a much loved mother, aunt, grandmother, and great-grandmother. The Isle of Man features very prominently in the view southwards from Little Ross, so it is reasonable to imagine that on a clear day she might have gazed across the north Irish Sea to her former home on the much smaller island that was the scene of such an idyllic childhood.

George Mackie was promoted to principal keeper at the Bell Rock Lighthouse in October 1929.

CHAPTER 11

The Keepers and their Families,
1920–1960

On George Mackie's departure from Little Ross in October 1919, his duties were taken over by a series of occasional keepers until his replacement was appointed. William Begg must have missed the presence of his daughter, son-in-law, and grandchildren, but occupied himself when not on duty by continuing to meticulously record his ornithological observations.

In 1920 principal keeper William Begg reported to *The Scottish Naturalist* the following birds sighted at Little Ross:

> Starling, Skylark, Goldcrest, Chiff chaff, Sedge warbler, Whitethroat, Lesser whitethroat, Fieldfare, Song thrush, Redwing, Ring ouzel, Blackbird, Wheatear, Whinchat, Redstart, Redbreast, Nightjar, Short-eared owl, Whooper swan, Storm petrel, Leach's fork tailed petrel, Oystercatcher, Ringed plover, Golden plover, Lapwing, Sanderling, Knot, Snipe, Common tern, Water rail.

> Information taken from 'Report on Scottish Ornithology in 1920', *The Scottish Naturalist*, No. 91/92, July/August 1921.

SPRING MIGRATION AT LITTLE ROSS IN 1920.

Winter has passed, and the severest I have experienced in all my lighthouse service as far as wind and rain storms, though there was very little frost and snow, which has caused a great mildness, bringing in a very early spring. In the open on the 14th March, the primrose could be gathered in bunches, wild daffodils were bursting out here and there, the daisy and violet, all appearing in their simple beauty. Now along with these early wild flowers come other spring scenes, namely, the appearance of our summer birds. After putting in the winter in more genial and cheerful homes than they could have found here, they have left this southern home and seek again their northern summer quarters.

Passing by hedgerow, gorse-bank, wood, and field, we find bird-life getting very animated, where a short time ago appeared only desolation.

On St Valentine's Day I heard the first sweet notes of the Song-thrush, which in itself makes one forget the dreary past months. On our island of Little Ross there is a gun-socket for firing signals for the lifeboat, and on top of this for the last six years a Thrush sits from the middle of February up till the end of March every morning and evening piping his tuneful lays. Other advance-guards have made an early appearance; it is still February, and we have nightly visits of Pipits, Fieldfares, Missel-thrushes, Blackbirds, and Starlings passing in great numbers. With the entry of March we expect a greater influx of our migratory birds, and on suitable nights we are rarely disappointed; round the lanterns, closely packed, are numerous Goldcrests, Wheatears, Larks, Redwings, Thrushes, Blackbirds, Ring-ouzels, and Starlings. I may make here a particular mention as regards Ring-ouzel. I have at other stations met with them occasionally, but here I have counted over a dozen flying against the lantern at one time. Between the 22nd March and the 11th April we have had nightly visits of these beautiful birds; one especially had the white ring very prominent round the neck, extra deep and snowy white, and back, breast, underparts prominently speckled with white, in fact the most magnificent Ouzel I have ever seen. Redwings made their first appearance on the 17th January, accompanied by several Skylarks and Starlings.

On the 7th February (S.E. strong haze), at 8 P.M., came a rush of Lapwings, Larks, and Knots.

14th February (S.E. fresh, rain).—Curlews, Oyster-catchers, Terns, Redshanks, and Larks.

16th February (S.E. haze, rain).—At 9 P.M. came another rush of the above-mentioned, with the addition of Song-thrushes, flying round the lantern until daylight the following morning, when they took their various courses.

18th February (S.E. haze, rain).—The various different species made their appearance again: all the above, with, in addition, Missel-thrush, Blackbirds, Robins, and Short-eared Owl; a great many were killed. The Owl had a great night; every time he made his appearance he took away a Starling; whether the same owl I can't say, but one visited us for four successive nights.

25th February (calm, haze).—Fresh arrivals at 10 P.M.; several Turnstones, Ring-plover, and Snipe; several Turn-stones and Ring-plover were killed.

15th March.—An excellent night for migration; thick haze, with light airs, but got a great disappointment; only a rush of Starlings.

20th March (N.E. light, haze and fog).—Great animation; the rays were closely packed with circling birds of various species; we had again Curlews, Lapwings, Starlings, Wheat-ears, Larks, Fieldfares, Thrushes, Redwing, Oystercatchers, Knots, Redshanks, Ring-plover, Ring-ouzel, and although none were seen, the call of the Snipe could be distinctly heard.

22nd March.—Another great night with same weather conditions; all the above again were represented; extras were Goldcrests, Robins, Turnstones.

8th April (E. fresh breeze, haze).—Curlews, Golden Plover, Ring-plover, Wigeon, Redshanks, Water-rails, Ring-ouzel ; several Ring-ouzel, Water-rail, and Redshanks were killed.

9th till 13th April.—From 10 P.M. nightly, and until break of day on the following morning, we had all the above species.

14th April.—At 11 P.M. came a rush of Fieldfares, there then coming on a drizzle of small rain which continued until 1 A.M. of the 15th. The rain clearing with a shift of wind from S.E. to S.W., they then all disappeared; several were killed.

15th April.—During the first two hours of darkness, only a few Wheatears with one Lesser Whitethroat; this night was excellent, it being a haze with very light breeze from S.E. At 11 P.M. I was out on the balcony walking round and taking notes: an odd Fieldfare came, but only flying round. At 11.20 P.M. a slight rain began to fall; then such a night I never witnessed. Fieldfares alone; every ray was filled with them; no one could form any idea as to their numbers-Although they were in such multitudes, the death-roll was not heavy, they merely flushing, not striking, the lantern; but when one did strike, instant death was the result. After breakfast on the 16th, I was down at the garden, and on the part of the island I walked down, the sight of Fieldfares was unprecedented for this station in my six years here. In the garden I found a male Redstart, several Lesser White-throats, one Redwing, and a few Blackbirds. At 5 P.M. I went for a turn of the island. At the north-east end I rose Fieldfares: I may without exaggerating put them at several thousands. I had a great sight in observing the attitude of this flock; they rose in spiral formation for I should say several thousand feet, against a background of clear blue sky. Although at such a height, owing to their great numbers they were quite easily followed. This circling continued until they got the desired altitude, when they made off in a northerly course. I found a Water-rail and a Nightjar lying dead. The Nightjar was badly destroyed by rats, otherwise I would have sent it to the Royal Scottish Museum. This is the third Nightjar I have found here.

18th April.—At midnight, resting round the lantern were several Chiffchaffs, Willow-wrens, and Wheatears. Three Chiffchaffs, one Wheatear, one Willow-wren, and one Fieldfare were picked up in the court below dead. Also were seen in the garden several wounded Fieldfares and Blackbirds.

19th April. — At 10 A.M. observed first Swallow busy chasing flies close to the grass in the garden.

20th April.—A very good night; light S.W. wind and slight rain. 11 P.M. arrivals began: several Chiffchaffs and Willow-wrens ; by midnight several Wheatears, one Fieldfare. Starlings as usual numerous, also several Redshanks, one Oystercatcher; these kept up a flight round the lantern until daylight began to break.

23rd and 24th April.—Willow-wrens, Chiffchaffs, Wheat-ears, Starlings, Robins, one Fieldfare: all the above well represented on both nights from 10.30 P.M. till daylight.

25th April.—At 4.30 P.M. Meadow-pipits. These were thickly scattered over the island; in general we don't have many during the night, the Meadow-pipit is more of a traveller during daytime. This date I have just located a Peregrine Falcon's nest with four eggs, and in close proximity is a Kestrel's nest, but neither can be reached as the cliffs are very rotten.

From the 26th April until the end of the month resident Wheatears are busy nesting: there are something like eight nests. One pair of Hedge-sparrows nest annually in the garden; in the cart-shed are four Starlings, and another in the smithy chimney, all with eggs. Meadow and Rock-pipits nest in goodly numbers. There must be a Blackbird's also, as there are a pair seen. Skylarks, we have several of them also nesting. Six pairs of Oystercatchers, one pair of Herring-gulls, a dozen pairs of Common Gulls nest on the island, but they have a hard time to get their young reared owing to rats and the Herring-gull, who steal eggs and young. There is an island in the Sound [Richardson's Rock], and upon it the Common Gulls' nests are very numerous.

How different now to sit on a quiet evening and see the life and bustle on an outlying skerry. A few months ago only a solitary Skart might have been seen; now the air is filled with circling birds, the cliffs all spotted with Gull, Razorbill,

Guillemot, and Black Guillemot, while high in the air sounds the cry of the stately Peregrine, the grunt of the Cormorant from their various colonies, also the croak of the Raven and sharp call of the Jackdaw. From the hill above these cliffs is heard the plaintive call of the nesting Peewits.

William Begg

From *The Scottish Naturalist*, No. 105 and 106, September–October 1920.

"Cormorants nested on Little Ross in 1833 and in 1920 Begg refers to the colonies of Cormorants there" (Baxter & Rintoul 1953). Mr. Poland, who was the official boatman to the lighthouse, informs me that in his experience they never did breed on Little Ross Island but only on the Big Ross cliffs. They were not nesting on Little Ross in 1967 (JGY). On 24th May 1964 there were 18 adults, but only 7 nests, near the Western end of the Meikle Ross cliffs, where the rocks are less steep. They were obviously much disturbed, with eggs seen in only one nest, and several large stones thrown into others. In 1967 entry to the area was being discouraged and there was a bull running in the fields. On 24th June we found 11 nests, 6 at the original site and 5 on small niches in the vertical face of the steep cliff. In 1968 there were 12 nests (RHM).

Scottish Cormorant Colonies by R. W. J. Smith, in *Scottish Birds The Journal of the Scottish Ornothologists' Club,* Vol. 5 No. 7, Autumn 1969.

R .W. J. Smith has perhaps been a little unfair to William Begg, who never actually claimed that there were colonies of cormorants nesting on Little Ross Island. He merely mentioned that he could both see and hear their activities from his vantage point on Little Ross, which is not inconsistent with Mr. Poland's account. See also Appendix V.

William Begg retired from his long and distinguished service with the Northern Lighthouse Board on 3 September 1921 after 6 years and 8 months on Little Ross. His stay at Little Ross was noteworthy as, quite apart from his professional abilities, his amateur ornithological skills enabled him to make a unique contribution to the island's history.

Kenneth Taylor took over as principal keeper on 13 September 1921. He had entered the lighthouse service on 8th December 1897, aged 21, having been previously employed as a carpenter. He married Catherine Sinclair Dunnet in 1900 when he was an assistant keeper at Noss Head lighthouse in Wick. Catherine was the daughter of David Dunnet, a retired lighthouse keeper living in Janetstown, Wick. Sadly, their marriage only lasted for ten years as Catherine died in 1910 from tuberculosis, aged only 34, while she and her family were stationed at Holburn Head lighthouse near Thurso. Kenneth was left with two small children to look after, and to assist him in this task, Catherine's sister Elizabeth apparently joined Kenneth's household. In 1914 Kenneth married Elizabeth Sinclair Dunnet while he was a keeper at Kinnaird Head Lighthouse, Fraserburgh. Elizabeth Sinclair Dunnet died in Edinburgh in 1929, aged 56, and four years later in 1933, while stationed at the Isle of Ornsay, in the Sound of Sleat, Kenneth Taylor married his third wife

Dolina Gordon, from the Isle of Skye. This marriage took place in Dingwall at the same time as his daughter's marriage to John Ritch, yet another lighthouse keeper, stationed at Start Point lighthouse, Sanday, in Orkney. Seventeen years later John Ritch was to follow in the footsteps of his father-in-law, taking on his job and occupying his former home at Little Ross.

K. Sutherland was appointed as assistant keeper at Little Ross on 15 June 1920 and served for three years and nine months there before being transferred to Bressay in Shetland on 10 March 1924. On 19 July 1921, he married Gracie Begg, daughter of former Principal Keeper William Begg, at Borgue Manse!

John Blackhall Middlemiss was the son of a lighthouse keeper, Thomas Middlemiss, and was appointed assistant keeper at Little Ross on 2 April 1924. A year later, on the 3 April 1925, in the Free Church at Callinish on the west side of the Isle of Lewis, he married Margaret Maclean, a laundry maid who was the daughter of a crofter. John had been born in Leith in 1901 while his father was stationed at the Mull of Galloway, so his posting to Galloway would be a return to the area of his early upbringing. Once again, Little Ross was to provide a first home for a newly-wed couple. They did not however have a great deal of time to enjoy life on the island, for on 4 October 1926 John was transferred to the rock station of Dubh Artach, south west of Iona and west of Colonsay. One does not imagine that the transfer to a rock station would have been welcomed, as it inevitably meant lengthy and indeterminate periods of separation for the young couple, but that was an aspect of the job to which they would have had to become accustomed.

Alex Nicholson replaced John B. Middlemiss as assistant keeper on 12 October 1926 and was transferred to Fair Isle, Shetland, on 8 May 1927 after seven months on Little Ross.

Peter Murray Gow was appointed as assistant keeper at Little Ross on 6 May 1927. The son of a ploughman, with no background in nautical matters, Peter was nevertheless a dedicated lighthouse keeper who loved his job and was very proud to be employed by the Northern Lighthouse Board. Few of the young lighthouse keepers and the children of older keepers had much opportunity to meet young women or men during their stays on rock or island stations, which must at times have been frustrating and disappointing for them. Peter Gow, at 29 years of age would therefore have looked forward with particular enthusiasm to the weekly visits of the attendant boatman William Stitt, who occasionally brought with him his daughter Margaret Jessie Stitt when she had time off from domestic service in Kirkcudbright. The Stitt family was very prominent in all matters related to Kirkcudbright harbour and the River Dee, and Margaret lived with her parents in Shore House, a picturesque cottage jutting into and almost surrounded by the sea at the west end of the harbour. On her visits to Little Ross, Margaret was often given the important but rather less than glamorous task of carrying bags of coal on her back from the boat, up the slipway, to a handcart. She was however soon noticed by the quiet assistant keeper, and on 1 August 1929, Peter, aged 31, and

Margaret, aged 23, were married at Borgue Manse, following the example of many previous keepers and their fiancées, in setting up their first home together on Little Ross. Their son John Ross Gow's birth was registered at Borgue in 1930.

Peter, Margaret, and John Gow at Little Ross. This torn and tattered photograph is cherished as it is the only such image that exists. Lighthouse keepers rarely owned cameras due to the difficulty they would have in processing film, courtesy of Nancy Muirhead, née Gow.

On 4 June 1931, Peter Gow and his wife, together with their baby son John, were involved in an incident off the island which could have become very serious, had it not been for prompt action by principal keeper Kenneth Taylor, who raised the alarm. The *Galloway News* of 6 June 1931 reported the incident as follows:

THE MORISON WATSON'S FIRST OUTING

On Thursday night information was received from His Majesty's Coastguard at Portling that a message had been communicated to him from the Ross Island that the assistant lighthouse keeper, his wife and child, had proceeded in a small dinghy to the Big Ross, presumably for provisions, and were unable to return as the weather had become stormy and cold, and the occupants suffering from exposure.

It was thought advisable to launch the lifeboat. The crew were assembled by maroon signal, and under command of 2nd Coxswain F. Gallacher (in the absence of Coxswain Parkhill who was down the river fishing) proceeded to the lifeboat house where the lifeboat was launched and set out to the assistance of the small boat. Its occupants, who were found to be suffering from the intense cold and exposure, were taken on board and landed safely at the Ross Island.

The crew returned at 10.04pm. This was the first call to service of the new boat, the *Morison Watson*. A strong easterly wind was blowing at the time, and under sail and motive power the new boat behaved splendidly.

Principal keeper Kenneth Taylor was transferred to Start Point, Sanday, in Orkney on 11 June 1928 after six years and nine months on Little Ross. James Thomas McDonald Matheson then took over as principal keeper on 23rd June 1928. James Matheson had married Annie McLeod in Glasgow in 1897, when he was 27 and she was 23. When he got married, he was a lighthouse keeper on Fair Isle, and she was the daughter of a hotel keeper in Glasgow.

Peter M. Gow was transferred to the Mull of Galloway lighthouse in Wigtownshire on 15 July 1931. He later served at Dubh Artach, south west of Iona and west of Colonsay; Tod Head, Kinneff, near Stonehaven; and St. Abbs Head in Berwickshire, before his untimely death aged only 50. His daughter Nancy, born at Erraid, the shore station for Dubh Artach lighthouse, remembers a kind and quiet man who spoke little, but was never known to be angry. He loved his work, and even when not on duty, spent much of his time in the lighthouse or its workshop. He was an avid reader and also followed his wife's example in knitting Fair Isle jerseys. The making of rag rugs was another useful hobby, and must have provided welcome insulation from some of the lighthouse cottage's cold stone-flagged floors. In the long dark winter evenings, the family mastered every board game they could find and Peter often entertained them with music played on his box accordion as he puffed contentedly at his pipe. Duty was never absent from his thoughts though, and Nancy remembers him spending long hours cleaning and polishing the glasses of their many Tilley lamps.

Robert Thomson was appointed as assistant keeper on 17 July 1931 and James T. Matheson retired a few months later on 13 October 1931.

Peter Gow (centre) at an unknown lighthouse station, courtesy of Nancy Muirhead, née Gow

Charles J. McNish was appointed as principal keeper on 13 October 1931. A carpenter to trade, he was the son of a Royal Navy seaman and had been born in Donegal in 1868 while his father was with the coastguard service based near the island of Inishcoo. He had married Catherine Macnish of Carradale in 1893 during his first posting as assistant keeper at the Isle of May in the Firth of Forth (Charles and Catherine shared a great-grandfather). Charles and Ann then served at Fidra, Chicken Rock, and the Point of Ayre. Their son Archibald was born in Rushen, Isle of Man, in 1895, and their daughter Janet Margaret was born in March 1899 at Port St Mary, Isle of Man. Sadly, Janet Margaret died in infancy in 1900. A second son, Neil, was born at Bride in the Isle of Man in January 1903 while Charles was stationed at the Point of Ayre lighthouse, and a second daughter, Elizabeth, was born at Coldingham in Berwickshire in 1907. Charles was a keeper at St Abbs Head at that time. Charles then served at Buchan Ness before becoming the first principal keeper at the new station of Copinsay in the Orkneys in 1915. When he left Copinsay, he sailed through Scapa Flow only 24 hours before the German fleet arrived there. He then served at Turnberry, and spent ten years on Ailsa Craig before his final posting to Little Ross. It is assumed that by the time Charles and Catherine were at Little Ross, their children were independent of them. Charles retired in 1933, after one year and eleven months at Little Ross and a total of 40 years of service with the Northern Lighthouse Board. He was regarded as an expert authority on seabirds, an enthusiastic gardener, and a fan of 'the wireless'.

Joseph Tulloch was appointed as principal keeper on 21 September 1933. Joseph had been born in the Isle of Man in 1872. The fact that his father had been born at North Ronaldsay and his mother at Corsewall lighthouse gives a strong indication of the nature of his background. His father, Thomas Tulloch, and his maternal grandfather, had both been lighthouse keepers. Joseph was unmarried and his elder sister Ellen had accompanied him as housekeeper on a previous posting to Stroma in the Pentland Firth. It is not known whether or not she accompanied him to Little Ross.

Only three days after Joseph's arrival at Little Ross, he and his assistant keeper were involved in a minor incident which was duly reported in the local newspaper. Yet again, the vigilance of the keepers had resulted in the authorities being alerted at the earliest possible moment to a situation which had the potential to be life-threatening:

YACHTSMEN'S EXPERIENCE

On the return voyage from Garlieston on Sunday, two Tongland electricity engineers, Mr. Geoffrey Connor and Mr. William Young had rather a curious experience. After rounding the Ross lighthouse they dispensed with sails and started up the outboard motor. The engine suddenly ceased to function, and the stiff breeze drove them towards Richardson's rocks. By careful manoeuvring they positioned the boat in such a way that it came to rest comfortably on two pinnacles where they remained high and dry. With the aid of semaphore signalling they requested the lighthouse keeper to communicate with Coxswain Parkhill, and the lifeboat and full crew were soon on the scene. As the men were in no danger they decided to stay aboard. The lifeboat returned to its station, but came alongside again at full tide in the early hours of the morning, when the yacht was re-floated and taken in tow.

Galloway News, 30th September 1933.

The two men involved in the foregoing incident would have been engaged on the construction of the Galloway hydro-electric power scheme, and particularly involved with the new power station sited at the village of Tongland, north of Kirkcudbright.

On 30 August 1934, principal keeper Joseph Tulloch was transferred to Corran, Ardgour, near Fort William, and Allan MacMillan was appointed as principal keeper. Assistant keeper Robert Thomson was transferred to the Mull of Galloway in Wigtownshire on 8 December 1936 and William Learmonth was appointed as assistant keeper on the following day. Principal keeper Allan MacMillan retired on 16 November 1937 and was replaced by Basil Mackenzie, a Kirkcudbright man, who was appointed on 24 November 1937. Basil, who was a shipwright and joiner to trade, had entered the lighthouse service on 23 February 1904.

Margaret Taylor married Basil Mackenzie on 21 July 1904 in Fortrose. Basil was then an assistant keeper at Lismore lighthouse, Argyllshire. He died in Kirkcudbright on 28 February 1938.

THE LATE BASIL MACKENZIE, KIRKCUDBRIGHT

Many friends in Kirkcudbright learned with deep regret of the death of Mr. Basil Mackenzie, principal Keeper at the Ross Lighthouse, which took place in Kirkcudbright Cottage Hospital at an early hour on Monday Morning. Deceased, who was a brother of ex-provost William Mackenzie, Kirkcudbright, belonged to an old Kirkcudbright family who were at one time prominent shipbuilders in the town. This business which was at one time a flourishing industry in the town, was carried on by two brothers, Homer and James Campbell, the former being the grandfather of the deceased. They came from Cumberland, their place of business being on the Moat Brae, and from there they launched not a few vessels, probably the best known being the schooner *Lynch* [*Lynx*]. Mr. Mackenzie was the youngest son of the late Mr. William Mackenzie, who was a well-known pilot on the Dee, and relief boatman to the Ross Lighthouse.

Before entering the service of the Northern Lights Commissioners he served his apprenticeship as a joiner with the late Mr. James Campbell, and during his long service he was stationed at various lighthouses round the coast of Scotland, including the lonely Skerryvore and other lighthouses in the Outer Hebrides. It was only in November last that he was transferred to the Ross Lighthouse, when he renewed acquaintance with his old Kirkcudbright friends. Fifty-six years of age, he is survived by Mrs. Mackenzie, and a family of three sons and one daughter.

The funeral took place on Wednesday afternoon to St. Cuthbert's Churchyard and was largely attended.

Galloway News, 5 March 1938.

Alexander Scott was appointed as principal keeper on 23 April 1938. He had previously served at Bell Rock, the Isle of May, Tiumpan Head, Bass Rock, Whalsey Skerries, and Ardnamurchan.

On 13 December 1939, a ship's lifeboat was reported by one of the lighthouse keepers to be adrift, three miles off Little Ross. In poor visibility, the lifeboat crew found the vessel with no one on board and saved it by towing it back to the lifeboat station. The keepers at that time were Alexander Scott, principal, and William Learmonth, assistant. Alexander Scott was a married man with at least two children, one of whom, Ernest Gordon Scott, was also in the service of the Northern Lighthouse Board and was stationed at Fidra lighthouse when he married in June 1940.

Alexander Scott Senior retired on 16 October 1940 and settled in Arbroath. Robert M. Pearson was appointed as principal keeper on the same day that Alexander Scott departed. He had previously been the principal keeper at Tarbatness. Assistant keeper William Learmonth was transferred to Kinnaird Head, Fraserburgh, on 7 October 1941. His replacement, David Rendall, was appointed and took over his duties on the same day. David Rendall was transferred to Whalsey Skerries in Shetland on 19 June 1944.

Charles John Fordyce Gifford was appointed as assistant keeper on 13 September 1944 at the age of 20. In a long career with the Northern Lighthouse Board, he served in eight different lighthouses, and records that he really liked Little Ross and thoroughly enjoyed his stay there. He describes growing all kinds of vegetables in the walled garden, and enjoying some of the apples that grew there in the shelter of the protecting wall. He remembers rowing across the Sound to Ross Farm on the mainland to collect milk and eggs in a small dinghy, and also attending at least one dance in the village hall at Borgue. On one of his passages to fetch milk, he remembers losing one of the boat's rowlocks while rowing, and explains that as a Shetlander, he was unfamiliar with rowlocks, always having rowed a Shetland model fitted with thole pins and lanyards. With neither a rowlock nor a thole pin, he was forced to paddle with one oar and was making no headway against the ebbing tide. Fortunately, he was seen by the principal keeper, who succeeded in throwing him a line before he drifted past the island. In a relatively short stay at Little Ross, he made good friends both in Borgue and in Kirkcudbright. Clearly it was still possible, even on a remote island, for a determined young man to enjoy a social life. In Charles Gifford's own words, these were 'wonderful days'.

Charles J.F. Gifford, courtesy of the Gifford Family

In late 1944, Charles Gifford was an eye-witness to events which led to the loss of the well-known three-masted topsail schooner *Mary B. Mitchell*, which was one of the very last commercial sailing ships to come to Kirkcudbright Bay. His accurate interpretation of the situation led to a timely call-out of Kirkcudbright lifeboat and the rescue of the captain and crew of the stricken vessel:

> It was on the 15th of December 1944. I was out and about at the lighthouse about 2pm that day. The weather was bad. A gale from a southerly direction with rain and low cloud. I was looking in a southerly direction when I saw this sailing ship emerge out of the mist. I observed that all her sails were furled and there was no sign of any person on deck. In my opinion the ship was just drifting. I went in and told the principal keeper and after himself seeing the ship he phoned the appropriate authorities. The ship then disappeared from our view. Later we learned that the ship grounded and the crew were taken off the ship.
>
> Some days later we took our small boat and rowed over to the ship. The hulk was intact. We went on board to have a look round but found that the wreckers had been early on the scene and removed everything that was movable. The masts, sails and the rigging had all been completely removed. I went down below and looked in the toilet. The toilet and washbasin were smashed and all the brass or copper fittings taken away. I did not find one thing that I could keep.
>
> Some time later I had had a few days leave in Kirkcudbright, and on returning to the Ross by the lighthouse tender (run by a Mr. Gourlay) we got stuck on a sand bank. The tide was out so we just waited about an hour till we floated off. During that time Mr. Gourlay was looking around the side of the boat, when he saw something in the seabed. It was an anchor with the anchor chain piled up on top of it. We assumed that this was the anchor from the *Mary B. Mitchell*. The ship was said to have dragged her anchor, which would not have left the chain in the situation we found it; and how did it get detached from the ship?
>
> Rumour had it that it was the first time at sea for the crew except for the master and the mate, and when the lifeboat took them aboard, they were all standing fully dressed ready to jump aboard.

An inquiry was made and the findings were 'shipwreck — cause unknown'.

Charles J. F. Gifford (2014).

Hugh Gourlay, courtesy of the Stewartry Museum

Charles Gifford was transferred to Whalsay Skerries in Shetland on 18 May 1945. Being a Shetlander, he must have been happy to return to Shetland, and despite being stationed at the extremely remote and difficult to access Out Skerries, he was soon engaged to a Shetland girl. Charles tells a good story of how he used the resourcefulness of a lighthouse keeper to overcome the poor communications of the day, and to successfully arrange his wedding. The Out Skerries lighthouse had at its base two large tanks containing paraffin and water, which were both painted black. Charles would write messages for his fiancée in lime wash on the sides of the tanks, and she would read them from Grunay Island, in the Skerries group, with the use of a telescope! The arrangements made in such an ingenious manner were successful, and Charles married Williamina Barbara Anderson in Lerwick on 6 May 1947. Charles and Williamina celebrated their seventieth wedding anniversary in 2017.

Principal keeper Robert M. Pearson retired on 14 September 1945 and Alex Gilmour was appointed to replace him at Little Ross on the same day. Only two months later, his son, also Alexander, was the subject of an article in *The Sunday Post* on 18 November 1945, which provides rare information about what it was like to be a child of school age living on Little Ross Island:

ENVY OF ALL HIS SCHOOLMATES

Alexander Gilmour, Kirkcudbright Academy schoolboy, lives on the Little Ross lighthouse which stands on rocks away out in the Solway Firth. After he dismisses his boat on the Borgue shore, Alex boards a bus which is waiting to take him to the Academy. When he goes to school in the morning he has to be rowed over at high tide while he sails across at nights. It is only natural that Alex should be the envy of all his companions. As a result of a bursary award which he has gained, young Gilmour, who came South from

Wick a few months ago, will only in future leave his lighthouse on Monday mornings and return on Friday nights. The bursary will enable him to lodge in Kirkcudbright. At the weekends he will have time to assist his father with the lights, whose warning signals prevent ships from foundering on the rocky Solway Coasts.

Published by kind permission of *The Sunday Post.*

David F. Mitchell was appointed as assistant keeper on 27 February 1946 and was transferred to Barns Ness, Dunbar on 4 May 1949. On the same day V. L. W. Hill was appointed to replace him. Less than a year later, he was transferred to Auskerry, south of Stronsay in Orkney, on 18 October 1950. A. I. Walker was then appointed assistant keeper on 2 November 1950. Principal keeper Alex Gilmour was transferred to Loch Indaal, Islay, on 2 December 1950.

John Ritch was appointed principal keeper on 2 December 1950, having been promoted from his previous position as assistant keeper at the Mull of Galloway. He had a family connection with Little Ross in that his father-in-law Kenneth Taylor had been principal keeper there between 1921 and 1928. John Ritch had married Catherine Eliza Taylor in Dingwall in 1933 when he was a lighthouse keeper at Start Point, Sanday, in Orkney. Catherine's grandfather, David Dunnet, had also been a lighthouse keeper, and her mother had been born when her father was at the rock station of Skervuile lighthouse off Jura. The closeness of the family relationships that were one of the greatest strengths of the Northern Lighthouse Board become even more evident when one considers that Kenneth Taylor's sister Margaret had married Basil Mackenzie (later to become principal keeper at Little Ross) on 21 July 1904, at Fortrose, in Ross and Cromarty, when he was assistant keeper at Lismore in Argyll.

Assistant keeper A. I. Walker was dismissed on 19 December 1952, and A. R. McGaw was appointed as his replacement on 1 May 1953.

On 20 February 1954 another minor incident at sea was saved from perhaps turning into a disaster by the vigilance of the lighthouse keepers at Little Ross. Distress signals from a small lobster-fishing boat were reported by the keepers and Kirkcudbright lifeboat was launched at 6.15 p.m. The lifeboat returned at 11.00 p.m., with the fishing boat in tow and its two-man crew safely aboard the lifeboat:

LIFEBOAT'S FIRST RESCUE
KIRKCUDBRIGHT YOUTHS SAVED

When 21 year old Arthur Dinnell, son of Mr. and Mrs. Arthur Dinnell, St Mary Street and Raymond Clacherty also 21, Dovecroft, both of Kirkcudbright went out on a lobster fishing expedition on Saturday afternoon, little did they realise the furore their escapade would create.

All went well with the lads till shortly before darkness fell when on the return journey the engine of their small motor boat broke down near Torrs

Point and they were left helpless at the mercy of a fast ebbing tide. They tried to scull the boat forward, but so strong was the tide that they were in grave danger of being blown back out to sea or of their boat being smashed against the rocks which surround the coast.

A strong gale was blowing at the time, but fortunately their plight was noticed by the lighthouse keepers on Ross Island, who at once phoned the Kirkcudbright police and they in turn summoned out the Kirkcudbright lifeboat. The two maroons went off at the harbour about 6 o'clock and the crew under Coxswain George C. Davidson made a prompt response. When the frail craft was sighted the two lads were taken on board and their motor boat was taken in tow....

.....This was the first rescue the new lifeboat, the J. B. Couper has had since it was placed at Kirkcudbright in the early summer of last year.

Galloway News, 27 February 1954.

The men stationed at Little Ross at the time of the foregoing incident were principal keeper John Ritch and assistant keeper A. R. McGaw.

A. R. McGaw was transferred to Point of Ayre, Isle of Man on 10 February 1955. W. A. Howard was an 'occasional' who acted as an assistant keeper on Little Ross for a period of about nine months in 1955. John Ritch was principal keeper at the time, and George and John 'Hubby' Poland were attendant boatmen. Mr. Howard recalled being treated by Dr. R. N. Rutherfurd in Kirkcudbright after suffering lime burns in an attempt at whitewashing the lighthouse. W. A. Howard had also served as a supernumerary keeper at St Abb's Head where he met Robert Dickson, a young man who was destined to play an infamous part in the history of Little Ross lighthouse.

John Ritch transferred to Maughold head, Isle of Man on 15th December 1955, and Harry Manson came to the Ross on 16th December 1955, taking over as principal keeper.

George Poland, courtesy of the Stewartry Museum

W. D. McGhie was appointed as assistant keeper on 16 March 1956, and was transferred to Ushenish, South Uist, on 19 October 1957. R. Johnstone was appointed to replace him on 6 November 1957 but resigned only a few weeks later on 24 December 1957. Ian Summers was subsequently appointed as assistant keeper at Little Ross on 1 March 1958.

Ian Summers enjoyed his time on Little Ross and devoted great energy both to his work and to fishing for lobsters around the island's shore. He recalls painting the entire lighthouse tower himself from a bosun's chair slung from the balcony. He and principal keeper Harry Manson had arranged to share the task, but on the appointed day, Ian got up early and finished the entire job before Harry Manson appeared. He also worked very hard at his hobby of lobster fishing, handling forty creels and selling his catch to John King, a Kirkcudbright fisherman who had a lucrative contract to supply a chain of local hotels. One evening, Ian was short of bait for his creels and went out to sea in a small dinghy with an outboard motor to ask the skipper of a passing Whitehaven trawler if he could spare any bait. The skipper concerned had often enjoyed hospitality and home baking at Little Ross, so was happy to oblige. He suggested that if Ian came out to meet him next morning, he would be able to give him some bait from the night's catch. Next morning, Ian, having asked Harry Manson if he would like to come with him, put to sea again but was disconcerted to find that the trawler was lying six miles from the island. After a few miles of feeling rather vulnerable in their tiny vessel so far from land, the two keepers considered turning back, but Ian's need for bait eventually spurred them on to continue the voyage. On reaching the trawler, they were invited below decks for a ham and egg breakfast and on returning to the deck, found their dinghy to be so full of bait that the thwarts were covered. Their journey back to the Ross was an anxious one, with only a few inches of freeboard, and bailing almost impossible because of the cargo of bait. Only on reaching the Ross and noticing his principal's pallor, did Ian discover that Harry Manson could not swim.

Jimmy Thomson (James D. Thomson) came to Kirkcudbright in 1959 to set up in business as an electrical contractor and retailer of electrical goods in partnership with Douglas Dunbar. Jimmy had been born at Duncansby Head lighthouse station and his father, grandfather, great-grandfather and several others among his relatives had been in the lighthouse service. His wife Kathleen was from Shetland and they were proud of their connections with their lighthouse and island homes. Jimmy was an enthusiastic sea angler and later became an able second coxswain of Kirkcudbright lifeboat after some years as a crewman.

Jimmy and Kathleen Thomson soon made contact with the keepers on Little Ross Island, principal keeper Harry Manson being an Orkney man, and assistant keeper Ian Summers being known to Mrs. Thomson because his sister had been in her class at the Nicholson Institute in Lerwick. Ian Summers's father had also been a lighthouse keeper and had served with Jimmy's father at Bell Rock. The Thomsons were surprised and pleased to learn that on the transfer of Harry Manson to Turnberry in Ayrshire on 26 November 1959, the new principal keeper, starting work on the same date, was to be John Thomson. He was Jimmy's uncle and had previously been stationed at Rattray Head, Cape Wrath, North Unst (Muckle Flugga), Ailsa Craig, St Abbs Head, Noss Head, Bass Rock, Cantick Head, and Turnberry. (John Thomson's father had also been a lighthouse keeper and had served at St Abbs Head for over ten years.)

Members of the Thomson family at Little Ross - John Thomson, his wife Meg behind him, and their daughter Ailsa seated. Their nephew's wife Kathleen stands behind the sundial with her daughter Shona. The Thomsons' dog Cora is also in the picture, courtesy of the Thomson family.

Not long after the birth of Jimmy and Kathleen's daughter, the family all travelled to Little Ross by small boat from Ross Bay to spend Hogmanay there in 1959 with John Thomson and his wife Meg, Ian Summers, his mother and sister, and Hugh Clark, a relief keeper who lived in Dalry, Kirkcudbrightshire. They had a memorable time, celebrating Hogmanay in style, unaware that it would be the last such celebration at Little Ross for many years, and the last ever while it was a manned lighthouse station.

Jimmy Thomson, in conversation during November 2006, recalled that his uncle and aunt thought Little Ross to be a convenient and comfortable posting and that they enjoyed their time there. John Thomson was a keen gardener and grew large amounts of vegetables, including potatoes, cabbages, lettuces, and Brussels sprouts. Mrs. Thomson came from Maidens in Ayrshire, where her brothers were involved in herring fishing. She was a great baker and produced excellent scones on her coal-fired Rayburn. There was still no electricity on the island and the houses were lit with paraffin-fuelled Tilley lamps. Ian Summers however had his own small petrol generator and Jimmy supplied him with a television set in 1959 or 1960. Reception from the BBC was very poor, but reception from Border Television's transmitter just across the water was excellent. The only indication of a leisure activity other than watching television was the existence of a small putting green of five holes or so, close to the drying green, just west of the houses.

New thinking in the lighthouse service encouraged the keepers and their families to have a few days 'respite' from time to time, which is where 'occasional' keeper Hugh Clark came in to the story of Little Ross. Jimmy remembered his aunt and uncle coming up the river to Kirkcudbright harbour for 'respite' in a 'silly wee boat', she dressed in a fur coat, and 'wrapped up like an eskimo'.

The wedding of Ian and Isabel Summers, with the late John King MBE as best man, courtesy of Ian and Isabel Summers

The smack 'Young John' lying alongside the quay at Kirkcudbright, circa 1960

During the time Ian Summers spent at Little Ross as a single man, he was frequently visited by his girlfriend Isabel, who was given the use of a room in principal keeper Harry Manson's house. Isabel was soon initiated in the ways of the Northern Lighthouse Board and fell in love, not only with Ian, but also with Little Ross and life in a lighthouse station. Ian and Isabel were married in Edinburgh in March 1960, with John King, skipper of the Kirkcudbright smack *Young John,* as best man. Ian was transferred three months later to Neist Point, Isle of Skye, in the early summer of 1960 and later left the lighthouse service to become a boatman/ handyman on Colonsay.

Ian and Isabel Summers have kindly provided the following brief account of their stay at Little Ross from March until August 1960:

We were married in Edinburgh on 5th March 1960 and returned to Little Ross two weeks later. Johnny Thomson was Principal Keeper, Ian Assistant Keeper and Hugh Clark the 'Occasional', the latter having a room in our home.

Hugh had had to stay at the lighthouse a week longer than he expected, as Ian developed sinusitis and when we reached Kirkcudbright the doctor pronounced that it was inadvisable for him to return to The Ross, as his temperature was dangerously high. We were invited by Bob and Maisie Maxwell to stay with them until Ian was better, and that hospitable couple even gave us their own bed. [Bob Maxwell was the dairyman at Ross Bay farm, and a renowned cheesemaker.] Newly married as we were, we became the object of many raucous earthy jokes, but we were made to feel part of their own happy uproarious family of seven of their own children and one lad who was fostered. During that week, and until we were transferred from The Ross, they were unfailingly kind and generous to us and, although Maisie and Bob have now passed away, we are still in touch with one of their daughters who still lives in Kirkcudbright. We cannot write about Little Ross without awarding this tribute to that wonderful Maxwell family.

There was of course no electricity, the lighthouse being powered by paraffin and the houses lit by Tilley lamps. Our paraffin fridge was forever a mystery, with milk either going sour when turned too low, or having 'candles' protruding from the bottles when too high, but we were never able to achieve the right balance.

Our sole means of contact with the world was by means of letter, the telephone, which was reverently kept in the Thomson's home, being kept solely for emergencies and for passing our weekly order to the Co-op. Telephone calls to and from family were discouraged and letter-writing was essential to retain contact with friends and families. We looked forward to the mail, together with our groceries, arriving by Geordie Poland's boat each Wednesday, weather permitting - and what disappointment if delayed for any reason! We had a battery operated radio and allowed ourselves a battery once a month (such luxury!); this was used very sparingly and usually lasted two weeks, so we had to wait for another two weeks to catch up with world events. However, being young and newly married, that did not seem a priority.

Ian had already made friends locally, quite apart from the jolly and always welcoming Maxwell family. Johnny Thomson (already known by Ian's parents, as his Dad too was a keeper and Ian was brought up within the service) had a nephew, Jimmy, who had a flourishing electrical shop in Kirkcudbright. Ian, having previously been a marine engineer (admittedly only partly qualified) had acquired a generator, we rented a television set from Jimmy and eventually had the first television reception—erratic as it was – on Ross Island.

Ian had made friends with Johnny King, who was at that time a modest lobster fisherman based in Kirkcudbright and who often called at Ross and did us the honour of being Ian's best man at our wedding. He had a spaniel that eventually had pups, all brought up on Johnny's boat, the *Young John*, and Ian had chosen one, a black and white beauty, who he called Judy. Ian's faithful companion for almost two years, Judy initially demonstrated her resentment of me, this interloper, who sent her packing to her 'own' bed and did not allow her on the settee.... But we did eventually reach a compromise.... If she reached either before I spotted her, there she stayed!

In April and May we collected seagull eggs from the many nests around the island, carefully removing only one from each. What we couldn't use for baking was preserved in *isinglass* to be used over the winter months. Otherwise, eggs were bought from Mrs. Thomson who had her own flock of hens. We had a garden and tried, in vain, to grow a few vegetables but in spite of all our efforts, the over-population of rabbits beat us every time a longed-for green shoot made an appearance.

Ian had his lobster creels, we watched seals and otters at play, fished from the rocks, and on one occasion, a deer swam across the channel to investigate – and quickly swam back when it spotted us.

These were happy carefree months, and after Ian having been on Little Ross for just over two years, we were informed that a transfer was imminent and we were aware, through Ian's dad, who religiously kept a diary of all movements within the Lighthouse Service, that there were a number of vacancies and, alarmingly for us, that most of these were what was named as 'Rock Stations' (i.e. keepers being posted to such as the Bell Rock, The Flannans, the Bass Rock, etc. and many more of those outlying areas, the families being housed in the nearest towns). Lighthouse keepers, no matter the length of time within the service were permitted to argue against transfer – either accept it or leave, so it was a scary day for us when eventually the letter arrived to inform us that – thankfully – it was not a 'Rock' station, but our transfer was to Neist Point, on the west-most point of Skye (which, incidentally, because of its inaccessibility, eventually became a 'rock' station a few years later).

We regretfully began to pack our few belongings in preparation and eventually the day came for us to leave our first home on Little Ross. The lighthouse steamer arrived, depositing Robert Dickson, to whom we were introduced and had a cup of tea with him and the Thomsons, before departing from our beloved island. We thought that, this being his first position and a bachelor, Robert Dickson was not best pleased by the prospect of living on an island for the next few years. There was an outboard motor boat for the use of the keepers, but with the vagaries of weather and tide, it was not always possible to reach the mainland or Kirkcudbright.

Following an arduous journey aboard the *Pole Star* lighthouse ship, we eventually arrived on Skye…. Which is another episode in our lives and from which, after two and a half years, we departed the Lighthouse Service and made our way to the beautiful verdant Island of Colonsay in the Inner Hebrides, the next episode in our lives' journey…. Thence to Aberdeen…. To Brunei, in Borneo…..Back to Aberdeen….. To Blairgowrie to host a Guest House… And now, eventually, considering total retirement but within this beautiful area of Perthshire where we have made our home for the past 12 years.

Isabel and Ian Summers 18 May 2011

Ian Summers's replacement at Little Ross was Robert Dickson, who was appointed as assistant keeper on 18 July 1960. His stay was to be short and traumatic and he was destined to dramatically focus public attention on both Little Ross lighthouse and on the process of automation. He departed from the island on 18 August 1960, and was dismissed from the service of the Northern Lighthouse

Board at the end of November 1960, following events that are described in detail in the next chapter.

It is perhaps fitting to close this last chapter on the lives of the keepers and their families at Little Ross with the following short piece of poetry, written by Ian Summers while he was assistant keeper at Little Ross:

THE NORTHERN LIGHTHOUSE KEEPER

High upon my balcony, view unimpaired, the spirit free;
Above the stars and clouds in tune, the rising wind and drifting spume
Indicates the Devil's brood soon will rear with raging mood.
The thunder rolls, the crashing beat of sea on rocks beneath my feet;
Gusting wind upon the panes, the rattle of sleet and driving rain.
But through the darkness, a glimpse of light - the welcome on this raging night.
A guide to all - depart Dark Reaper! I'm proud to be a lighthouse keeper.

Ian Summers, assistant keeper at Little Ross Lighthouse, 1958–1960.

CHAPTER 12

Murder, Mystery,
and
Melodrama

In the summer of 1960, I was enjoying a welcome break from my study of architecture at Edinburgh College of Art, spending much of my time sailing in Kirkcudbright Bay in an elderly 13 ft. dinghy. I usually sailed alone, enjoying the solitude and open air after a hard year of work in the city, but on Thursday, 18 August 1960, my father, Thomas R. Collin, decided to come with me, hoping for a day out on Little Ross Island. Though coming from many generations of Eyemouth fishermen, my father was not an experienced sailor, having been well-warned by both his mother and his grandmother to stay away from the sea. They had very good reason to give this warning, as my great-grandfather and his three brothers were among the 14 people bearing the surname Collin who drowned in the Eyemouth fishing disaster of 1881. A total of 132 men died when almost the entire Eyemouth fishing fleet and many boats from other nearby ports were lost. Thanks to the advice of his mother, my father escaped from the crushing poverty of post-disaster Eyemouth, and was apprenticed to the Commercial Bank of Scotland's Ayton branch. He came to Kirkcudbright in the 1930s as branch manager, and never seemed to regret leaving Eyemouth behind him. Ironically, from the earliest age, I was drawn to the sea and ships and enjoyed nothing more than a holiday in Eyemouth, watching fishing boats being built in the open air, gazing wistfully at the fishing fleet putting to sea, attending the fish market, and listening to the fishermen's conversations.

When still in my early teenage years I began to build my first boat and by the time I was 16, I had successfully built a small sailing dinghy. My father realised that I was not going to be easily deterred from pursuing nautical interests, and being a conscientious parent, sought to make sure that I would be properly trained in seamanship. The formation of Kirkcudbright Sailing Club in 1956 provided an ideal opportunity for me and many other local youths to be given instruction in all matters concerning small boats by the RNLI coxswain George Davidson, the second coxswain Joseph Sassoon, and by two very experienced local yachtsmen,

Dr. R. N. Rutherfurd and Mr. John (Jock) Mitchell. A little later, when my aspirations began to extend to making passages in cruising yachts, my father arranged that he and I would attend a Scottish Council of Physical Recreation course on sailing, based at Blairmore on Loch Long, near the mouth of the Holy Loch. The course was a great success and as a result, my father, who had always been fond of hill-walking and other land-based sporting activities, strayed a little from his upbringing and began to enjoy sailing. It was not however something he took to naturally, and he was also perhaps a little late in life to take up an activity to which all his instincts were averse.

I was a fairly frequent visitor to Little Ross, but my father, like many other local people, saw the island as a pretty but largely inaccessible component of a much-loved view. But with his new-found interest in sailing, he looked forward to exploring Kirkcudbright Bay in general and Little Ross Island in particular. The weather forecast had been reasonably good and 18 August dawned fresh and fair. My father had taken a day off work, and it being neap tides, we had decided to leave Kirkcudbright with the morning ebb tide and to return on the evening flood.

High tide was at about 9.30 a.m., and at the earliest opportunity we left from the old Kirkcudbright Sailing Club slipway at the Castledykes and took the ebbing tide down the river and into the estuary. There was very little wind and the weather was warm with a mixture of bright sunshine and occasional heavy showers, so with no outboard motor we made slow progress southwards. As we eventually neared Little Ross Island, we noticed a dinghy near the mouth of Ross Bay beached or washed up high on the rocks, and we made a mental note to look more closely at it on our way home. We reached Little Ross Island at about 12.30 p.m., leaving our boat at the east quay, which was then in good repair. We walked over to the west quay, where a dilapidated shelter that had served as a garage for the island's motor van provided a place for us to light our Primus stove and enjoy our lunch. After lunch, we walked up to the lighthouse, intending as a courtesy to let the keepers know who we were and what we were doing. There was nobody about and no response to our knocks on the doors of either of the two houses. A friendly excited dog appeared and seemed very pleased to see us, and followed us everywhere from that point on. We were not concerned by not having seen anyone, and were more anxious that we might have disturbed the keepers while they were off-watch.

As the day progressed however it became a little puzzling that there was no sign of human activity. The only sound on the island was the repeated ringing of a telephone. We stood outside the keepers' cottages, wondering what to do, and were startled by a sudden noise coming from under a wooden box on top of the courtyard wall. I lifted the box, and a trapped rabbit ran from underneath it, where it must have been suffering greatly in the hot sunshine between showers. Something was not right.

By mid to late afternoon it was time for us to prepare to take the flood tide up to Kirkcudbright. Our boat drew only a few inches of water, so during neap tides, it would be possible for us to leave shortly after the flood tide started to run (about 4.30p.m.). Before leaving, we made a last attempt to contact the keepers, but again received no response. My father peered through one of the rear windows of the two houses and thought he could see someone lying in bed. He decided to enter the houses to check that everything was all right but I stood outside, embarrassed by his well-intentioned intrusion. All was peaceful and orderly in the empty principal keeper's house, but my father quickly emerged from the assistant keeper's house and shouted for me to see if I could get help, as he had found a man, apparently ill or injured, in his bed. I ran down to the shore at the east side of the island, off which I knew that Robert Milligan and his father were fishing from the smack *Young John*. I had also seen John Poland hauling creels there from the *Lavinia*. By the time I got within earshot, the *Lavinia* was heading for Torrs point, but Robert Milligan on the *Young John* heard my shouts and quickly rowed ashore in his dinghy.

Robert and I went up to the assistant keeper's house and entered with my father, who guided us to a small bedroom at the west side. A man lay in bed with his head wrapped in a towel and his feet and legs protruding from the bed covers. There was some blood near his head and, rather oddly, some lengths of rope lay on the bed. We all thought that he was probably dead, but having no experience of such matters, our priority was to seek medical help. At about 4.30 p.m. my father telephoned both a doctor and the police, summoning urgent assistance. Our suggestion that they went by road to the mouth of Ross Bay where Robert Milligan could pick them up immediately was not taken up, and instead they contacted George Poland, the attendant boatman for the Northern Lighthouse Board, to request passage to the island. George Poland, whose boat was based at Kirkcudbright harbour, explained to them that he could only take them to the island when the tide had risen, and that it would take some time to get there due to the speed of the incoming tide. This was exactly the situation we had tried to avert, but to no avail. Robert Milligan returned to his boat to be with his elderly father, and my father and I began what was to prove to be a long wait for assistance.

We did not talk much. We were both disturbed and saddened to find that a man was apparently dead in the heart of a beautiful island, the charms of which we had been enjoying so much. Perhaps he had taken ill or fallen and struck his head. Perhaps his fellow keeper had gone to get assistance, abandoning the dinghy on the rocks in his haste. Why had he not returned? None of it quite made sense. We wandered around the buildings, not quite sure what we were looking for but feeling vaguely ill at ease. The principal keeper's house was a little haven of normality – spotless and extremely comfortable with a budgie contentedly chirruping in a cage by the kitchen window – but it felt wrong for us to intrude. In the lighthouse tower the logbook showed that the last entry had been made at 3.00 a.m. What had happened after that? Who was the man we had found and where was the other lighthouse keeper? On the stairs up to the top of the lighthouse tower, we noticed a small red stain on one of the treads, and wondered if perhaps someone had fallen in the early morning and injured his head (the stain was later found to be paint, perhaps from a dropped paintbrush). In the workshop at the base of the tower, the vice on the workbench gripped the sawn-off barrel of a rifle. All was not well.

Although it was the height of summer we began to feel cold, and we climbed to the top of the lighthouse tower where we could sit in the lantern room in the warm sunshine with a spectacular view all around us. Eventually, we saw George Poland's launch creeping past St Mary's Isle Point against the incoming tide, proudly flying the flag of the Northern Lighthouse Board. At about 7.00 p.m., we met the launch at the east quay and were relieved to greet two policemen, Inspector Garroch and Constable Thomson, Doctor R. N. Rutherfurd, and to our surprise, an Edinburgh-based official of the Northern Lighthouse Board, who had been on his way to inform the keepers on Little Ross Island that the station was about to become automated and would no longer need to be manned.

With the arrival of George Poland and his passengers, our role in the dramatic events of the day was over. We directed everyone to the assistant keeper's house and waited outside. The first person to emerge was the ashen-faced Northern Lighthouse Board official, who ran from the house and was violently sick. It was soon confirmed to us that the man in bed was the relief lighthouse keeper, Mr. Hugh Clark from Dalry in Kirkcudbrightshire, and that he was dead. Principal keeper John Thomson and his wife were on annual leave on the island of Ailsa Craig, and assistant keeper Robert Dickson was missing. We answered the policemen's few questions and showed them anything that we thought might be relevant, such as the dinghy on the shore and the sawn-off rifle barrel in the workshop. After that, we simply waited, becoming colder and hungrier, until we were told that nothing else was required from us and that we could go home.

Thomas R. Collin outside Little Ross Lighthouse shortly before discovering the murder on 18 August 1960

By the time clearance was given, daylight was fading and the wind had dropped, so Robert Milligan offered us a tow back to Kirkcudbright harbour from the *Young John*. Before George Poland and his passengers departed, a lone policeman was left on the island to guard the landing places, as the island, unknown to us, had now become a crime scene. Our return journey was a slow one as the tide was beginning to ebb and Robert Milligan was already towing his own small boat. By the time we reached the harbour at Kirkcudbright, it was dark. We edged gently alongside the quay wall but as we prepared our mooring lines for passing ashore, we were suddenly blinded by a series of flashes. These turned out to be from the cameras of press photographers, and gave us our first indication that we were part of a story that was to make headlines in many leading newspapers the following morning. It transpired that my father's conversations with the police and the doctor may have been overheard by linesmen who were checking the telephone line to Little Ross for faults, because of the lack of response to a routine daily call. The story had spread rapidly.

For the following 24 hours we were subjected to what then seemed an extraordinary degree of harassment by the press. We were virtually prisoners in our own home, leaving only by car to deliver my father to and from his office. We now knew from the radio news and other sources that what we had discovered was deemed to be a brutal, gruesome, and mysterious murder. We also faced the reality that in the minds of some people, particularly members of the press, we could be considered as suspects. Mercifully, nobody we knew, or had direct dealings with, ever made us feel that this might be the case.

Throughout the course of the day, missing parts of the story were beginning to emerge from local sources. Hugh Clark had indeed been murdered, his death having resulted from gunshot wounds to his head, which had been fired from a rifle at very close range while he lay asleep in bed. When Dr. Rutherfurd made his initial examination on arriving at the island he had turned Hugh Clark's body to look at the back of the head, whereupon a bullet had fallen from the left eye-socket. We then understood all too clearly the reason for the Northern Lighthouse Board official's sudden exit from the house. Death was estimated to have occurred at about 6.00 a.m. Robert Dickson had been seen leaving Ross Bay in Hugh Clark's 10 h.p. Wolseley car at 9.10 a.m., having used Hugh Clark's dinghy to row across to the mainland, where he had abandoned it on the rocks. He had then driven to Maxwelltown on the outskirts of Dumfries, where he was involved in a minor collision with another vehicle. In a polite exchange with the driver of the other vehicle, he gave his name as 'R. Dickson, Ross lighthouse', which seems a very bizarre action by a fugitive from justice. He then hired a Hillman Husky car in Dumfries using the name and driver's licence of Principal keeper John Thomson. Attendant boatman George Poland had made his weekly visit to the island on Wednesday 17 August and among the items he had delivered were two registered letters addressed to Robert Dickson, who was the senior keeper in charge of the

185

station during the principal keeper's holiday. One letter contained Hugh Clark's pay, and the other contained cash for payments to tradesmen. Neither had been found on the island.

Considering the facts and all the events of the day with the benefit of hindsight, it seems strange that neither my father nor I voiced any concerns about the possibility that we had discovered a murder. It did not occur to us that our slow passage to the island in the very light prevailing wind might have been watched carefully by the murderer and could even have precipitated his early departure from the scene of the crime. Nor did it cross our minds that he might have been in hiding on the island and our erratic wanderings might have put our lives in danger. The truth is that the finding of a man in his sixties tucked up in bed with a towel wrapped round his head was a sad but far from horrific event. Nothing in our minds linked the cut pieces of rope with sinister events – random bits of rope did not seem particularly out of place in a lighthouse station. We did not link the finding of the barrel of a rifle in the lighthouse workshop with gunshot wounds, as we had not seen any. The possibility that a murder might have taken place on that summer's day, on a beautiful island in the peaceful Stewartry of Kirkcudbright, was the furthest thing from our minds.

At 8.15 a.m. on the morning of 19 August, two policemen acting on impressively accurate information stopped Robert Dickson's hired Hillman Husky near Selby in Yorkshire. Dickson was taken by surprise and did not resist arrest. A loaded rifle with a sawn-off barrel lay between the car's front seats, and £80 in cash was found in his pockets. In response to questioning about events at Little Ross, Dickson calmly replied, 'All right, I know all about it'. After the arrest, press attention shifted from Kirkcudbright and following the provision of formal statements to the police, we were left alone to contemplate our strange adventure. I returned to my studies in Edinburgh, where I was disconcerted to find that so widespread was the press coverage of the incident, and so great was public interest in all aspects of the matter, that I was recognised in the streets on many occasions by people who obviously knew of my involvement in the mystery, but probably could not remember the nature of my role.

The story broke at a time when the press seemed to be particularly hungry for news; perhaps more importantly, it was a story that could be interpreted and related in distinctly different ways according to the preferences of editors. To some, it was essentially a mystery story, to be likened to the disappearance of the three lighthouse keepers at the Flannan Islands in 1900. To others, it was a tale of violent disharmony between two men, whose calling required them to live in close proximity to each other in an environment in which petty squabbles could easily have broken out and then been magnified beyond endurance. Other reports likened the situation that my father and I had found to that of the 'ghost ship' *Marie Celeste,* and one American magazine managed to weave gold from the Spanish Armada into a highly inaccurate account of the whole affair. Headlines such as

'Death Island' appeared, and reports were full of references to 'howling dogs' and to special reporters having climbed the 'seven steps' to the lighthouse door. The dog did not howl and there are no steps to the lighthouse door, but almost all press reports included these entirely fictional details. Perhaps the reporters deserve a little sympathy, as the policemen who guarded potential landing places on the island steadfastly followed their orders and refused to permit anyone to land. This did not prevent the less scrupulous of Kirkcudbright's mariners from charging large sums of money to convey members of the press to the island, at which they later found they could only stare from a distance. After some harrowing and intrusive coverage of the distress of Dickson's mother and that of the friends of Hugh Clark, the story began to fade from the front pages.

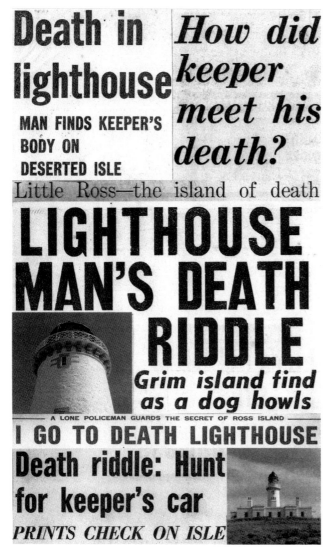

Collage of press headlines

A strange tale has been told by Ian and Isabel Summers, who left the island only two months before the murder, having been transferred to Neist Point on Skye. Isabel Summers, in writing about her stay at Little Ross, gives the following account:

> You will find mention of our spaniel Judy, who formed a great attachment to Hugh, and he to her. Hugh's wife was in a care home with what we now acknowledge to be dementia, they had no family, and Ian and Judy seemed to fill that gap. When we left, Hugh pleaded with Ian to leave Judy with him for company, but he could not bear to part with his friend. Weeks later, Judy seemed upset, and with head lifted, howled so painfully and so often that we decided we had to take her to the vet in Dunvegan the next day (a costly visit as we had to hire a car, having no transport of our own). Next morning however, she seemed to have settled. Then later that day, the devastating news came through to us at Neist Point about Hugh. We thought you would find this an interesting view of a dog's acute sense, in spite of the intervening miles and weeks since we had left Hugh on the Ross, of there being something terribly wrong.

Principal keeper John Thomson and his wife Meg returned from their holiday on Ailsa Craig to find that their professional and domestic lives had changed forever. Many strangers, including my father and I, had invaded the privacy of their home. Of their two neighbours and colleagues who had both regularly enjoyed afternoon tea and scones in their kitchen, one was dead, and the other was in prison accused of his murder. On top of all this they now also knew that with the imminent introduction of automation, they were to be the last of their highly-regarded profession to occupy the island. Their remaining time on the island must have been extremely sad and disturbing. It was also fairly short, as Little Ross lighthouse was automated on 17 November 1960 and the Thomsons were then posted to Ailsa Craig.

Robert McKenna Cribbes Dickson's trial for capital murder and the theft of his victim's car, boat, and wages commenced in the High Court in Dumfries before Lord Cameron on 27 November 1960. My father and I were both cited to appear as witnesses and had to give evidence to the court, together with a large number of other Kirkcudbright people, all of whom were known to us and many of whom were friends. I was a few days short of my 20th birthday when I made my one, and hopefully only, appearance in a court of law. I found the experience initially fascinating and impressive, but ultimately chilling and very disturbing. Like anyone else in my position would have been, I was unfamiliar with either the layout of the courtroom, or the form that the proceedings would follow. Since giving my formal statement immediately after the event, I had not been in communication with anyone regarding the case and had little idea of what to expect. It was a shock to find that as one of the first few witnesses, I was called from the witness room through a doorway which led directly into the witness box. To move so swiftly from chatting to many friends among my fellow witnesses to being confronted with the formality of the courtroom and a confusing array of bewigged figures was a shock. Before I was able even to distinguish the jury, prosecution counsel, and defence counsel, I found myself being asked to swear an unfamiliar oath, then having to give an account of the events of the day, before beginning, rather nervously, to answer questions. An 'exhibit' was displayed to me and I was asked 'Is this the log book you examined at little Ross Lighthouse on the 18th August?' My answer was a good deal less than decisive, as the page was swimming in front of my eyes, my hands were trembling, and I had no clear recollection of what the log-book in question looked like. Fortunately my evidence and that of my father was necessary merely to provide the context from which the case would emerge and I was kindly treated by my inquisitor. After giving evidence, I was able to go to the public gallery, and I found the case so interesting that I attended the court each day until judgement was made. I was not by any means the only witness to find the formality of the court proceedings overwhelming. A lady, when asked to identify the prisoner in court, pointed firstly at the foreman of the jury, and secondly at a gentleman in the public gallery. Lord Cameron promptly cut through the tittering that rippled incongruously through the courtroom and asked the prisoner if, in the circumstances, he would signify his presence and whereabouts. Robert Dickson gave a wave and a little smile to the much relieved lady who said words to the effect of 'Oh there ye are Robert – I couldn'ae see ye'.

The Crown's case against Robert Dickson was that he had carried out what the prosecution deemed to have been a 'cold calculated, deliberate, brutal, black hearted murder', the motive for which was alleged to be the theft of money, a dinghy and a car. No reference was made to the fact that violence was completely unnecessary to commit the theft, as Dickson could have helped himself to all these items and more at any time of the night or day. Robert Dickson and Hugh Clark were the only two people on the island, but because of the nature of their work and the watch-keeping system, they were rarely together other than for brief periods of time. For much of the time that one of them was awake, the other was fast asleep. The murder of Hugh Clark was to my mind utterly pointless, irrational, and inexplicable. It was carried out while Hugh Clark slept peacefully, and there was no evidence of any ill-feeling between the two men. The prosecution's case that it was among other things a 'brutal' murder seemed to display a convenient resort to the preconception of an inherently wicked perpetrator. Their theory extended to the suggestion that part of Dickson's plan had been to create a mystery reminiscent of infamous situations discovered at the Flannan Islands and on board the *Marie Celeste*. The claim that as part of this plan, he had intended to use the lengths of rope found beside the body of his victim to ballast it with rocks and then to dispose of it at sea seemed to me to be without foundation. Even the short time Dickson had spent on Little Ross would have left him well aware that any item deposited in the sea off the island, however well ballasted, was likely to be washed up on the shore within a very short time. The question of how Dickson's own disappearance was to be arranged was never touched on, and the circumstances that led up to his arrest hardly suggested that his escape plans were those of a criminal mastermind. My impression was that the murder of Hugh Clark was an act of such folly that it could have been undertaken only by someone who was suffering from a form of temporary mental illness. When a degree of reason returned to the perpetrator, he then committed the thefts in a half-hearted and completely ineffective effort to evade the consequences of his actions. It could be argued that all murders are by their very nature brutal, but it must surely be conceded that shooting a sleeping man, who would never know what had happened to him, was a lot less brutal than many murders, and in the circumstances described, an entirely irrational act.

The defence referred to Dickson's troubled history prior to his appointment as a lighthouse keeper, which included a period of time served in an approved school after the theft of a car, complaints of severe headaches after a fall from a horse, voluntary attendance as a patient at Aberdeen Royal Mental Hospital, and an attempted suicide on returning to the Royal Navy after a period of absence without leave. In 1957, an individual doctor at Aberdeen Royal Mental Hospital had certified Dickson as insane, but no action had been taken to formalise that certification as his condition had subsequently improved. Robert Dickson did not give evidence on his own behalf, so it was not possible to gain any direct insight to his character at the trial. He did however conduct himself with some dignity and appeared to follow events with close attention. John Thomson, the experienced principal keeper, who had shared the island with him during working hours and leisure time for four weeks prior to the murder, described him to the court as 'a good and responsible employee, on cordial terms with the murdered man.'

The result of the case was never really in any doubt, as the evidence against Robert Dickson was overwhelming. It was reported in some newspapers that, during a prison visit from his mother, he had said to her 'I know God's law — an eye for an eye, a tooth for a tooth.' He clearly had little doubt about what was going to happen to him. His mental fitness to be accountable for his actions however was another matter and it seemed to me and to many other people, both then and now, that the defence case claiming that he was a psychopath, episodically on the borderline of insanity, with reactions that were abnormal under conditions of stress, was well made. After the jury pronounced the prisoner guilty, a scene unfolded which no writer of Victorian melodrama could have outdone. As Lord Cameron donned the hideous black cap and prepared to pronounce a sentence of death by hanging, the courtroom, lit by a cupola, grew darker and darker, until coinciding with the Judge's awful words, the building and its occupants were both illuminated and shaken by an enormous flash of lightning and a colossal peal of thunder. Nobody who was present will ever forget that terrifying moment.

My views at the time were perhaps not in accordance with those of most other people, in that I found the verdict to be deeply disturbing, but I have remained of the same opinion ever since. I have no doubts whatsoever that Robert Dickson was responsible for the death of Hugh Clark and cannot do other than totally condemn his actions. I am equally sure however that Robert Dickson was suffering from some form of serious mental illness at the time of the crime. In 1960, both public opinion and the law of the land seemed to find it reasonable that retribution should be sought from a young man with a history of mental illness by fastening a rope round his neck and dropping him through a trapdoor. I found this to be completely unacceptable.

A few years ago, I took part in a television documentary programme about the murder at Little Ross, in the course of which I expressed my doubts about the appropriateness of the verdict and sentence. On seeing the finished documentary, I was surprised and moved to find that two other people interviewed, a reporter who had covered the case for a rather hawkish newspaper, and one of the local police constables involved in the initial investigation, shared my misgivings about the form that justice took on this occasion.

I am still a regular visit to Little Ross Island and have occasionally enjoyed a cup of tea in the much-altered room where the murder took place. I have seen no ghosts there and I have had no feelings of dread. Sadness does linger, but it is chiefly regret that one life was needlessly lost and another initially ruined and ultimately lost. The greater regret is the loss of the wonderful traditions of the Northern Lighthouse Board's resident keepers, and their dedicated professional vigilance on behalf of all seamen.

What does still fill me with horror is my memory of the trial in Dumfries, and the fact that my evidence and that of my father and our friends played a part, admittedly indirect, in bringing about the death of a physically healthy young man. Although Robert Dickson was reprieved five days before the execution planned for 21 December 1960, he took his own life in prison two years later by an overdose of drugs.

CHAPTER 13

A Lighthouse without Keepers

On 17 November 1960, while the last assistant keeper at Little Ross lighthouse languished in a prison cell awaiting his trial for the murder of relief keeper Hugh Clark, principal keeper John Thomson and his wife Meg packed their belongings and prepared to leave Little Ross with their dog and their budgie, bound for Ailsa Craig. That prominent rocky island in the Firth of Clyde was to be their new home and their last posting before retirement. When the embers finally died down in the stove in their kitchen at Little Ross, it was probably the first time in 118 years, apart from during the periods of its occupants' annual leave, that the kitchen had not been a source of warmth and comfort.

John Thomson had already witnessed the dismantling of the equipment which had been so diligently cared for by himself and all his predecessors. He may have approved generally of the modernisation process and been impressed by the relative simplicity of the new system, but he is also likely to have been saddened by the fact that his life's work, and that of all his predecessors, had so rapidly been rendered obsolete. The magnificent clockwork mechanism that had governed their lives had ceased to tick, its brass work would no longer need to be polished and the oil-burning lamp would no longer need to be lit.

The weight, which was the source of energy to drive the clockwork mechanism, was of course redundant after automation. One might reasonably wonder what became of this object that had travelled up and down the tower for so many years and had caused generations of lighthouse keepers not only stress but also considerable physical effort. It could easily have been forgotten and left in repose at the bottom of the chamber in which it had risen and fallen for so many years, but it was recovered by attendant boatman George C. Davidson, and used as a mooring weight for his motor launch. It is probably now lying at the bottom of Kirkcudbright harbour.

George C. Davidson, who succeeded George Poland as attendant boatman, provided, with his characteristic blend of accuracy and wit, the following description of the gas-powered system, which was installed in 1960:

The fuel is propane: two banks each of four 13kg bottles. One bank feeds the light and the other cuts in automatically if the first one fails. In addition there are four full bottles standing by. The light, flashing every five-seconds, burns day and night and consists of three small mantles with pilot flames and magnifying lenses. The flashing mechanism, the size of a pint jug, has no external moving parts: In fact the only visible moving component in the whole system is the attendant/boatman.

The flashing mechanism consisted of a cylinder containing a bellows/piston which moved under the influence of the incoming gas, taking five seconds to fill. On activation of a trip valve, the gas was then released to the mantles in such a way as to provide a flash every five seconds.

Gas bottle store, courtesy of Douglas Molyneux

After the process of automation was completed the lighthouse continued to function reliably, but the flash it emitted every five seconds was but a weak version of the original. The light powered by the original oil-fired lamp could be seen for 18 miles, but the new light from the gas-powered mantle that replaced it was only visible for about ten miles. This nevertheless complied with the reduced requirements of the Northern Lighthouse Board, reflecting the fact that many other navigational aids were available to mariners, who no longer depended quite so heavily on lighthouses.

In the weeks, months, and years that followed the departure of the keepers, the condition of the lighthouse station that had always been so typically clean, bright, and well cared for, began to slowly deteriorate. The Northern Lighthouse Board's staff continued to inspect and maintain the lighthouse regularly and their various attendant boatmen/keepers ensured that the light was always burning efficiently. However, the evidence of human care and attention that resulted from constant habitation of the island by the keepers and their families became daily less conspicuous. All the buildings on the island, with the exception of the lighthouse tower, reverted to the ownership of St Mary's Isle Estate and lay empty and unoccupied. The attendant boatman's task became a lonely one, with nobody to welcome his arrival, no warming cup of tea beside the kitchen stove, and no offer of a bed for the night if the weather worsened. The gardens became overgrown and the pathways less well defined. Winter storms damaged both the east quay and the slipway at the western side of the island, and nobody had either the time or the inclination to carry out anything other than the minimum maintenance. Passing mariners still visited the island, but were, for a time at least, more curious about it being the scene of a murder than they were about its general history or its natural attractions. Some minor vandalism took place, mostly resulting from efforts to find fuel for barbecues and bonfires, and local scallywags occasionally broke into the cart store and the lighthouse stores to investigate their contents. Seabirds became accustomed to the island's lack of human occupants and nested where they had never previously dared. Nettles and other weeds flourished and even invaded the 'inner sanctum' of the cobbled courtyard at the base of the lighthouse tower. The windows of the two houses were covered with galvanised steel plates, protecting them from souvenir hunters and opportunists, but giving the houses a rather sinister and depressing appearance.

In 1967 or 1968, storms caused extensive damage to the slipway on the west side of the island and the Northern Lighthouse Board engaged Kirkcudbright builder W. Whan to carry out repairs. The late Ian McNeillie, one of the tradesmen who did the work, provided in 2015 the following account of his experiences at Little Ross:

> George Poland [attendant boatman] took me, Andy Broll, James 'Toosh' Hamilton and Robert 'Bing' McKie to the island in the Lighthouse Board's motor launch, together with provisions, building materials and our tools. We got access to the former Principal Keeper's house, the kitchen of which was still furnished with a table and chairs, and we made our home there for the next few days. Conditions were a bit primitive with only the floor to sleep on, but we were glad to find that the Rayburn cooker was still in working order and that there was plenty of coal. Our food supplies soon began to run low however, as did our supplies of sand and cement. The work we did was difficult, as the sea had dislodged very large stones from the slipway, all of which had to be lifted and levered back into place and carefully pinned together. We were soon tired and hungry and were eventually forced to consider how we were going to cope with the daunting task of cooking a chicken, which was the only item remaining in our larder. 'Toosh' Hamilton volunteered for this important but challenging task, and was permitted to spend much of the day lighting the Rayburn, and keeping it up to temperature, while the rest of us used up the last of the dwindling supply of building materials.
>
> When the roasted chicken was eventually brought out from the oven, it seemed expertly cooked and we looked forward to a small but tasty dinner. Sadly however, when master chef 'Toosh' proudly carved and served the chicken, his lack of experience was made evident by the fact that he had failed to remove the polythene bag containing the giblets from the chicken's innards. The long hoped for meal, contaminated with liquid plastic, was completely inedible.

John King's fishing boat *Ranger* passed close to the island next day and after checking to see that we were all safe and sound, he and his crew then willingly made a special trip up the channel to Kirkcudbright to put two of us ashore to procure fresh supplies and more building materials. We borrowed the dinghy that George Poland used as a tender to the Ross launch, and were towed back to the island by the *Ranger.* Having the dinghy meant that we could row across to Ross Bay when we finished the job, and phone from there for transport to take us back to Kirkcudbright. In all, we spent a memorable five days on the island.

The Northern Lighthouse Board's decision to proceed with automation, though much regretted by many people at the time, was readily justified by the fact that the new propane gas–powered system functioned efficiently at Little Ross for the surprisingly long period of 43 years, during which time it was refuelled and maintained on a weekly basis by three different attendant boatmen: George Poland, George C. Davidson, and Norman Parker. Norman's father Eddie had been attendant boatman at Hestan Island, and Norman had taken over that job when his father retired. It was therefore convenient for him to also take on responsibility for Little Ross when George Davidson retired in about 1995. Engineers from the Northern Lighthouse Board regularly inspected and maintained the apparatus and arranged any necessary repairs to the lighthouse tower. Over the years however, technology again advanced, and the gas-powered light system became obsolete as is explained in the following extract from 'The Northern Lighthouse Board's Notice to Mariners No 1' of 2006:

> Development of high-efficiency metal-halide lamps has allowed the replacement of the gas mantle to be achieved using solar-electric systems which charge batteries by generating an electric current directly from sunlight. In the northern latitudes of Scotland and Isle of Man, the solar panels can make use of the diffused light through the cloud cover and the battery is of a size to accumulate sufficient energy in the summer and autumn months to ensure winter operation. The power consumption for the typically required light range of 18 miles has decreased in the last decade from over 100 watts to 35 watts, making use of highly efficient lamp drivers operating directly from the 24 volt battery supply. Supplementary power for monitoring purposes is supplied from small wind powered generators.
>
> To ensure that all Aids to Navigation operate correctly, NLB aim to monitor the performance by using land-line and cellular telephone or radio links connecting the light to the NLB monitor centre in Edinburgh. Any malfunction can be immediately advertised to marine users using the Internet or maritime information systems.

The dismantling and removal of the propane gas–powered system and the installation of the new solar-powered system involved minor alterations to the lighthouse tower and the rooms at its base, which were carried out as part of a contract that included general refurbishment of the entire building. The Northern Lighthouse Board invited selected contractors to tender for the works in May 2003, and the successful firm was Conon Valley Builders of Dingwall. Their director, Mr. D. A. Morrison was responsible for undertaking all the necessary work under the watchful eyes of the Northern Lighthouse Board's engineer and project manager, and has provided the following description of the various tasks carried out by his firm:

> Following the acceptance of our tender, we started work on the 26th May 2003, preparing materials and plant for delivery to Oban where everything had to be weighed prior to loading on board the Northern Lighthouse Board's vessel *Pharos* for delivery to Little Ross Island. Thanks to a highly skilled helicopter pilot and the crew of the *Pharos,* everything arrived safely on the island on 7th June. Before we started work on site, a new camp was built which consisted of three cabins, each about 2.4 metres x 3.00 metres; two for sleeping accommodation and one for use as a kitchen. Power and water were provided through a generator and a special pump to give supplies just like at home, and a washroom/portaloo was erected separately from the cabins. Water and fuel was stored in 800-gallon and 600-gallon tanks respectively. When linked to our generator and pump, this system worked well. Our camp was fully functional by the end of the day and all materials had been transferred from the *Pharos* which was anchored off the island. We were ready to start work on site on the 8th June.
>
> For the duration of the main contract, we had four or five men on site but subcontractors brought the total workforce up to six men and one woman. The arrival of the young lady electrician put some stress on our humble living accommodation, but as she was the daughter of the subcontractor concerned, she shared a cabin with her father and the Boss happily slept in the tool-shed for the benefit and comfort of his contented workforce.
>
> Our first task was to build a scaffold over the quarterdeck and round the lighthouse tower, with no load bearing on the quarterdeck. This had to be done using pillars at the front and back of the building with long alloy beams spanning over three sides. The main scaffold was built on top and the jacks were screwed up so that no weight was put on the roof. After the scaffold was completed, we then fixed temporary lights at the front and back of the tower to be seen by vessels navigating in the area while the conversion and alterations were being carried out.
>
> After the scaffolding was erected and the temporary lights were working, we removed all fittings and gas bottles from the existing system and cleaned out all the rooms in the building. The store room on the right of the front entrance was turned into a battery room with the joints of all stone walls picked out and repointed, the floor was dug out and prepared for a new concrete floor and a well was formed with an outlet pipe draining to the outside in case of any fluid spills. After a new ceiling had been fitted, the walls and ceiling were painted white and the floor was painted red. New batteries were then installed on battery racks, and on the external south facing wall, solar panels were fitted and cables were run to connect them with the batteries.
>
> The middle room below the tower had its walls stripped back to the bare surfaces and then was lined with framing and water resistant plasterboard. A new concrete lintel was cast over the doorway and a new door was hung. The fireplace opening was built up, leaving a vent to permit the circulation of air in an effort to keep dampness at bay.

The storeroom on the left of the entrance had previously been used as a coal store and was retained as a general store after its ceiling had been renewed and its floor levelled out with a concrete screed.

New external doors were then fitted to each of the outside storerooms and metal grilles were fitted to both these doors and to the entrance to the tower.

Inside the light room at the top of the tower, work was already well underway to remove existing lights and old workings from previous lights. Some parts were crated and others were put into helibags, ready to be lifted by helicopter to Ross Farm. From there, they were collected by truck and taken to their new home at the Stewartry Museum in Kirkcudbright. Once the light room was cleared, we fitted a new floor at a different level, then all electrics were completed and the new light was installed and made ready for use.

At the exterior of the tower, defective pointing was raked out from joints in the stonework and new pointing was carried out. Once the new pointing had dried out, the whole exterior was repainted. The old door that gave access from the lamp room to the balcony was removed and a new door fitted, providing better access and a better seal from the weather. At the same time, many cracked panes in the light room glazing were replaced and the exterior of the dome was painted black. On completion of those works, the scaffolding was removed and the way was clear to put the new solar-powered system into operation. Our last task at the main buildings was to repair and paint the wall which bounded the courtyard between the houses and the tower.

After all the work was completed on the tower, we were instructed to renovate the beacon, lower down on the North side of the island. Our first task was to erect scaffolding round the beacon and then to remove the top stones. A new shuttering was then built and a concrete coping was cast. The beacon's masonry walls were then repointed and painted. A stainless steel ladder was fitted to the East wall of the beacon and handrails were fixed round the concrete cope at the top. The refurbished beacon was then painted white.

Our final task was to dismantle our cabins, tidy the site and ship all tools and surplus materials back to Oban via the *Pharos*. We then collected everything from Oban and returned to Dingwall by road. Work on site finished on 20th November 2003 and all plant and materials were returned to Oban by 27th January 2004.

Solar panels,
courtesy of Douglas Molyneux

Battery store,
courtesy of Douglas Molyneux

On completion of the installation of the solar-powered system, there was no longer any requirement to retain an attendant boatman, so despite the important role that Norman Parker and his boat *Westward* had played in ferrying men, materials, and equipment to the island, his services were dispensed with. In future, vessels were only to be chartered as necessary to carry Northern Lighthouse Board staff to and from the island for the few occasions on which visits were anticipated. One hundred and sixty one years of continuous employment of attendant boatmen at Little Ross had ended for good.

During 1971, in response to requests by Scottish Oils and Shell Mex, all buoys that defined the channel leading up the River Dee had been lit by battery-operated electric lights, to enable coastal tankers to arrive at and depart from Kirkcudbright during the hours of darkness. These lights were provided and maintained by the Town Council of Kirkcudbright until after 1974 when Dumfries and Galloway Regional Council came into being and took over responsibility for the port of Kirkcudbright. The lone remaining beacon on Little Ross Island was on land which was the property of St Mary's Isle Estate and, being technically out with the port of Kirkcudbright, it remained unlit.

In 2005, two years after the Northern Lighthouse Board altered the lighthouse at Little Ross to utilise solar power rather than bottled gas, it became obvious that a fairly small additional investment would enable the beacon to also be provided with a light. Consequentially, the many fishing vessels and pleasure boats using the harbour and marina at Kirkcudbright during the hours of darkness would also benefit:

NOTICE TO MARINERS

No 48 of 2005
Scotland West Coast
Little Ross Beacon
Northern Lighthouse Board Edinburgh, 4th October 2005

Lat: 54 deg 46.064 deg North WGS 84 datum   Long:
004 deg. 05.020 deg. West WGS 84 datum

ESTABLISHMENT OF LIGHT

Notice is given that on or about 19th October 2005 a permanent light, synchronised with the Little Ross Lighthouse, will be established at this location with the under noted characteristics:

Character: flashing (twice) white every five seconds

Elevation above MHWS: 21 metres
Nominal Range: 5 miles
Description of structure: stone beacon (Height 10 metres)
Leading line: 201 degrees (as charted)

J B Taylor
Chief Executive
Little Ross Lighthouse

At the time of writing (April 2016), the NLV *Pharos* has been lying off Little Ross Island for several days, unloading the necessary workforce, portable accommodation, and materials by helicopter, for another refurbishment of the lighthouse station that is expected to last for approximately ten weeks. Welcome minor repairs to the east quay are understood to be among the many tasks to be undertaken.

CHAPTER 14

Reoccupation, Restoration,
and
Recreation

An exciting new chapter in the history of Little Ross Island was opened in 1986, when plans were prepared to save the former lighthouse keepers' cottages from further deterioration and restore them to habitable condition. The brave and imaginative people who dared to take on this extremely ambitious task were Roger and Rosie Wild and their close friend Douglas Molyneux. To describe their intended course of action as merely daunting would undermine the extent of the difficulties that had to be overcome. Only people of the most exceptional skill, determination, and resourcefulness would be able to find solutions to the many problems that would confront them and the energy necessary to implement them. In addition, the ability to exercise great care and sensitivity would be essential to facilitate the reforming of a home on Little Ross without detriment to the island's unique character and charm. Roger, Rosie, and Douglas have conclusively proved themselves to possess all these qualities and many more in their patient, scrupulous, and practical restoration of the two little houses that had been much loved homes for so many families from the end of 1842 until 1960.

In early 1986, Rosie Wild, a community speech and language therapist in East Lothian, had become concerned for the wellbeing of her friend Douglas Molyneux. Douglas was a former automotive engineer who, because of a change in his personal circumstances, was in need of a new challenge to which he could apply his considerable practical skills. In conversation with Rosie, Douglas had expressed the view that what he would really like to do would be to find a dilapidated, remote, and distinguished property that he could save from further deterioration, and thereby feel that he had done something more useful than merely earning his own living. Rosie's husband Roger Wild, an extremely busy consultant radiologist in Edinburgh, was wrestling with vital changes in his profession's way of working. Adjusting to these changes was, in Rosie's opinion, causing him and many others in his situation to have to work for very long hours that were potentially prejudicial both to personal health and to general wellbeing. Rosie realised that if she was able to help Douglas find the property that he yearned for, it might also provide an escape for Roger and herself from the pressures of his work, the potential property's very remoteness being crucial to the concept of a complete escape from most professional obligations. Douglas and Rosie scoured the Inner and Outer Hebrides and the other islands from the Butt of Lewis southwards, looking at and considering many different opportunities, but initially failing to find anything that seemed to strike the necessary balance between character, seclusion, and reasonable accessibility. Eventually, and somewhat to their surprise, at the southernmost extremity of their search area, they found the island of Little Ross and learned that the houses there were uninhabited. Roger, Rosie, and Douglas came fairly quickly to the unanimous conclusion that they had found exactly what they were looking for, in an area that Roger and Rosie had already had happy experience of as a holiday destination, separated from Edinburgh by only a two and a half hour road journey and a very short sea passage from the mainland at Ross farm, over Ross sound to the island. Douglas takes up the story:

> I was working at the time (1985/86) as a labourer for a recently qualified architect friend based in Peebles, (having resigned my post as a Technician in the Fluid Dynamics Research Group at Edinburgh University's Kings Buildings). He had decided to open a branch office in Kirkcudbright. We were taking some office equipment from Peebles to Kirkcudbright one day and once we had off-loaded the car I was told to go off and explore the Ross Bay area as there was apparently an island nearby with empty property on it. This I did, and through binoculars observed a lighthouse tower and adjacent buildings. On our way back to Peebles later that day we called at the local Council Offices and found out who owned the island and property on it. Back home I communicated my findings to Roger and Rosie and we subsequently wrote to Sir David Hope Dunbar, Bt., expressing our interest in the cottages. He summoned us for interview and granted us a lease on attractive terms on condition that we brought the property up to habitable standard, as defined by the local authority. We agreed, and so started the adventure!

St Mary's Isle Estate includes Little Ross Island and the buildings thereon, but the lighthouse tower and associated stores, are occupied by the Northern Lighthouse Board. The lease offered by Sir David Hope Dunbar Bt. of St Mary's Isle Estate included the two former lighthouse cottages and the principal keeper's garden, and was to extend for an initial period of ten and three quarter years at a peppercorn rent, during which period the tenants were to be responsible for bringing the cottages up to a habitable condition and for maintaining them at their own expense. On 28 May 1997, the rent was to be re-assessed and rent reviews would be made every three years thereafter. Agreement was quickly reached, after which a jocular Sir David wished his new tenants well and confessed that he thought they must be a bit mad!

When Roger, Rosie, and Douglas finally took possession of their intended home they were confronted with a scene of devastation, which though not wholly unforeseen, was challenging to say the least. The lead work behind the parapet walls on the east side of both houses had either been damaged by wind and weather or had been vandalised; great amounts of water had therefore penetrated the structure, resulting in the windows and surrounding woodwork being severely affected by wet rot, dry rot and woodworm infestation. The ceiling joists, which also supported the lead–covered flat roofs, were severely rotted at their eastern ends, and many of the lath and lime-plastered ceilings were consequently in a precarious condition. The galvanised metal sheets which had kept the window openings secure had been deliberately fitted with gaps at their tops and bottoms to permit ventilation, but this had allowed swallows to nest throughout the houses for 25 years. The Rayburn cookers on which Mrs. Thomson had baked her beautiful scones and 'Toosh' Hamilton had prepared his infamous roast chicken were now rusted beyond restoration. The only sign of human habitation was a solitary and very disreputable blue jacket lying in the middle of the floor of one of the bleak, damp, and cheerless rooms.

Before work could seriously begin on repair and restoration, the nature of the original fresh water supply needed to be determined and, if possible, restored. A suitable boat had to be obtained to transport people, furniture, and building materials from the mainland and a means of transporting heavy loads from the landing places to the island's summit had to be devised. The existing drains would also have to be located, investigated, and probably renewed. Oil lamps would provide ample light initially, but a piped supply of bottled gas, or even the means of generating electricity, would be longer-term targets:

> Initially we had to find a boat and engine. We were lucky in finding an ex–diver's boat in Galashiels which came with a 40hp Johnson engine which had stripped its crankshaft splines but had a good gearbox. We then found another scrap engine which had a good crankshaft and by combining the two, which was not recommended procedure, ended up with a working outboard engine which served us well for some years. The rebuilding of this engine I did before moving to Little Ross while living in my rented cottage in Peebleshire, which had no mains electricity and only gas lighting!

> Douglas Molyneux.

Douglas commenced residence at Little Ross on 1 May 1987, virtually camping in what was from that date to be his permanent home, and Roger and Rosie Wild's 'holiday home'.

Shortly after Roger, Rosie, and Douglas's tenancy commenced, they were startled to learn from a press report brought by one of their visitors that their fine new home had been the scene of a murder. It seems that everyone had thought the story was so well known that they could not possibly have been unaware of it. With hindsight, it was perhaps better that they stumbled upon that potentially disturbing news after they had become accustomed to living there and developed a real affection for their island home, untainted by any macabre tales of past events.

After some time in residence and much careful thought, it was decided to make minor alterations to the two cottages, with the intention of combining them to form one larger house. This was partly necessitated by the fact that neither of the original houses had what would now be regarded as a living room. Lighthouse keepers and their families had usually been either asleep or at work and their kitchens provided the only communal spaces in which they could share domestic life with their families. One small bedroom was sacrificed in each cottage and the wall between them was demolished to form a large west-facing living room accessible from either house. Separate kitchens and bathrooms were formed in each cottage so that the occupants could have privacy and independence when required.

On an early visit to the converted houses, I recollect being asked to identify the room in which the murder had taken place. I was initially disconcerted when I entered the room in the former assistant keeper's house, because it was one of the two bedrooms that had been combined to form the new living room and therefore felt unfamiliar. Roger and Rosie however merely nodded wisely and said 'yes, that's what we guessed'. It transpired that they and Douglas had always found that particular room to have an eerie chill, no matter what measures were taken to raise its temperature. After formation of the new living room however, the problem vanished forever. As an architect, I usually like to think that I can provide a practical reason for such occurrences and I therefore tend to think that the very large wood-burning stove in the new living room might be a factor in this case. I must however report, in all fairness, that several residents in the houses have apparently reported the presence of a man in a blue 'beanie' hat, appearing and disappearing in unexpected places. One of Roger and Rosie's friends, while visiting Little Ross from the Isle of Skye, decorated the exposed beams of their living room ceiling with Celtic runes, and her work is now credited with having been successful in warding off any lurking evil spirits.

The three new tenants were fortunate to have large numbers of family, friends, relatives, and colleagues who were not only eager to visit their romantic and mysterious new home, but were also willing to help with a myriad of tasks ranging from those requiring great skill to those requiring, no less importantly, brute force and stamina. Little Ross Island attracts a surprising number of visiting yachts, fishing vessels, and miscellaneous other craft which use the anchorage off the island, and the crews of which often come ashore there for a stroll. On one wild and wet day, Roger and Douglas were engaged in pulling down the rotting lime ceilings in their new abode when, through the dense cloud of plaster dust, a dishevelled face appeared. It turned out to be that of a South African kayaker seeking refuge from the weather and permission to camp overnight on the island. He was promptly given food and a bed for the night and then, in gratitude, spent a whole week demonstrating his mastery of the crowbar and its application to rotten ceilings. The resulting mountain of timber laths was disposed of in a series of bonfires systematically dispersed all over the courtyard; flames destroyed the accumulated grass and nettles, exposing beautiful original cobblestones. Potatoes were baked daily in the embers of the many fires.

With the multi-skilled Douglas in permanent residence, progress was steady, and on summer weekends he was backed up by a squad of up to 20 friends, relatives, and conscripts brought by Roger and Rosie. A new UPVC fresh water supply pipe was laid in a trench which had been cut to expose the original cast iron pipe. It went through rough grassland and numerous rocky outcrops, extending more than 100 yards from a spring and catchment area close to sea level on the island's west coast, and up a steep slope to the cottages. This task, all carried out by hand over many weeks with picks and shovels, was particularly gruelling, back-breaking and seemingly never-ending. A concrete base had been found near the source of the fresh water, suggesting that at one time there might have been a pump located there. Enquiries to the Northern Lighthouse Board confirmed that such a pump had once existed. The following account by Douglas of the nature of the water supply and the steps that were taken to improve it demonstrates his skill in dealing with one of the most essential elements in his new home:

> As originally built in 1841/42 the cottages derived their water supply entirely from rainwater which was collected from both the cottages roof and the lighthouse storerooms roof. On the cottages, the flat roof was laid to a fall from west to east, and at the eastern (front) side a deep gutter behind the wall parapet collected the roof water and discharged it through pipes passing through the parapet which connected to vertical drainpipes which discharged into two large tanks located below the pavement in front of the cottages. (These tanks have large removable covers so it would have been easy to dip a container into them to extract water. However, there is some evidence that small lead pipes were subsequently fitted from the original kitchen sink areas to the tanks and these may have had a small lever-type hand pumps connected to them to make water extraction easier.) In a similar manner, roof water from the lighthouse stores was delivered through the wall parapet, down through vertical pipes then piped under and across the courtyard to discharge into the same large underground tanks. At the base of each vertical drainpipe was a lead gully with a removable vertical riser pipe. With the pipe installed, the roof water filled the gully and was piped through an overflow to the underground tanks. If the gully became contaminated with debris, removing the riser pipe allowed the sludge to escape to waste via culverts below the courtyard which were built to pass below the lighthouse tower base and discharge to waste some distance down the eastern slope of the island.
>
> Given that all the roof coverings were lead, a new fresh potable water supply source was required, and this had already been put in place before we arrived. A cast iron pipe ran from the house's south storeroom down to a pump house on the West side of the island. On top of the South storeroom, above its roof, a sectional steel water tank was once fitted and this tank was connected, by small-bore pipes to the two kitchen sink areas. Adjacent to the pump house on the West coast, but at a slightly higher level, was a spring which fed fresh water to a sedimenting tank located in a small stone

building, and from there the it was piped to an engine-driven lift pump to be pumped up to the house as required.

This last system had all but been removed when the lighthouse was de-manned in 1960, so we replaced it and made it semi-automatic. We were lucky enough to fall heir to a fifty year old Petter powered Lister ram pump unit, which still provides the fresh water to the cottages.

We did not replace the rather ugly sectional steel tank which sat atop the South store of the cottages. Instead we installed new plastic storage tanks just below roof level over the bathrooms. Two tanks with a capacity of 25 gallons each are supplied by the engine driven pump at the pump house on the West coast. These feed fresh water to both kitchen sinks. An electric pressure pump is also installed at the pump house and, when we had a working generator, we were able to pump up fresh water at the push of a button! However, this exercise required at least 4kVA output from the generator in order to start the pump. The generator broke down and at present we rely on the old Petter/Lister engine pump system to raise water. As a visit is required to the pump house to start this engine it is also a healthy exercise routine! Float switches in the storage tanks kill the engine's ignition when the tanks are full.

Another two tanks of around 50 gallons each, and also in the roof space, are supplied by electric lift pumps (actually bilge pumps) located inside the courtyard underground tanks. The roof tanks supply collected rainwater by gravity feed to the toilet cisterns, baths, hot water tanks (the heat comes from boilers in the kitchen ranges) and other basins. This system works automatically from the 24volt DC supply, again using float switches to start and stop the pumps.

Interestingly, we did have to arrange for the fresh water to be tested before we were allowed to use it. The quality was fine except for a slightly raised salt level. Hardly surprising when the source was rainwater draining down through many feet of coastal grassland frequently showered by sea spray!

Drains were laid from the cottages to a new septic tank sited to the east side of the lighthouse and a track was cut through very rocky ground for the outfall from that tank. The hole in which the septic tank was to be placed was cut from solid rock, with the help of a hired hydraulic drill. Weeks of absolutely exhausting work were necessary to achieve what can be written about in a mere two sentences. Delivery of the new plastic septic tank was in itself a challenge involving its transport by lorry to Ross Bay on the mainland, from where it was safely floated across to the island, despite its apparent determination to capsize and sink. On completion of the drainage work, which had caused some inevitable damage to the cobblestones in the courtyard, Rosie's mother, at the age of 90, spent many hours on her hands and knees, helping to neatly restore them in accordance with the original pattern:

Many friends and relatives willingly gave of their time and or expertise in the early days of the project. Digging the trench uphill from the fresh water source on the West side required many weekends of hard labour throughout one summer. The greatest enthusiast for this task was Rosie's cousin's partner who, on each visit would turn up with a different implement which he convinced us was the right one for the job. One day he seemed to be having a problem with a foot which really annoyed him. Two years later, in his early 50s, he died of Motor Neurone Disease. Having witnessed the relentless advance of this tragic condition, we were determined to do something to mark his passing and this led to the establishment of a sponsored Charity Swim in relays round the island in aid of Motor Neurone Disease Research. Each year, over I think a six year period, different groups of relatives, friends and on one occasion, a bunch of colleagues from my X-Ray department, collected much money for the cold wet circumnavigation of the island. One or two managed the whole way, approximately one and a half miles. The Charity was grateful to receive over six thousand pounds in total and we felt we had done justice to the memory of the redoubtable Les.

Roger Wild.

A Kirkcudbright plumber, the late Donald Clement, repaired the defective lead work behind the parapets and all the windows on the east elevation were renewed. These were the only two tasks that were undertaken by commercial firms, everything else being tackled by Douglas, Roger, Rosie, and their team of volunteers. Ceiling joists were repaired or renewed as necessary, timber flooring was replaced, and plaster was either patched or renewed by a relative of Rosie who was experienced in that trade. The same relative willingly came forward to deal with a second-hand Aga range that had to be dismantled in Ross Bay, shipped across to the island in pieces, and then reassembled in the new kitchen that was being fitted out by Douglas. The person responsible, Alan George Armitage, felt that his initials indicated that it was a task that he was destined to undertake.

Three young goats introduced to the island during the 1980s were named May, Little Fidra, and Bell, after lighthouses on the east coast of Scotland. But their presence had unforeseen consequences, as they soon demonstrated their ability not only to jump over the stone walls of the garden which Rosie was struggling to develop and maintain, but also to devour everything she had planted. They were nevertheless tolerated and permitted to spend the rest of their natural lives on the island.

Throughout the early years of Douglas's residence on the island, the Northern Lighthouse Board's attendant boatman George C. Davidson also acted as non-

George C. Davidson DSM BEM,
courtesy of the Henry family

resident lighthouse keeper, and was responsible for both the maintenance of the light and the regular supply and replacement of the necessary gas cylinders. George was the former coxswain of Kirkcudbright lifeboat, pilot to the River Dee, and an authority on all nautical matters, as well as having an extensive general knowledge of local and natural history. Douglas developed an excellent relationship with him, and also with the various officials of the Northern Lighthouse Board who regularly inspected the lighthouse station. By this time, the slipway was once more in need of repair, and the Northern Lighthouse Board, recognising that having a functional slipway was in both their interest and that of their attendant boatman, provided the necessary sand and cement, while Douglas and other volunteers supplied the labour to complete the task. Roger, Rosie, and Douglas acquired a dumper truck, a cement mixer, and a generator, all of which were brought to the island on their own small boat with the assistance of Richard Finlay of Ross farm and his forklift truck. The dumper truck made light work of the task of taking goods, materials, and sometimes people up the path to the lighthouse, and was a particularly welcome innovation to anyone who had ever carried a gas cylinder or a bag of coal to the island's summit. Obtaining supplies of fresh food and other necessities of life was often problematical and always required careful planning to take into account weather and tidal conditions. This was particularly important when Douglas was alone on the island:

> Every victualling trip depends on tide and weather conditions; even more so if you are single handed and risk-averse! I owe my survival to a lot of luck and the good advice and examples of the late George Davidson, whose local knowledge of the vagaries of access and egress from Little Ross, so generously given, was essential. I remember just before Easter one year, when the wind so often becomes a strong easterly, we attempted to row out of Ross Bay on a fairly low tide and could not get the dinghy into deep enough water to get the outboard engine running. Our rowing effort was not enough against the wind, and the sea was getting increasingly vicious until eventually we were swamped and rolled over, losing our Easter provisions to the tide, and apparently losing our Spaniel too as it had disappeared! We were able to stand up in the sea as it was quite shallow and right the dinghy, below which was our frantically paddling hound!
>
> We learned, both from advice and experience, what our own limits were, what our various boat limits were and what combination of sea and wind conditions were safe for our activities.

Douglas Molyneux.

In 1992/1993, on what was deemed to be the 150th anniversary of the completion of the lighthouse's construction, a party was held at Little Ross to celebrate the occasion. The guests included many people who had been involved in the restoration work, as well as other friends and colleagues of Roger, Rosie, and Douglas. Among the guests was the late Jimmy Thomson, nephew of John

Thomson (the last principal keeper to serve at Little Ross), and son of a lighthouse keeper. Jimmy brought with him as a gift for the island's residents a very large Northern Lighthouse Board flag which had belonged to his father, and it is still proudly flown on the island to commemorate important events. Spirited attempts are also reported to have been made to perform, on this and other suitable occasions, the dance 'Little Ross Light'.

As a result of the truly Herculean efforts of Douglas, Roger, and Rosie, the terms of their lease of the cottages on Little Ross were met within the stipulated ten and three quarter years, and a completion certificate was issued by the local authority confirming the buildings to be officially habitable. For that to be possible, repairs had been done to render them wind and watertight, a fresh water supply had been re-established and tested, new drainage had been installed, kitchens and bathrooms in keeping with the character of the houses had been fitted, and gas lighting had been provided. A small wind turbine had been installed which, supplemented by a generator, provided a modest supply of electricity until a wind of 96 mph caused the turbine to shed a blade. The resulting imbalance led to its self-destruction and the distribution of its parts northwards over the island. The Northern Lighthouse Board, despite having no further responsibility for their former lighthouse keepers' cottages, continued to offer much encouragement, advice, and support to Roger, Rosie, and Douglas, with whom they have now enjoyed a happy and productive relationship for 30 years.

Despite occasional setbacks, like the need to replace the wind turbine, it was now possible for Douglas, Roger, and Rosie to begin to escape from the constant need to wield pickaxes, sledgehammers, wrenches, and paintbrushes. Life on an isolated island was never going to be easy, but the daily chores could now become a matter of domestic routine rather than being a never-ending series of new and unforeseen challenges. Roger and Rosie were able to accommodate friends and family in some degree of comfort during the summer months, and Douglas was able to enjoy their company, in contrast to the isolation he endured throughout the winter months. In his new-found spare time, among other things, he began to develop an interest in family history with consequences that were almost surreal:

> I was adopted soon after birth in 1945 by a wonderful couple. My father, Austin Charles Molyneux, was English, born in Leominster, and my mother, Margaret Agnes Dixon Douglas, was Scottish, born in Edinburgh. We lived in a suburb of Manchester where my father had a garage business and my mother was a teacher. We regularly spent our summer holidays in Taynuilt, Argyllshire where cousins of my mum had a farm, and later on Arran. My childhood holidays were idyllic!
>
> For reasons still only known best to them, they only advised me that I was adopted when I reached the age of 11, and it somewhat surprised me. It was clear that they found discussing the matter difficult so I put the matter away in my head!
>
> In 1997, after my parents had died, I felt ready to investigate my origins

and with the help of my now ex-wife Vicky (we divorced amicably in 1981) who is an excellent researcher, discovered that I had an actual mother called Elizabeth Mary Stevenson Gass, and that she was still alive. Through the medium of an intermediary acting for a charity which supports adopted people, contact with my mother was established and I ended up meeting her in her home near Chester, where she was living alone after the death of her husband (who incidentally was not my father!). During the 1938/45 war my mother was working as a technician at Metropolitan Vickers in Trafford Park, Manchester. She did a lot of number crunching for the boffins and remembered working on Frank Whittle's jet engine project. She had lodgings in Old Trafford which she shared with another Metrovickers employee called Freddie, who I believe may be my father! My Mum hinted, but never confirmed this.

Elma, as my mum was known, came from Kirkconnel. Her family Gass were previously agricultural workers from Kirkpatrick Durham but had relocated to Kirkconnel to take advantage of the growth of the coal mining industry and a better life. This was probably around the turn of the century. While they were based at Kirkpatrick Durham my great great-Grandfather, John Gass, lived in Durhamhill Cottage, Kirkpatrick Durham and worked at Balmae House, Kirkcudbright as a gardener. This would have been at the same time as Little Ross Lighthouse was being built. Both John and his son William are buried in Kirkpatrick Durham churchyard.

Douglas Molyneux.

For Douglas, who believed himself to be a Manchester boy, to discover firstly that his mother came from Dumfriesshire, and secondly that his great-great-grandfather not only came from Kirkcudbrightshire, but was a gardener at Balmae House, must have been uncannily strange. Ever since the lighthouse station had gone into service in 1843, the occupants of Little Ross Island have gazed across to the mainland, where the most prominent and closest of the few buildings that could be seen, was Balmae House. Sadly, by the time of Douglas's residency, Balmae House had been demolished and little evidence now exists of its once beautiful gardens:

> Elma's family in Kirkconnel were not sympathetic to her pregnancy which was why I was adopted in Manchester. It could be a quirk of fate, or something to do with the way the health service, such as it was in 1945, deals with these matters, but the nursing home where I was born was next door to my adoptive father's house on Edge Lane, Stretford. I like to think that my childless parents got to hear of the plight of a Scottish lass and somehow arranged my adoption which was formalised at Strangeways Court early in 1946.
>
> Elma herself went on to marry a lovely Irish man called Patrick Nugent who worked for the Ordnance Survey. They were married at St. Bede's Church in Silloth Street, Carlisle, and later moved to Belfast where they had four children, three of whom live in England and one in France. Elma died soon after I had met her. I am so glad I was able to see her and thank her for my life, for she still carried a sense of guilt. I hope I was able to assuage at least some of it.

Douglas Molyneux.

Douglas finally came 'ashore' to the mainland in 2007 following an operation to alleviate spinal stenosis. The operation was successful but he felt that, given his age and condition, living alone on an island was probably not going to be the most sensible option for the future. He describes the 20 years he spent on Little Ross Island as the best years of his life, and it is easy to imagine how difficult it must have been for him to take the decision to finally depart from such a beautiful and inspiring place. He has however the distinction of being the longest known inhabitant in the history of the island, and has gained a unique understanding of and rapport with the natural elements that control all aspects of life in that idyllic location. He still visits the island regularly, helping Roger and Rosie with general maintenance of the fabric of the buildings and giving particular care to the mass of technological innovations he introduced and installed. When questioned about the highlights of his long stay on the island, Douglas provided the following characteristically thoughtful account, ranging from the poetic to the practical:

> Where to begin! Being at close quarters to mountainous seas in gale force winds while watching from the security of our island home is awe inspiring. The sound of the wind alone is incredible. The bluebells which colour the island in spring, and when viewed from the sea, make it seem totally blue. The satisfaction of getting the fresh water supply working so water could be obtained from a tap, without the need to carry a bottle down to the spring and back. The joy of abandoning a chemical toilet, or a dash to the shore, in exchange for a flushing toilet and working drains. The excitement of being able to flick a switch and have light without need to refuel and pump up the Tilley lamp, though I do miss the gentle hiss and the smell! The visit(s) of the NLB Commissioners and the *Fingal* and *Pharos*. The occasional trips in the Bond helicopter when it helped us with deliveries of materials. The visit of HRH Princess Anne. The arrival of the Stalwart HMLC, although it proved to be a white elephant. The list is endless, probably because to succeed in anything on the island requires so much planning, coordination and often assistance from others that when it all comes together the result is incredibly satisfying!

The above reference to the 'arrival of the Stalwart HMLC' requires some further explanation. A large and once impressive amphibious vehicle is now parked or berthed on the west side of the cart-house/store at Little Ross. It is sadly in a deteriorating condition, and in response to enquiries about its origins, Douglas has provided a full account of its history, which can be found in Appendix IV.

The home that has been given new life by Roger, Rosie, and Douglas is now comfortable and welcoming to their many friends, relatives, and visitors. Outwardly, it is almost exactly as Thomas Stevenson and Robert Hume left it at the end of 1842, protected by its status as a category 'B' listed building. The minor alterations that have been necessary in its conversion from two cottages to a single dwelling all comply fully with the listed building inspectorate's requirements. No efforts have been made to prettify the immediate surroundings of the building by the introduction of a suburban approach to landscaping. The tower and its adjacent cottages continue to appear to be a traditional lighthouse station: stark, bold, functional, and completely unspoiled. There are no extensions, porches, conservatories, or outhouses to upset either the lighthouse station's symmetry or its simple elegance. Care has also been taken to ensure that the introduction of the technology necessary to achieve officially approved habitable status has made a minimal impact on the lighthouse station's surroundings. In updating the fresh water supply and drainage, almost all covers to valves, drains, and rodding eyes have been retained exactly as fitted into the beautiful stone paved areas to the east of the building, by Robert Hume.

Internally, the accommodation is neither decorated in a currently fashionable style, nor does it indicate that any attempt has been made to recreate a spurious mid-19th century character. The fact that all furniture has to be transported by small boat and carried to the island's summit tends to dictate modesty and efficiency and to curb any aspirations to grandeur. All attractive features such as the surviving original windows, doors, and ironmongery have been retained and restored, and in many areas, natural stone walls have been exposed and original timber beams and flooring have been varnished. The fine Caithness flagstones in the hallways and kitchens have been retained, and the former storerooms are still fitted with their original sturdy pine shelving, removing the need for much furniture to be added to turn these rooms into bedrooms.

If any of the 61 keepers that lived in the houses were to return, they would find many details of their former homes to be exactly as they remembered them, but they would also perhaps be overawed by the benefits of modern kitchens and bathrooms, gas, electricity, television, and radio communications. Life at the summit of Little Ross has many similarities to life aboard a ship, spared only from violent motion. One is always conscious of weather conditions and particularly of the speed at which the sea state can change from tranquillity to a violent and threatening force. As on board a ship, the technology needed to support a reasonable degree of comfort is readily visible. Should the wind turbine be blown down and the generator run out of fuel, the piping and fittings for emergency gas lighting are there for all to see, and should gas supplies run out, rows of Tilley lamps hang on racks, waiting to be brought back into service. One of the house's two kitchens bristles with radio equipment and twinkling lights that are reminiscent of the equipment seen on a ship's bridge, and a glance out of the kitchen window at the surrounding sea does nothing to dispel the illusion.

When standing at the summit of the island at the doors to the lighthouse and its cottages, no visitor could fail to be impressed by the grandeur of the sweeping seascape and landscape, and the potential that exists there for the forces of nature to assert their maximum influence. The many people who love Little Ross Island are extremely grateful to all those who have worked so hard to restore and maintain the former lighthouse cottages that have been such an attractive feature of the way of life on the island for so many years.

APPENDIX I

Duties of Light-Keepers

I. Each Lighthouse shall in every case be placed in charge of two Keepers appointed by the Board, the one denominated the Principal Light-keeper, and the other the Assistant Light-keeper.

II. Each principal Light-keeper shall be, from the Assistant Light-keepers, regularly promoted according to their seniority, as vacancies occur, unless the Engineer shall report that any obstacle exists to such promotion, which obstacle, if sanctioned by the Board, shall be specially noticed in the Minute making an appointment not according to seniority.

III. Before any individual can be received into the service as a Light-keeper, he must be duly qualified by six weeks' attendance at the Bell-Rock Lighthouse, and one month's attendance at Inchkeith Lighthouse, for instruction.

IV. No individual shall be sent for instruction as a Light-keeper until his case and recommendations shall have been submitted to and approved of by the Board.

V. When an individual ordered for instruction shall have attended at the Lighthouse Stations for the prescribed period, the respective Principal Light-keepers at each station shall grant him a certificate setting forth the general conduct of and progress in instruction made by such individual during his residence at the Lighthouse (which the Light-keepers are hereby required to grant), and upon such certificate being laid before the Board, he shall, if the Board see fit, then be placed upon an 'Expectant List,' which list shall not contain more than twelve names.

VI. Upon vacancies occurring among the Light-keepers, these vacancies shall be filled up from the Expectants in order according to seniority of qualification, unless the Engineer shall report that any reason to the contrary exists, which, if sanctioned by the Board, shall be specially noticed in the Minute making an appointment not according to seniority; and as individuals, though placed upon the Expectant List, are not in the service of the Board, nor in any way under its cognisance, it is understood that they are to satisfy the Engineer (who will report to the Board) of the respectability of their character and employment from the period of their having been placed on the Expectant List, in terms of the preceding Rule.

VII. No individual shall be promoted from the Expectants' List to be a Light-keeper, who at the time of such promotion is under 21 or above 30 years of age.

VIII. All Light-keepers shall at the time of their appointment, or as soon thereafter as convenient, appear before the Board and receive a regular certificate of their appointment, which certificate shall in every case bear the same date as the Minute making the appointment.

IX. On a vacancy occurring, by the death or incapacity of a Light-keeper, or other cause, the Engineer shall forthwith report the same to the Secretary of the Board.

X. The Engineer may make such temporary arrangements for supplying a vacancy as he may find most suitable to the convenience of the service, but no permanent change shall take place in the station of Light-keepers until the Engineer shall have submitted the same to the Board for approval.

XI. In all cases where an 'Occasional Keeper' (see Introduction, p. 13) is called for, in terms of the 27th Instruction to Light-keepers, and shall be retained longer than six weeks at any station, the Engineer is to report the special cause of his being so retained. The Occasional Keeper to be annually called in for a fortnight, in the month of January, to do duty, so as to keep him in the practice thereof.

XII. Upon a Light-keeper being superannuated, in terms of the Regulations on that subject (Chap. VIII. Rule X.), the meeting of the Bell-Rock Committee, to which the Superannuation Committee shall report, on the report being approved of, shall fill up the vacancy caused by such superannuation.

XIII. The Light-keepers may have occasional leave of absence for necessary business or for health, and the Engineer may grant such leave, but he shall immediately make a report to the Secretary stating the circumstances, the period for which such leave has been granted, and the arrangement made for supplying the place of the Light-keeper on leave.

XIV. The Monthly Returns hereinafter required to be made (Instructions, No. 12) by the Light-keepers to the Engineer, are to be by him laid before the Board as the same are received.

XV. There shall be hung up in the Board-room, a List of the Principal and Assistant Light-keepers; shewing their names — the date of their entering the service - their ages - the Stations at which they act - the date of Promotion in the case of Principal Light-keepers. This List shall also contain the names of the Principal and Assistant Light-keepers respectively, in order according to seniority, - a similar List of the Expectants, according to seniority of qualification, and also a List of superannuated Light-keepers, with the date of their superannuations, the period of their services, and their retiring allowances.

XVI. Light-keepers shall observe the following Instructions:-

1. The Lamps shall be kept burning bright and clear every night from sunset to sunrise; and in order that the greatest degree of light may be maintained throughout the night, the Wicks must be trimmed every four hours, or oftener if necessary; and the Keeper who has the first watch shall take care to turn the oil valves so as to let the oil flow into the Burner a sufficient time before lighting.

2. The Light-keepers shall keep a regular and constant Watch in the Light-room throughout the night. The First Watch shall begin at sunset. The Light-keepers are to take the watches alternately, in such manner that he who has the first watch one night, shall have the second watch next night. The length or duration of the watch shall not, in ordinary cases, exceed four hours; but during the period between the months of October and March, both inclusive, the first watch shall change at eight o'clock. The watches shall at all times be so arranged as to have a shift at midnight.

3. At stations where there is only one Light-room, the daily duty shall be laid out in two departments, and the Light-keepers shall change from one department to the other every Saturday night.

4. FIRST DEPARTMENT. - The Light-keeper who has this department, shall immediately after the morning Watch, polish or otherwise cleanse the Reflectors or Refractors till they are brought into a proper state of brilliancy; he shall also thoroughly cleanse the Lamps, and carefully dust the Chandelier. He shall supply the Burners with cotton, the Lamps with oil, and shall have every thing connected with the Apparatus in a state of readiness for lighting in the evening.

5. SECOND DEPARTMENT.-The Light-keeper who has this department shall cleanse the glass of the Lantern, lamp-glasses, copper and brass work and utensils, the walls, floors, and balcony of the Light-room, and the apparatus and machinery therewith connected; together with the Tower stair, passage, doors and windows, from the Light-room to the Oil cellar.

6. For the more effectual cleansing of the glass of the Lantern, and management of the Lamps at the time of lighting, both Light-keepers shall be upon watch throughout the first hour of the first watch every night, during the winter period, between the first day of October and last day of March, when they shall jointly do the duty of the Light-room during that hour. These changes to and from the double watch shall be intimated by the Keepers in the Monthly Returns for October and April.

7. At those stations where there are two Light-rooms, each Light-keeper shall perform the entire duty of both departments in that Light-room to which he may be especially appointed. But after the first hour of the first Watch, the Light-keeper who has charge of this watch shall perform the whole duty of trimming and attending the Lights of both Light-rooms till the expiry of his watch; and in like manner, his successor on the watch shall perform the whole duty of both Light-rooms during his watch.

8. The Light-keeper on duty shall on no pretence whatever, during his watch, leave the Light-room and balcony, or the passage leading from one Light-room to another, at stations where there are two Lights. Bells are provided at each Light-room to enable the Light-keeper on duty to summon the absent Light-keeper; and if at any time the Light-keeper on duty shall think the presence or assistance of the Light-keeper not on duty is necessary, he shall call him by ringing his bell, which should be immediately answered by the return signal, and

213

the Keeper so called, should repair to the Light-room without delay. In like manner, when the watches come to be changed, the bell shall be rung to call the Light-keeper next in turn. After which the Light-keeper on duty shall, at his peril, remain on guard till he is relieved by the Light-keeper in person who has the next watch.

9. Should the bell of the Light-keeper whose turn it is to mount guard, happen to be in an unserviceable state, the other house-bell shall be used, and some of the inmates of that house shall call the Light-keeper not on duty, so as by all means to avoid leaving the Light-room without a constant watch during the night.

10. The Principal Light-keeper is held responsible for the safety and good order of the Stores, Utensils, and Apparatus of what kind soever, and for every thing being put to its proper use, and kept in its proper place. He shall take care that none of the stores or materials are wasted, and shall observe the strictest economy, and the most careful management, yet so as to maintain in every respect the best possible light.

11. The Principal Light-keeper shall daily serve out the allowance of Oil and other Stores for the use of the Light-room. The oil is to be measured by the Assistant, at the sight of the Principal Light-keeper.

12. The Light-keeper shall keep a daily Journal of the quantity of Oil expended, the routine of their duty, and the state of the Weather, embodying any other remarks that may occur. These shall be written in the Journal-Books to be kept at each station for the purpose, at the periods of the day when they occur, as they must on no account be trusted to memory. On the first day of each month they shall make up and transmit to the Engineer a return, which shall be an accurate copy of the Journal for the preceding month.

13. The Light-keepers are also required to take notice of any Shipwreck which shall happen within the district of the Lighthouse, and to enter an account thereof - according to the prescribed form, in a Book furnished to each Station for this purpose; and in such account he shall state whether the Light was seen by any one on board the shipwrecked Vessel and recognised by them, and how long it was seen before the vessel struck. A copy of this entry shall form the Shipwreck Return, to be forthwith forwarded to the Engineer.

14. A book containing a note of the Vessels passing each Lighthouse daily shall be kept; and an annual Schedule, shewing the number of vessels in each month, shall be sent to the Engineer in the month of January.

15. The Monthly and Shipwreck Returns are to be written by the Assistant, and the accompanying letters by the Principal Light-keeper. The whole shall be carefully compared and signed by both Light-keepers, as directed by the printed form, and dispatched by post to the Engineer as soon as possible.

16. For the purpose of keeping up the practical knowledge of the 'Occasional Keeper,' he shall be annually called in by the Principal Light-keeper to do duty for a fortnight in the month of January; and the same shall be stated in the Monthly Letter.

17. The Principal Light-keeper is held responsible for the regularity of the Watches throughout the night, for the cleanliness and good order of the Reflecting or Refracting Apparatus, Machinery, and Utensils, and for the due performance of the whole duty of the Light-room or Light-rooms, as the case may be, whether performed by him personally, or by the Assistant.

18. The Principal Light-keeper is also held responsible for the good order and condition of the Household Furniture belonging to the Lighthouse Board, as well in his own as in the Assistant's house. This duty extends also to the cleanliness of the several apartments, passages, stairs, roofs, water-cisterns, storerooms, workshops, privies, ash-pits of the dwelling-houses, offices, court, and immediate access to the Lighthouse.

19. The Light-keepers shall endeavour to keep in good order and repair the Dykes enclosing the Lighthouse grounds, the Landing-places, and Roads leading from thence to the Lighthouse and the Drains therewith connected, together with all other things placed under their charge.

20. When stores of any kind are to be landed for the use of the Lighthouse, the Light-keepers shall attend and give their assistance. The Principal Light-keeper must, upon these occasions, satisfy himself as far as possible, of the quantity and condition of the stores received, which must be duly entered in the Store-book and Monthly Return-book.

21. The Light-keepers are to make a Report of the quality of the Stores, in the Monthly Return for March annually, or earlier should circumstances render this necessary; and this Report must proceed upon special trial of the several Cisterns of Oil and of the other Stores in detail, both at the time of receiving them and after the experience of the winter months.

22. At all stations where Peat Fuel is in use, there must be such a quantity of Peats provided, that the Stock of the former year shall be a sufficient supply to the end of the current year.

23. Should the supply of any of the Lighthouse Stores at any time appear to the Principal Light-keeper to be getting short, so as thereby to endanger the regular appearance of the Light, he shall immediately intimate the same to the Engineer, and he must be guided by prudence in reducing the stated number of Burners until a supply be received.

24. The Light-keepers are prohibited from carrying on any trade or business whatever. They are also prohibited from having any boarders or lodgers in their dwelling-houses, and from keeping dogs at the Lighthouse establishments.

25. The Light-keepers are also directed to take care that no smuggled goods are harboured or concealed in any way in or about the Lighthouse premises or grounds.

26. The Light-keepers have permission to go from home to draw their salaries, and also to attend church. The Assistant Light-keeper, on all occasions of leave of absence, must consult the Principal Light-keeper as to the proper time for such leave, and obtain his consent; in like manner, the Principal Light-keeper shall duly intimate his intention of going from home to the Assistant Light-keeper; — it being expressly ordered that only one Light-keeper shall be absent from the Lighthouse at one and the same time.

27. While the Principal Light-keeper is absent, or is incapacitated for duty by sickness, the full charge of the Light-room duty and of the premises shall devolve upon the Assistant, who shall in that case have access to the keys of the Light-room stores, and be held responsible in all respects as the Principal Light-keeper; and in the case of the incapacity of either Light-keeper, the assistance of the Occasional Light-keeper shall be immediately called in, and notice of the same given to the Engineer. Notice of any such occurrences to be taken in the Monthly Return, or by special letter to the Engineer, should circumstances render this necessary.

28. The Light-keepers are required to be sober and industrious, cleanly in their persons and linens, and orderly in their families. They must conduct themselves with civility to strangers, by shewing the premises, at such hours as do not interfere with the proper duties of their office; it being expressly understood, that strangers shall not be admitted into the Light-room after sunset. But no money or other gratuity shall be taken from strangers on any pretence whatever.

29. The Light-keepers are to appear in their Uniform-dress when any of the Commissioners or Principal Officers visit a station, and also on Sunday;- on which day, at noon, the weather permitting, the Lighthouse flag shall be hoisted by the Assistant Light-Keeper, or in his absence by the Principal Light-keeper, when it shall remain displayed until sunset.

30. These Instructions are to be read in the Light-room by the Principal Light-keeper, in the hearing of his Assistant, on the term days, before drawing his salary; and notice thereof taken in the Monthly Returns.

31. In the event of any neglect occurring in the performance of any part of the duties required from a Light-keeper, the offending party shall, jointly with the other Light-keeper or Light-keepers at the station, send immediate notice of the circumstance to the Engineer; and in the event of one party refusing or neglecting to concur in giving this intimation, the others (whether Principals or Assistants) shall proceed to give the notice in their own names.

32. The breach of any of the foregoing Rules and Instructions shall subject the Light-keepers to dismissal, or to such other punishment as the nature of the offence may require.

33. It is recommended that the Principal Light-keeper, or other Principal Officer at the respective Lighthouses for the time being, shall, every Sunday, perform the service pointed out for the inmates, by reading a portion of the Scriptures, and any other religious book furnished by the Board, and the Prayer composed for their use by the Rev. Dr. Brunton, one of the Ministers of Edinburgh, or other Prayers in any work furnished by the Board. For this purpose, the Principal Light-keeper shall invite the families to assemble at noon in the Visiting Officer's room.

34. The Light-Keepers are to observe that the above general Regulations are without prejudice to any more special Instructions which may be made applicable to any particular Lighthouse, or to such orders as may from time to time be issued by the Engineer.

Taken from a transcription of the 1847 'Bye-laws and Rules and Regulations of the Commissioners of Northern Lighthouses', by kind permission of Frances Coakley, http://www.isle-of-man.com/manxnotebook/.

APPENDIX II

Principal Keepers
at
Little Ross Lighthouse
1842–1960

Thomas Ritson, 22 June 1842
Hugh Fitzsimons, 18 February 1852
Alexander Craib, 23 February 1859
James Pithie, 11 March 1863
John Fullarton, 5 February 1868
William McKay, 15 March 1871
James Ferrier, 18 January 1884
Neil McDonald, 5 March 1886
Peter Nicholson, 7 July 1893
Donald Georgeson, 19 December 1895
George Irvine, 14 June 1900
Robert Brown, 11 December 1906
James Mercer McCulloch, 2 November 1910

William Begg or Beggs, 22 December 1914
Kenneth Taylor, 13 September 1921
James Thomas McDonald Matheson, 23 June 1928
Charles J. McNish, 13 October 1931
Joseph Tulloch, 21 September 1933
Allan MacMillan, 30 August 1934
Basil Mackenzie, 24 November 1937
Alexander Scott, 23 April 1938
Robert M. Pearson, 16 October 1940
Alex Gilmour, 14 September 1945
John Ritch, 2 December 1950
Harry Manson, 16 December 1955
John Thomson, 26 November 1959

Twenty six principal keepers – average stay at Little Ross was just over four and a half years.

APPENDIX III

Assistant Keepers
at
Little Ross Lighthouse
1842–1960

Alexander Law, 2 November 1842
Richard Cumming, 17 November 1846
Robert Burnett, 19 May 1847
Thomas Saunderson, 15 July 1857
Robert Watson, 20 March 1861
Archibald Turner, 18 May 1864
Murdoch Morrison, 26 April 1867
Joseph Dick, 10 July 1867
Donald McKerrell, 12 August 1869
John Martin, 18 July 1872
George Craig, 22 October 1873
William Gilmour, 8 August 1879
Robert McIntosh, 2 February 1883
Simon Fraser, 12 March 1891
James Gair, 18 May 1893
Robert M. Anderson, 3 August 1898
R. Watt, 19 May 1904
John H. McLeod, 2 December 1904

George Mackie, 26 May 1910
K. Sutherland, 15 June 1920
John Blackhall Middlemiss, 2 April 1924
Alex Nicholson, 12 October 1926
Peter Murray Gow, 6 May 1927
Robert Thomson, 17 July 1931
William Learmonth, 9 December 1936
David Rendall, 7 October 1941
Charles J. F. Gifford, 13 September 1944
David F. Mitchell, 27 February 1946
V. L. W. Hill, 4 May 1949
A. I. Walker, 2 November 1950
A. R. McGaw, 1 May 1953
W. D. McGhie, 16 March 1956
R. Johnstone, 6 November 1957
Ian Summers, 1 March 1958
Robert McKenna Cribbes Dickson, 18 July 1960

Thirty five assistant keepers – average stay at Little Ross was just under three and a half years.

APPENDIX IV

Alvis Stalwart Mk2
High Mobility Load Carrier

You asked about my poor old amphibious vehicle — well, it's a long tale. The vehicle is an Alvis Stalwart Mk 2 high mobility load carrier. These vehicles were made initially as a private development initiative by Alvis Motors of Coventry until they succeeded in persuading the Ministry of Defence to place a contract for them. They were a development of earlier Alvis fighting vehicles such as the Saladin armoured car and Saracen armoured personnel carrier, both of which were made from the 1950s into the early 1970s. The Stalwart was not armoured and its principal use was moving supplies of fuel, ammunition and other stores over land and water to service the army front line. They were manufactured throughout the 1960s in Mk1 and Mk2 forms which differed in detail, and variations of the Mk2 were produced for more specialised forms of cargo handling.

All Stalwarts were amphibious and were powered in the water by vectored thrust water jets. The port and starboard jets could be directed independently for ahead or astern propulsion, and anywhere in between, making the vehicle quite interesting to control. On land a permanent six-wheel drivetrain with a spin-limiting centre differential and both pairs of front wheels being steered, provided excellent traction.

The engine was a 6.522 litre petrol fuelled Rolls Royce B80 series developing around 240 b.h.p. in its final production form. Transmission was through a five-speed gearbox with a crawler first gear ratio and all five speeds were available in both forward and reverse gears, which were separately selectable!

The vehicles saw most of their service with the British Army of the Rhine, and once the cold war was over they became pretty much redundant and were sold out of service. I have often marvelled at the creative accountancy with which Government makes purchases (with 'our' money) of goods, uses them, and then sells them back to us. Whether the goods are vehicles, or more recently banks, it seems a weird device?

The firm of A. F. Budge in Retford bought many retired 'Stollys' and also produced a diesel version, hoping to maintain sales of Stalwarts with this modification but by that time other weaknesses in the Stalwart's design due primarily to its complexity, high maintenance costs and inability to travel any distance on hard surfaces without endangering its permanent 6 wheel drive system made the project fail.

I bought the beast from Budge on 17th December 1998, had it freighted by low-loader to Kirkcudbright where it was left on the harbour front until a day or two later when I summoned the courage to drive it to Ross Bay, much to the amusement and interest of Brian Finlay. It was some time later that I gathered sufficient friends to form a potential rescue party prior to swimming the Stalwart over to Little Ross!

Buying the 'Stolly' was a whim, encouraged by my late father who was with me when I first saw one of these vehicles while staying with him in Manchester. Indeed, it was a good part of his legacy that purchased the Stalwart. I thought it might be useful for transporting coal, building materials and other bulky goods. It did transport our solar panels, some coal deliveries and the lawn tractor but with a fuel consumption of around 4 m.p.g. and the ravages of salt water on the thinner parts of the superstructure, its service life was not long on Little Ross. The 4 m.p.g. refers to road use and on water this increases by approximately a factor of four! Hence the unusually large fuel tank capacity of 100 gallons. I remember filling the monster at Crosbie and Bateman's garage on the day I drove it to Ross Bay but chickened out of a complete fill after the pump was displaying over £150 worth of two star. Those were the days!

The thought of leaving the decaying hulk disquiets me but until I can find a means of either refloating her and returning her to the mainland where she could be scrapped or rebuilt, I cannot think of a solution.

Perhaps she will remain as a monument to over-ambitious dreams, for which I plead guilty!

Douglas Molyneux, 2015

APPENDIX V

Ross Island, Borgue Coast S.S.S.I.

Site monitoring and vegetation mapping 17.05.1989

The 30 acres of the island rise to marginally over 100 feet, with cliffs of around 50 feet in the SW and S; the SE side of the island has a more sloping coastline but with several rock outcrops and small cliffs; a number of deep clefts cut into the island. Around White Bay on the northern end a steep shingle beach with two berms occurs (according to DW the shape and number of the berms changes with weather conditions). The attached map shows the location of existing structures and old/existing tracks [N.B. it has not been possible to include the map referred to].

Vegetation

Being an exposed, maritime island the basic vegetation is *Festuca rubra* dominated, over large parts of the island being the only (or dominant) plant. It is extremely rank with about 12"-18" depth of mat and would greatly benefit from burning or grazing. Within this vegetation there are however a number of small areas of different communities:-

1. *Endymion non-scriptus* variant, on the western side between the southern walled garden and a point due E of the barns and byres (NVC community MC12).
2. Short *Holcus lanatus* grassland on the eastern side where a fire last year (?) cleared the *F. rubra* and allowed a gull colony to settle (MC9 community).
3. Small areas of more neutral, damper ground where *Alopecurus pratensis* has established again largely on the western side.
4. Seeps and flushes with *Oenanthe croccata*, usually near the heads of the clefts.
5. Obviously disturbed ground with weeds of cultivation appearing, namely *Urtica dioica*, *Heracleum sphondylium*, *Cirsium arvense*, *Chamaenerion augustifolium* and *Galium aparine*. It was notable that no *Pteridium* was recorded and only 1 small bush of *Rubus fruticosus*.

The *F. rubra* community contained few species, the more obvious ones being *Ranunculus ficaria*, *Rumex acetosa* and *Conopodium majus*. (*Ranunculus ficaria* sub-community). A path has been closely mown between the slipway and the lighthouse and the vegetation contains abundant *Trifolium repens*. Throughout the grassland, the snail *Cepaea nemoralis* in all colour forms and bands was abundant.

The cliff vegetation was of the *Armenia maritima-Cerastium diffusum* maritime community (NVC MC5). It is difficult to assign the vegetation to say particular sub-commuity because of the apparent absence of a number of diagnostic species. On the NE coastline, a short turf with *Lotus corniculatus*, *Trifolium dubium* and *Thymus drucei* occurred, with around the large beacon a single plant of *Pimpinella saxifraga*. Further species found here and not elsewhere on the island included *Achillea millefolium* and *Glechoma hederacea*.

Within the generator/workshop, a single tree and two seedlings of *Sambucus nigra*, the only naturally occurring woody perennials, were found (A single *Aesculus hippocastaneum* had been planted beside the mown track).

The shingle beach at White Bay held *Atriplex hastata* and *Sonchus arvensis*, but on the edge of the *F.rubra* turf, patches of *Valerianella locusta* and *Myosotis arvensis* were found. Insufficient time may have precluded the finding of other species and communities as well as the avoidance of disturbing the seabird colonies.

Birds

A colony of Cormorants (numbers unknown, but of the order of 30) occupied the tallest cliffs on the SW of the island; clutch size in the nests observed varied from 1-5 with most at 3-4. From this colony round the S and E of the island to the large beacon was occupied by a colony of Herring Gulls (total numbers unknown, but of the order of 200-300) and about 14 prs. of lesser black-backed gulls. Again of the nests visible, clutches varied from 1-4 with the majority being of 3. Considerable colour variation existed between nests and in a few cases, there was a single lighter egg in with two dark eggs. Common gulls were seen in small numbers around the island with a nest at White Bay, where an oyster-catcher's nest with 3 eggs was found (a second nest may have been close by). According to the occupier, a pair of shelduck and a number of pairs of mallard breed regularly on the island. Rock pipits were common, with a pair of swallows breeding in the Lighthouse Cottages. Other species seen were goldfinch, linnet and meadow pipit.

(There appear to be mink on the island, which may be responsible for the disappearance of mallard clutches/broods. A programme to eradicate the mink would be appropriate)

The approximate extent of the breeding colonies and of some of the plant communities is shown on the attached map.

Future Management

It would be of benefit to the plant community if small areas of rank <u>Festuca</u> were burned to allow other plants to develop; this would be best undertaken on a rotational basis. Failing that limited grazing would be an alternative, but there would be the additional problem of keeping the grazers away from breeding seabirds (I believe the island was grazed in the past). Care would also need to be taken that such invasive species as nettle, rose-bay and bramble, already present on the island, did not spread rapidly into the burned/grazed areas.

Plant Species

Achillea millefolium	Yarrow
Aesculus hippocastaneum	Horse chestnut
Aira praecox	Early hair-grass
Alopecurus pratensis	Timothy
Anthoxanthum odoratum	Sweet vernal grass
Arctium lapponum	Burdock
Armeria maritima	Thrift
Atriplex hastata	Spear-leaved orache

Cardamine flexuosa	Wavy bittercress
C. hirsuta	Hairy bittercress
Cerastium diffusum	Sea mouse-ear
Chamaenerion angustifolium	Rose-bay
Cirsium arvense	Creeping thistle
C. vulgarus	Spear thistle
Cochlearia officinalis	Common scurvy-grass
Conopodium majus	Pignut
Dactylis glomerata	Cocksfoot
Endymion non-sciptus	Bluebell
Festuca rubra	Red fescue
Galium aparine	Cleavers
Glechoma hederacea	Ground-ivy
Heracleum sphonylium	Hogweed
Holcus lanatus	Yorkshire fog
Juncus gerardii	Saltmarsh rush
Lathyrus pratensis	Meadow vetchling
Leontodon hispidus	Rough hawkbit
Lotus corniculatus	Common bird's-foot-trefoil
Matricaria marítima	Sea mayweed
Oenanthe croccata	Hemlock water-dropwort
Pimpinella saxifraga	Burnet-saxifrage
Plantago coronopus	Buck's-horn plantain
P. lanceolata	Ribwort plantain
Potentilla anserina	Silverweed
Ranunculus ficaria	Lesser celandine
Rubus fruticosus	Bramble
Rumex acetosa	Sorrel
R. crispus	Curled dock
Sambuc us nigra	Elder
Sedum anglicum	English stonecrop
Silene maritima	Sea campion
Sonchus arvensis	Perennial sow-thistle
Spergularia rubra	Sand spurrey
Stellaria media	Chickweed
Taraxacum agg.	Dandelion
Thymus drucei	Thyme
Trifolium dubium	Lesser trefoil
T. repens	White clover
Urtica dioica	Nettle
Valerianella locusta	Common cornsalad
Vicia cracca	Tufted vetch
V. sativa	Common vetch

David M. Hawker,
Notification Assistant,
Stewartry District
19th May 1989

Information
Sources

Books, Journals, and Articles

A Natural History of Lighthouses, by John A. Love (2015).

Accounts and Papers of the Commissioners of Northern Lights (28 January 1843).

Circuit Journeys, by Lord Cockburn (1889), referring to a visit made in 1844.

Diary of George Mackie 1916-1919.

Dictionary of National Biography, Volume 18, Fergusson, Robert Cutlar, by Francis Watt (1885–1900).

Frances Groome's Ordnance Gazetteer of Scotland (1882-4).

From the Galloway Lifeboat Service, by Dr. J. Maxwell Wood in the *Gallovidian* (circa1906–1908).

Kirkcudbright, an Alphabetical Guide to its History, by David R. Collin (2003).

Kirkcudbright Shipping, 1300 – 2005, by David R. Collin (2007).

Mineralogy of Scotland Vol II by M. Forster Heddle, M.D., F.R.S.E. Emeritus Professor of Chemistry, St. Andrews, edited by J. G. Goodchild (1901).

Minute Books of St Cuthbert's Lodge, Kirkcudbright, in the care of the Stewartry Museum, Kirkcudbright.

Minute of Meeting of the Shipowners, Mariners, Merchants, and other traffickers of the Town and Port of Kirkcudbright. Kirkcudbright 30 March 1835.

Pocket Book and Manual of Thomas Stevenson (circa 1859), courtesy of The Royal Commission on the Ancient and Historical Momuments of Scotland, and The Stevenson Society of America.

Rambles in Galloway, by Malcolm McL. Harper (1896).

Remarks on the Geology of the Island of Little Ross, Kirkcudbrightshire, by Thomas Stevenson, Esq., Civil Engineer. Communicated by the author (read before the Wernerian Natural History Society, 8 April 1843). *Records of the Wernerian Natural History Society,* two volumes of minute books (Jan 1808– Apr 1858) GB 237 Coll-206 loc. Dc.2.55-56.

Image from the Biodiversity Heritage Library. Digitised by Edinburgh University Library. www.biodiversitylibrary.org

Report of the Parliamentary Select Committee regarding administration and management of lighthouse stations in all parts of the British Isles (1845).

Scottish and Manx Lighthouses, by Ian Cowe (2015).

Species point records from 2000 Reach, Little Ross Island (Kirkcudbright bay) Littoral survey. Published by Joint Nature Conservation Committee (JNCC) (custodian).

The Breeding Birds of the Solway Islands, by Richard and Barbara Mearns, published in the *Transactions of the Dumfriesshire and Galloway Natural History and Antiquarian Society,* Third Series, Vol LXXXI (2007).

The History of Parliament: The House of Commons 1820-1832, edited by D. R. Fisher (2009).

The Lighthouse Stevensons, by Bella Bathurst (1999).

The Scottish Gallovidian Encyclopedia, by John Mactaggart (1824).

The Stockbridge Baby Farmer and other Scottish Murder Stories, by Molly Whittington-Egan (2001).

The Scottish Naturalist, No. 61 (January 1917).

The Scottish Naturalist No. 43 (July 1915).

The Scottish Naturalist No. 54 (June 1916).

The Scottish Naturalist, Nos. 105–106, Sept–Oct 1920, *Spring Migration at Little Ross Island,* by William Begg (1920).

The Story of Kirkcudbright Lifeboat Station, 1862-1991, by Dr R. N. Rutherfurd and T. R. Collin (1991).

Topographical Dictionary of Scotland: and of the islands in the British Seas, by Nicholas Carlisle. (1813).

Tribute to James Skelly, by John C. Mackenzie, (1880).

True Police Cases, Volume 13 No. 141, U.S.A. (June 1961).

UK & Eire Marine Turtle Strandings & Sightings Annual Report, by R. S. Penrose (2003).

Newspapers and Periodicals

Belfast Banner of Ulster

British Newspaper Archive, The British Library, London.

Caledonian Mercury

Carlisle Journal

Carlisle Patriot

Cumberland Pacquet from *Naval Chronicle* in *The Nautical Magazine (1840).*

Daily Herald

Daily Mirror

Daily Record

Dumfries Courier

Dumfries and Galloway Courier

Dumfries & Galloway Standard & Advertiser

Evening Citizen

Evening Times

Hansard

Liverpool Albion

Manx Sun

Scottish Daily Express

Scottish Daily Mail

The Galloway News

The Glasgow Argus

The Morning Chronicle

The Scotsman

The Sunday Post

Westmoreland Gazette

Museums, Art Galleries, and Libraries

Archives of the Northern Lighthouse Board, in the National Archives of Scotland.
  Broughton House, Kirkcudbright.

Business records of Robert Stevenson and sons, civil engineers, in the National Library of Scotland.

The British Library, London.

The Ewart Library, Dumfries.

The National Archives of Scotland, Edinburgh.

The National Library of Scotland, Edinburgh.

The Stewartry Museum, Kirkcudbright.

Websites

A Manx Notebook, http://www.isle-of-man.com/manxnotebook/
  Kirkcudbright Community Website, http://www.kirkcudbright.com/index.asp

Credits

Collin Family Collection
1. *Venus* and *Marten*, circa 1900
2. Old harbour, Kirkcudbright, circa 1900

Dick Family Collection (per the late Alison Kay, John Dick, Roger Cliffe, Neil McKelvie, Jan and Keith Smith and Hiroshi Nakata)
1. Joseph Dick

Gifford Family Collection
1. Charles J. F. Gifford

Alistair C. Gillone
1. The author's boat *Speedwell* and Little Ross Island from the north east

Henry Family Collection
1. George C. Davidson DSM BEM

Mackie and Begg Family Collection
1. George Mackie
2. George and Eva Mackie
3. William Begg
4. Eva Mackie and children

Robert Mitchell's Collection
1. John (Hubby) Poland

Douglas Molyneux's Collection
1. Gas bottle store
2. Battery store
3. Solar panels

Muirhead Family Collection
1. Peter M. Gow and Colleagues
2. Peter, Margaret and John Gow at Little Ross

Museum of Scottish Lighthouses, Fraserburgh
1. Little Ross. Douglas Molyneux standing against rock, 1996. Photograph by Keith Allardyce.
2. Little Ross. Lantern and Keeper, 1996. Photograph by Keith Allardyce.

National Trust for Scotland, Broughton House, Kirkcudbright
1. Photographic portrait of John C. Mackenzie

Northern Lighthouse Board Collection
1. Elevation of Tower and House. Item DC9333, External Reference 90/L1/2
2. Elevation of Tower. Item DC 9334, External Reference 90/L1/3
3. Sketch Portrait of Alan Stevenson
4. Control panel ref: Graeme Macdonald, LRO 2003-10-14-GAM DSCF 0046

5. Plaque ref: Graeme Macdonald, LRO 2004-01-25 GAM DSCF 0126
6. Cellar ref: Graeme Macdonald, LRO 2002-09-26-GAM 09240005
7. Bottom of duct for weight ref: Graeme Macdonald, LRO 2002-09-26-GAM 09240010
8. View down duct for weight ref: Graeme Macdonald, LRO 2003-11-11-GAM 04220024

Photoactive.co.uk

1. Sunset over Little Ross Island. Photograph by Philip Dunn

Scottish National Portrait Gallery

1. Portrait of Thomas Stevenson, 1818–1887, Lighthouse and harbour engineer, ID No. PG 568, by   Sir George Reid
2. Portrait of Robert Stevenson, 1772–1850, Lighthouse engineer, ID No. PG 657, by John Syme

Daniel Shackleton Collection

1. Portrait of Robert Cutlar Fergusson, by Sir George Haytor

Stewartry Museum

1. Design for Captain Skelly's original beacons
2. Oil painting of the ketch *Windward*
3. RNLB *Hugh* and *Ann*
4. Hugh Gourlay
5. George Poland

Summers Family Collection

1. The Wedding of Ian and Isabel Summers

Thomson Family Collection

1. John Thomson and family on Little Ross

Wellcome Library London, Wellcome images, images@wellcom.ac.uk

1. Joseph Hume, wood engraving by (T.G.) 1855.
2. Advert for the Allenbury's Milk Foods for infants (L0040453) made by Allen and Hanbury's Ltd, London.1905 Ephemera Collection.

Glossary

Aboon Above

Berm A term for land forming an edge or border of the sea

Blochans Young coal fish

Bothy A simple and basic shelter, often built of stone and shared by farm labourers or other workers

Broe Sap or juice

Claise Clothes

Depone To give evidence as a witness

Farkage A confused untidy ravelled heap or bundle

Feckless Weak in body and/or mind

Gurly Blustery

Frith The old Scots form of the word firth

Heughs Steep and rocky shores, sometimes consisting of a mix of rocks and grass, but slightly less precipitous than cliffs

Jambs The sides of openings such as doorways or fireplaces.

Na'el Navel

Partons Edible crabs

Pirr-eggs Sea bird's eggs

Porgy A name applied to various sea fish, perhaps American in origin.

Powkfu Pocketful

Quoins Masonry blocks forming the corner of a wall.

Roadstead A place where ships may lie at anchor

Roup A sale by auction

Shanks Legs

Stewartry The area of land that later became the County of Kirkcudbrightshire. Its name was derived from the fact that it was administered by a Steward, appointed by the Monarch.

Tack A lease, tenancy, especially the leasehold tenure of a farm, mill, mining or fishing rights, tax- or toll-collecting, etc.

Wherries These small boats, often built in the Isle of Man, were shapely little vessels with pronounced sheer, pointed sterns and finely modelled hulls of moderate draft that gave them a good performance under sail. They were mostly open boats, the smaller ones rigged as sloops or cutters and the larger occasionally rigged as schooners. It is most likely that the term wherry was used in Kirkcudbright merely to describe a wide variety of small and fairly rugged open vessels of shallow draft, each controlled by one or two men, capable of carrying modest loads, doing some fishing, and perhaps making just the occasional foray into smuggling.

Index